Homespun Heroines and Other Women of Distinction

THE SCHOMBURG LIBRARY OF
NINETEENTH-CENTURY BLACK WOMEN WRITERS

General Editor, Henry Louis Gates, Jr.

Titles are listed chronologically; collections that include works published over a span of years are listed according to the publication date of their initial work.

Phillis Wheatley, *The Collected Works of Phillis Wheatley*

Six Women's Slave Narratives: M. Prince; Old Elizabeth; M. J. Jackson; L. A. Delaney; K. Drumgoold; A. L. Burton

Spiritual Narratives: M. W. Stewart; J. Lee; J. A. J. Foote; V. W. Broughton

Ann Plato, *Essays*

Collected Black Women's Narratives: N. Prince; L. Picquet; B. Veney; S. K. Taylor

Frances E. W. Harper, *Complete Poems of Frances E. W. Harper*

Charlotte Forten Grimké, *The Journals of Charlotte Forten Grimké*

Mary Seacole, *Wonderful Adventures of Mrs. Seacole in Many Lands*

Harriet Jacobs, *Incidents in the Life of a Slave Girl*

Collected Black Women's Poetry, Volumes 1–4: M. E. Tucker; A. I. Menken; M. W. Fordham; P. J. Thompson; C. A. Thompson; H. C. Ray; L. A. J. Moorer; J. D. Heard; E. Bibb; M. P. Johnson; Mrs. H. Linden

Elizabeth Keckley, *Behind the Scenes. Or, Thirty Years a Slave, and Four Years in the White House*

C. W. Larison, M.D., *Silvia Dubois, A Biografy of the Slav Who Whipt Her Mistres and Gand Her Fredom*

Mrs. A. E. Johnson, *Clarence and Corinne; or, God's Way*

Octavia V. Rogers Albert, *The House of Bondage: or Charlotte Brooks and Other Slaves*

Emma Dunham Kelley, *Megda*

Anna Julia Cooper, *A Voice From the South*

Frances E. W. Harper, *Iola Leroy, or Shadows Uplifted*

Amanda Smith, *An Autobiography: The Story of the Lord's Dealings with Mrs. Amanda Smith the Colored Evangelist*

Mrs. A. E. Johnson, *The Hazeley Family*

Mrs. N. F. Mossell, *The Work of the Afro-American Woman*

Alice Dunbar-Nelson, *The Works of Alice Dunbar-Nelson*, Volumes 1–3

Emma D. Kelley-Hawkins, *Four Girls at Cottage City*

Pauline E. Hopkins, *Contending Forces: A Romance Illustrative of Negro Life North and South*

Pauline Hopkins, *The Magazine Novels of Pauline Hopkins*

Hallie Q. Brown, *Homespun Heroines and Other Women of Distinction*

Homespun Heroines
and
Other Women of Distinction

HALLIE Q. BROWN

With an Introduction by
RANDALL K. BURKETT

New York Oxford
OXFORD UNIVERSITY PRESS
1988

Oxford University Press

Oxford New York Toronto
Delhi Bombay Calcutta Madras Karachi
Petaling Jaya Singapore Hong Kong Tokyo
Nairobi Dar es Salaam Cape Town
Melbourne Auckland

and associated companies in
Beirut Berlin Ibadan Nicosia

Published by Oxford University Press, Inc.,
200 Madison Avenue, New York, New York 10016

Library of Congress Cataloging-in-Publication Data
Homespun heroines and other women of distinction /[compiled] by
Hallie Q. Brown; introduction by Randall K. Burkett.
p. cm.—(The Schomburg library of nineteenth-century black
women writers)
Previously published: 1926.
1. Afro-American women—Biography. I. Brown, Hallie Q. (Hallie
Quinn) II. Series.
E185.96.H65 1988 920.72'08996073—dc19 87-24149
ISBN 0-19-505237-4
ISBN 0-19-505267-6 (set)

2 4 6 8 10 9 7 5 3 1

Printed in the United States of America
on acid-free paper

The
Schomburg Library
of
Nineteenth-Century
Black Women Writers
is
Dedicated
in Memory
of
PAULINE AUGUSTA COLEMAN GATES

1916–1987

PUBLISHER'S NOTE

Whenever possible, the volumes in this set were reproduced directly from original materials. When availability, physical condition of original texts, or other circumstances prohibited this, volumes or portions of volumes were reset.

FOREWORD
In Her Own Write

Henry Louis Gates, Jr.

> One muffled strain in the Silent South, a jarring chord and a vague and uncomprehended cadenza has been and still is the Negro. And of that muffled chord, the one mute and voiceless note has been the sadly expectant Black Woman, ...
>
> The "other side" has not been represented by one who "lives there." And not many can more sensibly realize and more accurately tell the weight and the fret of the "long dull pain" than the open-eyed but hitherto voiceless Black Woman of America.
>
> . . . as our Caucasian barristers are not to blame if they cannot *quite* put themselves in the dark man's place, neither should the dark man be wholly expected fully and adequately to reproduce the exact Voice of the Black Woman.
>
> —ANNA JULIA COOPER, *A Voice From the South* (1892)

The birth of the Afro-American literary tradition occurred in 1773, when Phillis Wheatley published a book of poetry. Despite the fact that her book garnered for her a remarkable amount of attention, Wheatley's journey to the printer had been a most arduous one. Sometime in 1772, a young African girl walked demurely into a room in Boston to undergo an oral examination, the results of which would determine the direction of her life and work. Perhaps she was shocked upon entering the appointed room. For there, perhaps gathered in a semicircle, sat eighteen of Boston's most notable citizens. Among them were John Erving, a prominent Boston merchant; the Reverend Charles Chauncy, pastor of the Tenth Congregational Church; and John Hancock, who would later gain fame for his signature on the Declaration of Independence. At the center of this group was His Excellency, Thomas Hutchinson, governor of Massachusetts, with Andrew Oliver, his lieutenant governor, close by his side.

Why had this august group been assembled? Why had it seen fit to summon this young African girl, scarcely eighteen years old, before it? This group of "the most respectable Characters in *Boston*," as it would later define itself, had assembled to question closely the African adolescent on the slender sheaf of poems that she claimed to have "written by herself." We can only speculate on the nature of the questions posed to the fledgling poet. Perhaps they asked her to identify and explain—for all to hear—exactly who were the Greek and Latin gods and poets alluded to so frequently in her work. Perhaps they asked her to conjugate a verb in Latin or even to translate randomly selected passages from the Latin, which she and her master, John Wheatley, claimed that she "had made some Progress in." Or perhaps they asked her to recite from memory key passages from the texts of John Milton and Alexander Pope, the two poets by whom the African claimed to be most directly influenced. We do not know.

We do know, however, that the African poet's responses were more than sufficient to prompt the eighteen august gentlemen to compose, sign, and publish a two-paragraph "Attestation," an open letter "To the Publick" that prefaces Phillis Wheatley's book and that reads in part:

> We whose Names are under-written, do assure the World, that the Poems specified in the following Page, were (as we

> verily believe) written by Phillis, a young Negro Girl, who was but a few Years since, brought an uncultivated Barbarian from *Africa,* and has ever since been, and now is, under the Disadvantage of serving as a Slave in a Family in this Town. She has been examined by some of the best Judges, and is thought qualified to write them.

So important was this document in securing a publisher for Wheatley's poems that it forms the signal element in the prefatory matter preceding her *Poems on Various Subjects, Religious and Moral,* published in London in 1773.

Without the published "Attestation," Wheatley's publisher claimed, few would believe that an African could possibly have written poetry all by herself. As the eighteen put the matter clearly in their letter, "Numbers would be ready to suspect they were not really the Writings of Phillis." Wheatley and her master, John Wheatley, had attempted to publish a similar volume in 1772 in Boston, but Boston publishers had been incredulous. One year later, "Attestation" in hand, Phillis Wheatley and her master's son, Nathaniel Wheatley, sailed for England, where they completed arrangements for the publication of a volume of her poems with the aid of the Countess of Huntington and the Earl of Dartmouth.

This curious anecdote, surely one of the oddest oral examinations on record, is only a tiny part of a larger, and even more curious, episode in the Enlightenment. Since the beginning of the sixteenth century, Europeans had wondered aloud whether or not the African "species of men," as they were most commonly called, *could* ever create formal literature, could ever master "the arts and sciences." If they could, the argument ran, then the African variety of humanity was fundamentally related to the European variety. If not, then it seemed clear that the African was destined by nature to be a slave. This was the burden shouldered by Phillis Wheatley when she successfully defended herself and the authorship of her book against counterclaims and doubts.

Indeed, with her successful defense, Wheatley launched two traditions at once—the black American literary tradition *and* the black woman's literary tradition. If it is extraordinary that not just one but both of these traditions were founded simultaneously by a black woman—certainly an event unique in the history of literature—it is also ironic that this important fact of common, coterminous literary origins seems to have escaped most scholars.

That the progenitor of the black literary tradition was a woman means, in the most strictly literal sense, that all subsequent black writers have evolved in a matrilinear line of descent, and that each, consciously or unconsciously, has extended and revised a canon whose foundation was the poetry of a black woman. Early black writers seem to have been keenly aware of Wheatley's founding role, even if most of her white reviewers were more concerned with the implications of her race than her gender. Jupiter Hammon, for example, whose 1760 broadside "An Evening Thought. Salvation by Christ, With Penitential Cries" was the first individual poem published by a black American, acknowledged Wheatley's influence by selecting her as the subject of his second broadside, "An Address to Miss Phillis Wheatly [*sic*], Ethiopian Poetess, in Boston," which was published at Hartford in 1778. And George Moses Horton, the second Afro-American to publish a book of poetry in English (1829), brought out in 1838 an edition of his *Poems By A Slave* bound together with Wheatley's work. Indeed, for fifty-six years, between 1773 and 1829, when Horton published *The Hope of Liberty*, Wheatley was the *only* black person to have published a book of imaginative literature in English. So central was this black woman's role in the shaping of the Afro-American literary tradition that, as one historian has maintained, the history of the reception of Phillis Wheatley's poetry *is* the history of Afro-American literary criticism. Well into the nineteenth century, Wheatley and the black literary tradition were the same entity.

But Wheatley is not the only black woman writer who stands as a pioneering figure in Afro-American literature. Just as Wheatley gave birth to the genre of black poetry, Ann Plato was the first Afro-American to publish a book of essays (1841) and Harriet E. Wilson was the first black person to publish a novel in the United States (1859).

Despite this pioneering role of black women in the tradition, however, many of their contributions before this century have been all but lost or unrecognized. As Hortense Spillers observed as recently as 1983,

> With the exception of a handful of autobiographical narratives from the nineteenth century, the black woman's realities are virtually suppressed until the period of the Harlem Renaissance and later. Essentially the black woman as artist, as intellectual spokesperson for her own cultural apprenticeship, has not existed before, for anyone. At the source of [their] own symbol-making task, [the community of black women writers] confronts, therefore, a tradition of work that is quite recent, its continuities, broken and sporadic.

Until now, it has been extraordinarily difficult to establish the formal connections between early black women's writing and that of the present, precisely because our knowledge of their work has been broken and sporadic. Phillis Wheatley, for example, while certainly the most reprinted and discussed poet in the tradition, is also one of the least understood. Ann Plato's seminal work, *Essays* (which includes biographies and poems), has not been reprinted since it was published a century and a half ago. And Harriet Wilson's *Our Nig*, her compelling novel of a black woman's expanding consciousness in a racist Northern antebellum environment, never received even *one* review or comment at a time when virtually *all* works written by black people were heralded by abolitionists as salient arguments against the existence of human slavery. Many of the books reprinted in this set experienced a similar fate, the most dreadful fate for an author: that of being ignored then relegated to the obscurity of the rare book section of a university library. We can only wonder how many other texts in the black woman's tradition have been lost to this generation of readers or remain unclassified or uncatalogued and, hence, unread.

This was not always so, however. Black women writers dominated the final decade of the nineteenth century, perhaps spurred to publish by an 1886 essay entitled "The Coming American Novelist," which was published in *Lippincott's Monthly Magazine* and written by "A Lady From Philadelphia." This pseudonymous essay argued that the "Great American Novel" would be written by a black person. Her argument is so curious that it deserves to be repeated:

> When we come to formulate our demands of the Coming American Novelist, we will agree that he must be native-born. His ancestors may come from where they will, but we must give him a birthplace and have the raising of him. Still, the longer his family has been here the better he will represent us. Suppose he should have no country but ours, no traditions but those he has learned here, no longings apart from us, no future except in our future—the orphan of the world, he finds with us his home. And with all this, suppose he refuses to be fused into that grand conglomerate we call the "American type." With us, he is not of us. He is original, he has humor, he is tender, he is passive and fiery, he has been

> taught what we call justice, and he has his own opinion about it. He has suffered everything a poet, a dramatist, a novelist need suffer before he comes to have his lips anointed. And with it all he is in one sense a spectator, a little out of the race. How would these conditions go towards forming an original development? In a word, suppose the coming novelist is of African origin? When one comes to consider the subject, there is no improbability in it. One thing is certain,—our great novel will not be written by the typical American.

An atypical American, indeed. Not only would the great American novel be written by an African-American, it would be written by an African-American *woman:*

> Yet farther: I have used the generic masculine pronoun because it is convenient; but Fate keeps revenge in store. It was a woman who, taking the wrongs of the African as her theme, wrote the novel that awakened the world to their reality, and why should not the coming novelist be a woman as well as an African? She—the woman of that race—has some claims on Fate which are not yet paid up.

It is these claims on fate that we seek to pay by publishing The Schomburg Library of Nineteenth-Century Black Women Writers.

This theme would be repeated by several black women authors, most notably by Anna Julia Cooper, a prototypical black feminist whose 1892 *A Voice From the South* can be considered to be one of the original texts of the black feminist movement. It was Cooper who first analyzed the fallacy of referring to "the Black man" when speaking of black people and who argued that just as white men cannot speak through the consciousness of black men, neither can black *men* "fully and adequately . . . reproduce the exact Voice of the Black Woman." Gender and race, she argues, cannot be conflated, except in the instance of a black woman's voice, and it is this voice which must be uttered and to which we must listen. As Cooper puts the matter so compellingly:

> It is not the intelligent woman vs. the ignorant woman; nor the white woman vs. the black, the brown, and the red,—it is not even the cause of woman vs. man. Nay, 'tis woman's strongest vindication for speaking that *the world needs to hear her voice*. It would be subversive of every human interest that the cry of one-half the human family be stifled. Woman in stepping from the pedestal of statue-like inactivity in the domestic shrine, and daring to think and move and speak,—to undertake to help shape, mold, and direct the thought of her age, is merely completing the circle of the world's vision. Hers is every interest that has lacked an interpreter and a defender. Her cause is linked with that of every agony that has been dumb—every wrong that needs a voice.
>
> It is no fault of man's that he has not been able to see truth from her standpoint. It does credit both to his head and heart that no greater mistakes have been committed or even wrongs perpetrated while she sat making tatting and snipping paper flowers. Man's own innate chivalry and the mutual interdependence of their interests have insured his treating her cause, in the main at least, as his own. And he is pardonably surprised and even a little chagrined, perhaps, to find his legislation not considered "perfectly lovely" in every respect. But in any case his work is only impoverished by her remaining dumb. The world has had to limp along with the wobbling gait and one-sided hesitancy of a man with one eye. Suddenly the bandage is removed from the other eye and the whole body is filled with light. It sees a circle where before it saw a segment. The darkened eye restored, every member rejoices with it.

The myopic sight of the darkened eye can only be restored when the full range of the black woman's voice, with its own special timbres and shadings, remains mute no longer.

Similarly, Victoria Earle Matthews, an author of short stories and essays, and a cofounder in 1896 of the National Association of Colored Women, wrote in her stunning essay, "The Value of Race Literature" (1895), that "when the literature of our race is developed, it will of necessity be different in all essential points of greatness, true heroism and real Christianity from what we may at the present time, for convenience, call American literature." Matthews argued that this great tradition of Afro-American literature would be the textual outlet "for the unnaturally suppressed inner lives which our people have been compelled to lead." Once these "unnaturally suppressed inner lives" of black people are unveiled, no "grander diffusion of mental light" will shine more brightly, she concludes, than that of the articulate Afro-American woman:

> And now comes the question, What part shall we women play in the Race Literature of the future? . . . within the compass of one small journal ["Woman's Era"] we have struck out a new line of departure—a journal, a record of Race interests gathered from all parts of the United States, carefully selected, moistened, winnowed and garnered by the ablest intellects of educated colored women, shrinking at no lofty theme, shirking no serious duty, aiming at every possible excellence, and determined to do their part in the future uplifting of the race.
>
> If twenty women, by their concentrated efforts in one literary movement, can meet with such success as has engendered, planned out, and so successfully consummated this convention, what much more glorious results, what wider spread success, what grander diffusion of mental light will not come forth at the bidding of the enlarged hosts of women writers, already called into being by the stimulus of your efforts?
>
> And here let me speak one word for my journalistic sisters

> who have already entered the broad arena of journalism. Before the "Woman's Era" had come into existence, no one except themselves can appreciate the bitter experience and sore disappointments under which they have at all times been compelled to pursue their chosen vocations.
>
> If their brothers of the press have had their difficulties to contend with, I am here as a sister journalist to state, from the fullness of knowledge, that their task has been an easy one compared with that of the colored woman in journalism.
>
> Woman's part in Race Literature, as in Race building, is the most important part and has been so in all ages. . . . All through the most remote epochs she has done her share in literature. . . .

One of the most important aspects of this set is the republication of the salient texts from 1890 to 1910, which literary historians could well call "The Black Woman's Era." In addition to Mary Helen Washington's definitive edition of Cooper's *A Voice From the South*, we have reprinted two novels by Amelia Johnson, Frances Harper's *Iola Leroy*, two novels by Emma Dunham Kelley, Alice Dunbar-Nelson's two impressive collections of short stories, and Pauline Hopkins's three serialized novels as well as her monumental novel, *Contending Forces*—all published between 1890 and 1910. Indeed, black women published more works of fiction in these two decades than black men had published in the previous half century. Nevertheless, this great achievement has been ignored.

Moreover, the writings of nineteenth-century Afro-American women in general have remained buried in obscurity, accessible only in research libraries or in overpriced and poorly edited reprints. Many of these books have never been reprinted at all; in some instances only one or two copies are extant. In these works of fiction, poetry, autobiography, biography, essays, and journalism resides the mind of the nineteenth-century Afro-American woman. Until these works are made readily available to teachers and their students, a significant segment of the black tradition will remain silent.

Oxford University Press, in collaboration with the Schomburg Center for Research in Black Culture, is publishing thirty volumes of these compelling works, each of which contains an introduction by an expert in the field. The set includes such rare texts as Johnson's *The Hazeley Family* and *Clarence and Corinne,* Plato's *Essays,* the most complete edition of Phillis Wheatley's poems and letters, Emma Dunham Kelley's pioneering novel *Megda,* several previously unpublished stories and a novel by Alice Dunbar-Nelson, and the first collected volumes of Pauline Hopkins's three serialized novels and Frances Harper's poetry. We also present four volumes of poetry by such women as Mary Eliza Tucker Lambert, Adah Menken, Josephine Heard, and Maggie Johnson. Numerous slave and spiritual narratives, a newly discovered novel—*Four Girls at Cottage City*—by Emma Dunham Kelley (-Hawkins), and the first American edition of *Wonderful Adventures of Mrs. Seacole in Many Lands* are also among the texts included.

In addition to resurrecting the works of black women authors, it is our hope that this set will facilitate the resurrection of the Afro-American woman's literary tradition itself by unearthing its nineteenth-century roots. In the works of Nella Larsen and Jessie Fauset, Zora Neale Hurston and Ann Petry, Lorraine Hansberry and Gwendolyn Brooks, Paule Marshall and Toni Cade Bambara, Audre Lorde and Rita Dove, Toni Morrison and Alice Walker, Gloria Naylor and Jamaica Kincaid, these roots have branched luxuriantly. The eighteenth- and nineteenth-century authors whose works are presented in this set founded and nurtured the black women's literary tradition, which must be revived, explicated, analyzed, and debated before we can understand more completely the formal shaping of this tradition within a tradition, a coded literary universe through which, regrettably, we are only just beginning to navigate our way. As Anna Cooper said nearly one hundred years ago, we have been blinded by the loss of sight in one eye and have therefore been unable to detect the full *shape* of the Afro-American literary tradition.

Literary works configure into a tradition not because of some mystical collective unconscious determined by the biology of race or gender, but because writers read other writers and *ground* their representations of experience in models of language provided largely by other writers to whom they feel akin. It is through this mode of literary revision, amply evident in the *texts* themselves—in formal echoes, recast metaphors, even in parody—that a "tradition" emerges and defines itself.

This is formal bonding, and it is only through formal bonding that we can know a literary tradition. The collective publication of these works by black women now, for the first time, makes it possible for scholars and critics, male and female, black and white, to *demonstrate* that black women writers read, and revised, other black women writers. To demonstrate this set of formal literary relations is to demonstrate that sexuality, race, and gender are both the condition and the basis of *tradition*—but tradition as found in discrete acts of language use.

A word is in order about the history of this set. For the past decade, I have taught a course, first at Yale and then at Cornell, entitled "Black Women and Their Fictions," a course that I inherited from Toni Morrison, who developed it in the mid-1970s for Yale's Program in Afro-American Studies. Although the course was inspired by the remarkable accomplishments of black women novelists since 1970, I gradually extended its beginning date to the late nineteenth century, studying Frances Harper's *Iola Leroy* and Anna Julia Cooper's *A Voice From the South,* both published in 1892. With the discovery of Harriet E. Wilson's seminal novel, *Our Nig* (1859), and Jean Yellin's authentication of Harriet Jacobs's brilliant slave narrative, *Incidents in the Life of a Slave Girl* (1861), a survey course spanning over a century and a quarter emerged.

But the discovery of *Our Nig,* as well as the interest in nineteenth-century black women's writing that this discovery generated, convinced me that even the most curious and diligent scholars knew very little of the extensive history of the creative writings of Afro-American women before 1900. Indeed, most scholars of Afro-American literature had never even read most of the books published by black women, simply because these books—of poetry, novels, short stories, essays, and autobiography—were mostly accessible only in rare book sections of university libraries. For reasons unclear to me even today, few of these marvelous renderings of the Afro-American woman's consciousness were reprinted in the late 1960s and early 1970s, when so many other texts of the Afro-American literary tradition were resurrected from the dark and silent graveyard of the out-of-print and were reissued in facsimile editions aimed at the hungry readership for canonical texts in the nascent field of black studies.

So, with the help of several superb research assistants—including David Curtis, Nicola Shilliam, Wendy Jones, Sam Otter, Janadas Devan, Suvir Kaul, Cynthia Bond, Elizabeth Alexander, and Adele Alexander—and with the expert advice of scholars such as William Robinson, William Andrews, Mary Helen Washington, Maryemma Graham, Jean Yellin, Houston A. Baker, Jr., Richard Yarborough, Hazel Carby, Joan R. Sherman, Frances Foster, and William French, dozens of bibliographies were used to compile a list of books written or narrated by black women mostly before 1910. Without the assistance provided through this shared experience of scholarship, the scholar's true legacy, this project could not have been conceived. As the list grew, I was struck by how very many of these titles that I, for example, had never even heard of, let alone read, such as Ann Plato's *Essays,* Louisa Picquet's slave narrative, or Amelia Johnson's two novels, *Clarence and Corinne* and *The Hazeley Family*. Through our research with the Black Periodical Fiction and Poetry Project (funded by NEH and the Ford Foundation), I also realized that several novels by black women, including three works of fiction by Pauline Hopkins, had been serialized in black periodicals, but had never been collected and published as books. Nor had the several books of poetry published by black women, such as the prolific Frances E. W. Harper, been collected and edited. When I discovered still another "lost" novel by an Afro-American woman (*Four Girls at Cottage City,* published in 1898 by Emma Dunham Kelley-Hawkins), I decided to attempt to edit a collection of reprints of these works and to publish them as a "library" of black women's writings, in part so that I could read them myself.

Convincing university and trade publishers to undertake this project proved to be a difficult task. Despite the commercial success of *Our Nig* and of the several reprint series of women's works (such as Virago, the Beacon Black Women Writers Series, and Rutgers' American Women Writers Series), several presses rejected the project as "too large," "too limited," or as "commercially unviable." Only two publishers recognized the viability and the import of the project and, of these, Oxford's commitment to publish the titles simultaneously as a set made the press's offer irresistible.

While attempting to locate original copies of these exceedingly rare books, I discovered that most of the texts were housed at the Schomburg Center for Research in Black Culture, a branch of The New York Public Library, under the direction of Howard Dodson. Dodson's infectious enthusiasm for the project and his generous collaboration, as well as that of his stellar staff (especially Diana Lachatanere, Sharon Howard, Ellis Haizip, Richard Newman, and Betty Gubert), led to a joint publishing initiative that produced this set as part of the Schomburg's major fund-raising campaign. Without Dodson's foresight and generosity of spirit, the set would not have materialized. Without William P. Sisler's masterful editorship at Oxford and his staff's careful attention to detail, the set would have remained just another grand idea that tends to languish in a scholar's file cabinet.

I would also like to thank Dr. Michael Winston and Dr. Thomas C. Battle, Vice-President of Academic Affairs and the Director of the Moorland-Spingarn Research Center (respectively) at Howard University, for their unending encouragement, support, and collaboration in this project, and Esme E. Bhan at Howard for her meticulous research and bibliographical skills. In addition, I would like to acknowledge the aid of the staff at the libraries of Duke University, Cornell University (especially Tom Weissinger and Donald Eddy), the Boston Public Library, the Western Reserve Historical Society, the Library of Congress, and Yale University. Linda Robbins, Marion Osmun, Sarah Flanagan, and Gerard Case, all members of the staff at Oxford, were extraordinarily effective at coordinating, editing, and producing the various segments of each text in the set. Candy Ruck, Nina de Tar, and Phillis Molock expertly typed reams of correspondence and manuscripts connected to the project.

I would also like to express my gratitude to my colleagues who edited and introduced the individual titles in the set. Without their attention to detail, their willingness to meet strict deadlines, and their sheer enthusiasm for this project, the set could not have been published. But finally and ultimately, I would hope that the publication of the set would help to generate even more scholarly interest in the black women authors whose work is presented here. Struggling against the seemingly insurmountable barriers of racism *and* sexism, while often raising families and fulfilling full-time professional obligations, these women managed nevertheless to record their thoughts and feelings and to *testify* to all who dare read them that the will to harness the power of collective endurance and survival is the will to write.

The Schomburg Library of Nineteenth-Century Black Women Writers is dedicated in memory of Pauline Augusta Coleman Gates, who died in the spring of 1987. It was she who inspired in me the love of learning and the love of literature. I have encountered in the books of this set no will more determined, no courage more noble, no mind more sublime, no self more celebratory of the achievements of all Afro-American women, and indeed of life itself, than her own.

A NOTE FROM THE SCHOMBURG CENTER

Howard Dodson

The Schomburg Center for Research in Black Culture, The New York Public Library, is pleased to join with Dr. Henry Louis Gates and Oxford University Press in presenting The Schomburg Library of Nineteenth-Century Black Women Writers. This thirty-volume set includes the work of a generation of black women whose writing has only been available previously in rare book collections. The materials reprinted in twenty-four of the thirty volumes are drawn from the unique holdings of the Schomburg Center.

A research unit of The New York Public Library, the Schomburg Center has been in the forefront of those institutions dedicated to collecting, preserving, and providing access to the records of the black past. In the course of its two generations of acquisition and conservation activity, the Center has amassed collections totaling more than 5 million items. They include over 100,000 bound volumes, 85,000 reels and sets of microforms, 300 manuscript collections containing some 3.5 million items, 300,000 photographs and extensive holdings of prints, sound recordings, film and videotape, newspapers, artworks, artifacts, and other book and nonbook materials. Together they vividly document the history and cultural heritages of people of African descent worldwide.

Though established some sixty-two years ago, the Center's book collections date from the sixteenth century. Its oldest item, an Ethiopian Coptic Tunic, dates from the eighth or ninth century. Rare materials, however, are most available for the nineteenth-century African-American experience. It is from these holdings that the majority of the titles selected for inclusion in this set are drawn.

The nineteenth century was a formative period in African-American literary and cultural history. Prior to the Civil War, the majority of black Americans living in the United States were held in bondage. Law and practice forbade teaching them to read or write. Even after the war, many of the impediments to learning and literary productivity remained. Nevertheless, black men and women of the nineteenth century persevered in both areas. Moreover, more African-Americans than we yet realize turned their observations, feelings, social viewpoints, and creative impulses into published works. In time, this nineteenth-century printed record included poetry, short stories, histories, novels, autobiographies, social criticism, and theology, as well as economic and philosophical treatises. Unfortunately, much of this body of literature remained, until very recently, relatively inaccessible to twentieth-century scholars, teachers, creative artists, and others interested in black life. Prior to the late 1960s, most Americans (black as well as white) had never heard of these nineteenth-century authors, much less read their works.

The civil rights and black power movements created unprecedented interest in the thought, behavior, and achievements of black people. Publishers responded by revising traditional texts, introducing the American public to a new generation of African-American writers, publishing a variety of thematic anthologies, and reprinting a plethora of "classic texts" in African-American history, literature, and art. The reprints usually appeared as individual titles or in a series of bound volumes or microform formats.

The Schomburg Center, which has a long history of supporting publishing that deals with the history and culture of Africans in diaspora, became an active participant in many of the reprint revivals of the 1960s. Since hard copies of original printed works are the preferred formats for producing facsimile reproductions, publishers frequently turned to the Schomburg Center for copies of these original titles. In addition to providing such material, Schomburg Center staff members offered advice and consultation, wrote introductions, and occasionally entered into formal copublishing arrangements in some projects.

Most of the nineteenth-century titles reprinted during the 1960s, however, were by and about black men. A few black women were included in the longer series, but works by lesser known black women were generally overlooked. The Schomburg Library of Nineteenth-Century Black Women Writers is both a corrective to these previous omissions and an important contribution to Afro-American literary history in its own right. Through this collection of volumes, the thoughts, perspectives, and creative abilities of nineteenth-century African-American women, as captured in books and pamphlets published in large part before 1910, are again being made available to the general public. The Schomburg Center is pleased to be a part of this historic endeavor.

I would like to thank Professor Gates for initiating this project. Thanks are due both to him and Mr. William P. Sisler of Oxford University Press for giving the Schomburg Center an opportunity to play such a prominent role in the set. Thanks are also due to my colleagues at The New York Public Library and the Schomburg Center, especially Dr. Vartan Gregorian, Richard De Gennaro, Paul Fasana, Betsy

Pinover, Richard Newman, Diana Lachatanere, Glenderlyn Johnson, and Harold Anderson for their assistance and support. I can think of no better way of demonstrating than in this set the role the Schomburg Center plays in assuring that the black heritage will be available for future generations.

INTRODUCTION

Randall K. Burkett

Church, school, and club constitute the triumvirate of associations central to the lives of the women chronicled in *Homespun Heroines and Other Women of Distinction*, compiled and edited by Hallie Quinn Brown. Originally published in 1926, this volume contains the biographies of sixty Afro-American women born in the United States or Canada between the mid-1740s and the end of the nineteenth century. Except for the six sketches reprinted from Delilah L. Beasley's *Negro Trail Blazers of California* and one essay reprinted from the *American Review*, all of the biographies were written expressly for this volume.

The principle author and editor, Hallie Q. Brown, had already passed her seventy-fifth year when the book was published; she was thus a contemporary of many of her subjects. Indeed, her own life is in many respects typical of the women whose lives are chronicled here. Though both her parents had been slaves, she was born free in Pittsburgh, Pennsylvania, on March 10, 1850. Her paternal grandmother, a Scottish plantation owner in Frederick County, Maryland, had permitted her son, Thomas Arthur Brown, to buy his own freedom on his twenty-fifth birthday. Hallie's mother, Frances Jane Scroggins, had been freed by her maternal grandfather, a Virginia planter and Revolutionary War soldier.

Hallie's parents were energetic, hard-working, and pious, and they strove to provide educational opportunity for their children. As is evident in *Homespun Heroines*' sketches of her mother (pp. 71–80) and an aunt, Eliza Anna Scroggins Austin (pp. 81–83), Hallie's youth was relatively privileged, though clearly it was not free from hardship. Bishops of the African Methodist Episcopal (AME) Church and travelers on the Underground Railroad frequented her family's home. Her older siblings attended Avery College in Pennsylvania, and in 1864 the family moved to Canada. In 1870 the family decided to move to Wilberforce, Ohio, so that Hallie and her younger brother could attend the college recently purchased for the AME Church by long-time family friend and bishop, Daniel Alexander Payne. Hallie graduated from Wilberforce University in 1873 and immediately responded to the call for teachers in the Reconstruction South. Over the next twenty years she alternated between South and North, teaching in Yazoo, Mississippi; Dayton, Ohio; Columbia, South Carolina; and Tuskegee, Alabama. In 1893 she was offered a faculty appointment at Wilberforce University, with which she was associated in a variety of capacities throughout the rest of her life.

She was an accomplished elocutionist, having graduated from the Chatauqua Lecture School in 1886. Her lectures were heard not only throughout the United States but also in England, Scotland, Wales, and elsewhere in Europe. She was actively engaged in temperance work, women's suffrage, and the demand for equal rights for Afro-Americans. Centrally involved in women's clubs at the local, state, and national levels, she was one of the founders of the National Association of Colored Women's Clubs, served as president of the Ohio Federation of Colored Women's Clubs from 1905–1912, and was president of the National Association from 1920–1924. Throughout her life she was active in the AME Church and was chosen to represent its Woman's Parent Mite Missionary Society at the 1910 World Conference on Missions in Edinburgh. Never married, she lived with her mother in Wilberforce. Her mother died there at the age of ninety-four in 1914; Hallie's own death occurred there thirty-six years later, in her one hundredth year.[1]

Although Hallie Brown herself wrote the largest number of essays (twenty-one) published in *Homespun Heroines*, a total of twenty-eight women were involved in the collaborative effort to create the book. Maritcha R. Lyons, the prominent Brooklyn educator and club woman, authored eight lengthy and valuable essays; Anna H. Jones and Ora B. Stokes each wrote three sketches; and Sarah L. Fleming wrote two. All the remaining authors contributed a single biography. Many of the writers knew their subjects personally, as mothers, grandmothers, or aunts; as teachers or mentors; or as friends; hence, the sketches are written with the special insight and appreciation that such familiarity can bring.

The essays are arranged in chronological order by date of birth of subject. Five of the subjects (Martha Payne, Catherine Ferguson, Phillis Wheatley, Sara Allen, and Sojourner Truth) were born during the eighteenth century. Though no more than a half dozen of the women included were born after Emancipation, only thirteen are identified as having themselves been slaves. Nearly forty percent of the women (22) were born in the upper southern states of Virginia (9), Kentucky (5), Maryland (5), Tennessee (2), and North Carolina (1); slightly more than thirty percent (a total of 17) were born in the northeastern states of New York (6), Massachusetts (4), Pennsylvania (3), Connecticut (1), New Jersey (1), Delaware (1), and Rhode Island (1). Four women were native to the deep South states of Louisiana, Mississippi, Georgia, or South Carolina; and two were born in the midwestern states of Indiana and Ohio. One woman, Fannie Jackson Coppin, was born in the District of Columbia; Lucy Smith Thurman was born in Canada; and Phillis Wheatley was born in Africa. None was born in the West Indies.[2]

Although nearly half the women were born in the South, only seven made their home there. Three women resided in Richmond, Virginia, while the others lived in South Carolina, Arkansas, Alabama, and Florida. It is not surprising, given the locus of Hallie Brown's own life and work, that the Midwest was the home of the largest number of women whose biographies are included. At least nine resided in the Dayton-Xenia-Wilberforce area, while four others lived elsewhere in Ohio. Three lived in Illinois (Chicago) and Michigan, while two were in Missouri and one in Keokuk, Iowa.

Only eight women appear to have lived all their lives in a single community; four of these were New Yorkers and two were Bostonians. A total of six women eventually resided in Boston and five in New York or Brooklyn, while others in the Northeast made their homes in Philadelphia (2), Pittsburgh (2), Providence (1), Kingston, Rhode Island (1), Worcester, Massachusetts (1), Auburn, New York (1), Buffalo (1), and Gouldtown, New Jersey (1). Two women resided in the District of Columbia, while one emigrated to Liberia and one went as a missionary to Haiti, where she died.

The women whose lives are chronicled here were extraordinarily talented, and they tended to be involved in so many different activities that it is often difficult to categorize them by occupation. At least nineteen were teachers at one time or another during their careers, while at least ten were distinguished for their church work. Others in the helping professions include nurses (4) and social workers (2). Among those who were noted for their public speaking, four could be characterized as antislavery activists and another four as professional elocutionists. Three were poets, while three others were musicians. Two were physicians, while two others were journalists, and one was a lawyer. Among businesswomen, one ran a boarding house, one was a cakemaker, and one (Madam C. J. Walker) made her fortune in the cosmetic business. At least five women were described as homemakers, while two were described as quilters or knitters, and one served as a maid in the White House. The latter, Elizabeth Keckley, also taught domestic arts at Wilberforce University.

Of the seven women who did not marry, five were teachers, one was a poet, and one was an antislavery activist who later became involved in temperance, club, and church work. The overwhelming majority of women had one or two children, while only six had eight or more offspring. Three of these women were among the five described in their biography as homemaker. Author Maritcha R. Lyons observed that among these women as a whole, though most were matrons, a fair number were unmarried. "Neither class [however] allowed the confines of the hearth to limit the extent of their reasonable ambitions" (p. 170).

In virtually all the biographies, it is evident that religion and church were central to the lives of these women. Fully twenty-five percent were members of the AME Church, while three were identified as being members of the Baptist, Episcopal, Presbyterian, or Methodist churches. Two were Congregationalists, and one was a member of the African Methodist Episcopal Zion Church. Much has been written about the centrality of the black church as the major institution that was owned and controlled by the black community. Far less has been written, however, about the role that black women played in the church's creation, development, and mainte-

1913); Mary Campbell Mossell Griffin, *Afro-American Men and Women Who Count* (n.p., 1915); Delilah L. Beasley, *Negro Trail Blazers of California* (Los Angeles, 1919); Elizabeth Ross Haynes, *Unsung Heroes* (New York, 1921); Elizabeth Lindsey Davis, *The Story of the Illinois Federation of Colored Women's Clubs, 1900–1922* (Chicago?, 1922); and Z. Annetta Rhone, *Oklahoma Historical and Pictoral Review* (n.p., 1925).

Homespun Heroines is distinguished in this list as a collaborative effort by a group of self-confident and historically self-conscious black women who were determined to preserve the stories of sacrifice and struggle that their forebears had endured. The book offers fruitful ground for research into female networks, patterns of voluntary association, work, family life, and black female culture of the nineteenth and early twentieth centuries. Of course, the essays also offer indispensable starting points for biographical research on a substantial number of extraordinary women.

NOTES

1. Biographical information is drawn from the essays by Charles H. Wesley in *Notable American Women*, vol. 1 (Cambridge, 1971), pp. 253–54, and by George T. Johnson in *Dictionary of American Negro Biography* (New York, 1982), pp. 67–68. Further details may be found in Charles H. Wesley, *The History of the National Association of Colored Women's Clubs; A Legacy of Service* (Washington, D.C., 1984); and in Annjennete S. McFarlin, "Hallie Quinn Brown: Black Woman Elocutionist," *The Southern Speech Communication Journal* 46 (1980):72–82. Secondary sources disagree concerning the year of Hallie Q. Brown's birth, a matter about which

she was secretive throughout her life. We have followed the date given by Charles H. Wesley, which is also the date appearing on her headstone in the Wilberforce cemetery.

2. For statistical purposes throughout, we have excluded the six women whose biographies are reprinted from Delilah Beasley's narrative. These biographies have a different format, origin, and purpose than the other essays in the volume. Total numbers in different categories vary, since not all information was known or presented by each writer.

3. Wesley, *History*, p. 12.

MISS HALLIE Q. BROWN
Hon. President of the N. A. C. W.

HOMESPUN HEROINES

AND OTHER

WOMEN OF DISTINCTION

COMPILED AND EDITED

By

HALLIE Q. BROWN

AUTHOR OF

"Bits And Odds" *"First Lessons In Public Speaking"*
"Tales My Father Told"
"Machile — The African"

Foreword By

MRS. JOSEPHINE TURPIN WASHINGTON

ILLUSTRATED FROM
PHOTOGRAPHS FROM WIDELY DIFFERENT SOURCES

Published at
THE ALDINE PUBLISHING COMPANY
Xenia, Ohio, U. S. A.

IN MEMORY OF THE MANY MOTHERS WHO WERE LOYAL IN TENSE AND TRYING TIMES, THIS VOLUME IS AFFECTIONATELY

DEDICATED

TO

THE NATIONAL ASSOCIATION OF COLORED WOMEN OF AMERICA AND CANADA

Through all the blight of slavery
They kept their womanhood,
And now they march with heads erect,
To fight for all things good,
Nor care for scorn nor seek for praise,
Just so they please their God.

—CLARA ANN THOMPSON.

FOREWORD

Interesting as are the facts recorded in this book, they do not constitute its chief value.

That is found in its reflection of the wonderful spirit which moved the women who strove and achieved, despite obstacles greater than any which have stood in the way of other upward struggles.

These sketches breathe aspiration, hope, courage, patience, fortitude, faith.

The youth of today and of other days will come under this influence. They will not relive those lives. That cannot be: conditions change; human beings differ; deeds cannot be duplicated. But the spirit of the noble dead may be enkindled in the hearts of those who live after.

It is said that one can appreciate only that to which he has some inner likeness. The author's spiritual kinship with the women of whom she wrote made possible the rare understanding brought to her subject.

The result is a work which not only furnishes useful information, but—what is even more—inspires to finer character growth and racial development.

—JOSEPHINE TURPIN WASHINGTON.

INTRODUCTION

To My Readers—Greeting:

This book is presented as an evidence of appreciation and as a token of regard to the history-making women of our race.

One chief object of these introductory sentences is to secure for this book the interest of our youth, that they may have instructive light on the struggles endured and the obstacles overcome by our pioneer women.

It has been prepared with the hope that they will read it and derive fresh strength and courage from its records to stimulate and cause them to cleave more tenaciously to the truth and to battle more heroically for the right.

The characters and facts herein set forth are veritable history.

In presenting this volume to the public, it is proper to remark that it has been prepared from a settled conviction that something of the kind is needed.

It is our anxious desire to preserve for future reference an account of these women, their life and character and what they accomplished under the most trying and adverse circumstances,—some of whom passed scatheless through fires of tribulation, only to emerge the purer and stronger,—some who received their commission even at the furnace door, the one moment thinking their all was lost forever, the next in secure consciousness of the Everlasting Arms.

We lack a complete record of these self-sacrificing heroines, but such as we have been permitted to gather we present through this medium to the public, hoping that it may find as much pleasure in its perusal as the writer had in its making.

—HALLIE Q. BROWN.

Homewood Cottage,
Wilberforce, Ohio.
1926.

ODE TO WOMAN

All to Woman! the mother of man,
Whose worth can never be measured.
Her moral and mental and physical life
As mother, or sister, or sweetheart, or wife,
And oft, too, as friend, is e'er treasured.
Her role is extensive and varied through earth;
Her service far-reaching and wide.
The Queen of the hearth and the home and the church;
While the club and the school come under her rule,
And all secular business beside.
The "Joy of Service," her fond heart endures,
From infancy, through many years
Of development; mingled with faith, hope and trust,
She builds to the great, the good and the just,
That the Future may fairly decide.
All hail to our Women! the welkin shall ring,
As the Queen of the Earth passes by.
'Tis her's to "Lift" as she "Climbs" to the heights;
'Tis her's to make day of the darkest of nights,
Let all earth sing her praises aloud.

—Sarah G. Jones,
Poet Laureate of Ohio State Federation.

MARTHA PAYNE
Mother of Daniel A. Payne
Founder of Wilberforce University

MARTHA PAYNE

The silhouette of Martha Payne as shown in this volume is probably one hundred and thirty years old. It represents the mother of Daniel Alexander Payne. We have meagre information of this mother and what we glean is told by her son after she had been dead more than fifty years.

We learn that London and Martha Payne were free born and lived in Charleston, South Carolina. They were earnest Christians and faithful observers of family worship. "Often," says this son, "their morning prayers and hymns aroused me from my infant sleep and slumbers." He was taught the alphabet by his father, but was bereft by death, of his paternal care at the age of four and a half years. When he was nine years old his mother died leaving him in charge of a grand aunt "whose godly lessons and holy example stimulated me to attain unto a noble character."

Of his father he says, he was one of six brothers who served in the Revolutionary War. Their father was an Englishman. Daniel had a clear recollection of the rejoicing after the close of the war of 1812 when the city of Charleston was illuminated and, that he might see the objects of interest more clearly, his father carried him through the streets on his shoulders. He describes his mother as a woman of light brown complexion, medium stature and delicate in frame. Her grandmother was of a tribe of Indians known in the early history of the Carolinas as the Catawba Indians. Her grandfather was remarkable for great bodily strength and activity.

Martha Payne was a woman of amiable disposition, gentle manners, and fervent piety. He remembers the custom of his mother which was to take "her little Daniel" by the hand and lead him to the house of God, seating him by her side. In this way he became early impressed with strong religious feelings. Again he says, "I was the child of many prayers. My parents prayed for a son and before my birth I was dedicated to the Lord. Afterward I was taken to the house of God and again consecrated to His service in the holy ordinance of baptism." When but a lad of eight years through that mother's godly example and early instruction he was converted and daily sought his closet "beseeching the Lord to make me a good boy."

Thus this mother, Martha Payne, early impressed her child with high, honorable impulses which were to develop into traits of noble character, making the name of Daniel Alexander Payne renowned on two hemispheres for eighty years as a man of deep piety, unsullied reputation, an educator of first rank, a champion for human rights and honorable prelate of the African Methodist Episcopal Church.

CATHERINE FERGUSON
Founder of the First Sunday School Movement in New York City

CATHERINE FERGUSON

1749 (?)—1854

FOUNDER OF THE FIRST SUNDAY SCHOOL MOVEMENT IN NEW YORK CITY

In the 1922 edition of Cubberley's History of Education we find this: "In 1793 Katy Ferguson's School for the Poor was opened in New York, and this was followed by an organization of New York women for the extension of secular instruction among the poor."

So meagre were opportunities for education of any sort for the poor that this effort is given significant place in the early beginnings of American education. The Sunday School movement, originated by John Wesley and worked out in England by Raikes in 1780, had two years previous made a start in Philadelphia. Katy Ferguson, with no knowledge of the Raikes' movement, with scant material, and with no preparation save her piety and her warm mother's heart, gave to New York City its first Sunday School; and because Sunday Schools at first gave secular as well as religious instruction, her name is recorded with other early American educators.

For the fact that Catherine Ferguson was an ex-slave, we are indebted to Lossing's Eminent Americans, published in 1883. She was well known and highly respected in New York City. The accompanying cut is from a daguerrotype "taken in 1850 at the instance of Lewis Tappan, Esq., and later owned by the Rev. Henry Ward Beecher."

From the historian Lossing we gain the facts given here. She was born a slave while her mother was on her passage from Virginia to New York. At the tender age of eight her mother was sold from her, "which taught her to sympathize with desolate children." She secured her freedom partly through her own efforts and partly through the benevolence of others. For fifty years she was held in high esteem as a professional cake-maker. At eighteen she was married. She lost her two children and from that time "put forth pious efforts for the good of bereaved and desolate little ones." In her ministrations she took from the almshouse and from dissolute parents forty-eight children, twenty of them white, rearing them herself or finding homes for them.

In her life of toil and sacrifice, there was not time for learning to read. She, however, attended Divine service regularly under the excellent Dr. Mason and, not content to enjoy this religious instruction for herself alone, she gathered into her humble dwelling in Warren Street the neglected children of the neighborhood, black and white. "Sometimes the sainted Isabella Graham would invite Katy and her scholars to her house, and there hear them recite the catechism, and give them instruction. Finally, Dr. Mason heard of her school, and visited it one Sunday morning. 'What are you about here, Katy?' he asked. 'Keeping school on the Sabbath?' Katy was troubled, for she thought his question a rebuke. 'This must not be, Katy; you must not be allowed to do all this work alone,' he continued; and then he invited her to transfer her school to the basement of his new church in Murray Street, where he procured assistants for her." Some of New York's most eminent divines were in later years proud to trace their experience to helping in Katy Ferguson's Sunday School. Among these may be cited the Rev. Dr. Ferris, sometime Chancellor of New York University.

And so it is that this humble handmaiden of the Lord has come into her own in the annals of educational achievement and is reckoned worthy to be named with Plato, Rousseau, Herbart, Pestalozzi, and Horace Mann.

PHILLIS WHEATLEY
First Poet of the Negro Race

PHILLIS WHEATLEY

1754—1783 (?)

'Twas mercy brought me from my Pagan land,
Taught my benighted soul to understand
That there's a God—that there's a Savior, too,
Once I redemption neither sought nor knew.

—PHILLIS WHEATLEY.

In the year 1761, a little slave girl about seven years old, stood in the market place in Boston, Massachusetts, with a number of others to be sold as chattel.

The little girl had been brought from far off Africa. She stood a pitiful looking object with no clothing save a piece of dirty, ragged carpet tied around her. Mrs. John Wheatley had several slaves, but they were growing too old to be active and she wished to purchase a young girl, whom she could train up in such a manner as to make a good domestic. For this purpose she went to the slave market and there she saw the little girl who appeared to be in ill health, which no doubt was due to the suffering she endured in the slave-ship on the long voyage. Mrs. Wheatley was a kind, religious woman and though she considered the sickly look of the child an objection, there was something so gentle and modest in the expression of her dark countenance and her large mournful eyes that her heart was drawn toward her and she bought her in preference to several others who looked more robust. She took her home in her chaise, gave her a bath and dressed her in clean clothes. They could not at first understand her and she resorted to signs and gestures for she spoke only her native African dialect and a few words of broken English. Mrs. Wheatley gave her the name of Phillis Wheatley, little dreaming that it, and the little slave girl she had rescued, would become renowned in American history.

Phillis soon learned to speak English, but she could tell nothing of herself nor when she was torn from her parents by the slave-traders, nor where she had been since that time. The poor, little orphan had gone through so much suffering and terror that her mind had become bewildered concerning the past.

The only thing that clung to her about Africa was seeing her mother pour out water before the rising sun which would indicate that the mother descended from some remote tribe of sun-worshippers. And that sight of her mother doing reverence before the great luminous orb coming as it did out of the nowhere, but giving light and cheer to the world, naturally impressed the child's imagination so deeply that she remembered it when all else was forgotten about her native land. In the course of a year and a half a wonderful change took place in the little, forlorn stranger. She not only learned to speak English correctly, but was able to read fluently in any part of the Bible. She possessed uncommon intelligence and a great desire for knowledge. She was often found trying to make letters with charcoal on the walls and fences. Mrs. Wheatley's daughter became her teacher. She found this an easy task for the pupil learned with astonishing quickness. At the same time she showed such an amiable, affectionate disposition that all the members of the family became much attached to her. Her gratitude to her motherly benefactress was unbounded and her greatest delight was to do anything to please her. At the age of fourteen she began to write poetry. Owing to such uncommon manifestations of intelligence, she was never put to hard household work. She became the companion of Mrs. Wheatley and her daughter. Her poetry attracted attention and friends of Mrs. Wheatley lent her books which she read with great eagerness. She soon acquired a good knowledge of geography, history and English poetry. After a while she learned Latin which she so far mastered as to be able to read it understandingly. There was no law in Massachusetts against slaves learning to read and write and Mrs. Wheatley did everything to encourage her love of learning. She always called her affectionately "My Phillis" and seemed to be as proud of her attainments as if she had been her own daughter. Phillis was very religious and at the age of sixteen joined the Orthodox Church that worshipped in the Old-South Meeting-house in Boston. Her character and deportment were such that she was considered an ornament to the church. Clergymen and other literary persons who visited Mrs. Wheatley's home took a great deal of notice of her. Her poems were brought forward to be read by the company and were often praised.

She was often invited to the homes of wealthy and distinguished people but she was not turned by so much flattery and attention. Seriousness and humility were natural to Phillis and she retained the same gentle, modest deportment that had won Mrs. Wheatley's heart when she first saw her in the market-place. Although tenderly cared for and not required to do any fatiguing work, her constitution never recovered from the shock it had received in early childhood. At the age of nineteen her health failed so rapidly that physicians said it was necessary for her to take a sea-voyage. A son of Mrs. Wheatley was going to England on commercial business and his mother proposed that Phillis should go with him. In England she received even more attention than had been bestowed upon her at home. Several of the nobility invited her to their houses and her poems were published in a volume with an engraved likeness of the author. Still the young poet was not spoiled by flattery. A relative of Mrs. Wheatley remarked that not all the attention she received, nor all the honors that men heaped upon her had the slightest influence upon her temper and deportment. She was the same simple-hearted, unsophisticated being. She addressed a poem to the Earl of Dartmouth who was very kind to her during her visit to England. Having expressed a hope for the over-throw of tyranny she says:

"Should you, my Lord, while you peruse my song,
Wonder from whence my love of Freedom sprung,—
Whence flow these wishes for the common good,
By feeling hearts alone best understood,—
I, young in life, by seeming cruel fate,
Was snatched from Afric's fancied happy state.
What pangs excruciating must molest,
What sorrows labor in my parent's breast!
Steeled was that soul, and by no misery moved,
That from a father seized his babe beloved.
Such was my case; and can I then but pray
Others may never feel tyrannic sway."

King George, the third, was soon expected in London and the English friends of Phillis wished to present her to their king; but letters from America informed her of the declining health of her beloved Mrs. Wheatley and she greatly desired to see her. No honors could divert her mind from the friend of her childhood. She returned to Boston immediately. The good lady died soon after. Mr. Wheatley soon followed and the daughter, the kind teacher of her youth, did not long survive. The son married and settled in England. For a short time Phillis remained with a friend of Mrs. Wheatley, then she rented a room and lived by herself. It was a sad change for her. The war of the American Revolution broke out. In the Autumn of 1776, General Washington had his headquarters at Cambridge, Massachusetts. The spirit of the occasion moved Phillis to address some complimentary verses to him. In reply, he sent her the following courteous note:

"I thank you most sincerely for your polite notice of me in the elegant lines you enclosed. However undeserving I may be of such encomium, the style and manner exhibit a striking proof of your poetical talents. In honor of which, and as a tribute justly due to you, I would have published the poem, had I not been apprehensive that, while I only meant to give the world this new instance of your genius, I might have incurred the imputation of vanity. This, and nothing else, determined me not to give it a place in the public prints.

"If you should ever come to Cambridge, or near headquarters, I shall be happy to see a person so favored by the Muses, and to whom Nature had been so liberal and beneficent in her dispensations.

"I am, with great respect,

"Your obedient, humble servant,

"GEORGE WASHINGTON."

The early friends of Phillis were dead, or scattered abroad and she felt alone in the world. About this time she formed the acquaintance of a colored man by the name of Peters who kept a grocery store. He was very intelligent, spoke fluently, wrote easily, dressed well and was handsome in appearance. He proposed marriage and in an evil hour she accepted him. He proved to be lazy, proud and high-tempered. He neglected his business, failed and became very poor. Though unwilling to do hard work himself, he wanted to make a drudge of his wife. She was unaccustomed to hardships, her constitution was frail and she was the mother of three little children with no one to help her in household labors and cares. He had no pity on her and increased her burdens by his ill temper. The little ones sickened and died and their gentle mother was completely broken down, by sorrow and toil.

Some of the descendants of her lamented benefactress heard of her illness. They found her in a forlorn situation, suffering for the common comforts of life.

The Revolutionary War was still raging. Everybody was mourning sons and husbands slain in battle. Currency was deranged and the country was poor. The people were too anxious and troubled to think of the African poet whom they once delighted to honor. And so it happened that the gifted woman who had been patronized by wealthy Bostonians and who had rolled through London in the splendid carriages of the English nobility, lay dying alone in a cold, dirty, comfortless room.

It was a mournful reverse of fortune; but she was patient and resigned. She made no complaint of her unfeeling husband.

The friends and descendants of Mrs. Wheatley did all they could to relieve her destitute condition but fortunately for her she soon went "Where the wicked cease from troubling and the weary are at rest."

Her husband was so generally disliked that she was never called Mrs. Peters, but went by the name bestowed upon her by her benefactress and by which she will be known to all posterity the name of PHILLIS WHEATLEY.

—L. Maria Child in Freedmen's Book to whom much of the above is due.

SARA ALLEN
Wife of the First Bishop
A. M. E. Church

SARA ALLEN

1764—1849

The subject of this sketch was born in Isle of Wight County, Virginia. At an early age she was taken to Philadelphia, Pennsylvania, where she remained until her death, July 16, 1849, which occurred at the home of her daughter, Mrs. Anna Adams.

When quite a young woman, Sara was united in marriage to Reverend Richard Allen. This young man rose to great and distinctive honors. From the works (1816) of Lorenzo Dow, who was connected with early Methodism in America, we learn the following facts: Richard Allen and a number of other colored people were members of the white Methodist Society. But they were placed around the walls and in corners, compelled to commune after their white brethren had partaken of the sacrament. Richard Allen led the colored members from the Meeting House. Being a blacksmith, he hammered at the forge through the week and on Sundays worshipped in this shop until they were able to build an "African Meeting House"—the first ever built in the Middle or Northern States. After this Richard Allen built a Meeting House with his own money, upon his own ground, and called the name of it, "Bethel."

The first General Conference of this infant child of God was held in the City of Philadelphia in 1816, at which meeting on April 11th, Richard Allen was elected Bishop—the first Bishop of the African Methodist Episcopal Church, his son, Richard Allen, Jr., was elected Secretary of the Conference.

One writer says: "Richard Allen belongs to the constellation of moral and religious reformers, he is to the

ISABELLA—SOJOURNER TRUTH

1777 (?)—1883

"Her parallel exisits not in history. She stood by the closing century like a twin sister. Born and reared by its side. What it knew, she knew; what it had seen, she had seen."

There was born late in the Eighteenth Century one of the most singular and impressive characters of pure African blood that has appeared in modern times in the person of the slave, Isabella. Of her early life little is known. Up to the time of her emancipation she served five masters and suffered all the hardships, deprivations and abuse common to slaves of that period.

She was married once and bore five children, all of whom were sold from her in their early life. We first see her as a slave in the state of New York. Her age is uncertain. The only event on which to build any substantial conclusion as to her age was her liberation in 1817. At this time an act went into force in the Northern States which freed all slaves who were forty years of age. Judging from this fact her birth year would probably have been 1777. According to this she was more than one hundred years old, but she lived not so much in years as in great deeds. She was called Isabella until she gained her freedom then she tells us that she asked God for a new name. She was given *Sojourner* because of her many wanderings and *Truth* because she was to preach the truth as to the iniquity of slavery, and because, as she says, "God is my master and His name is Truth and Truth shall be my abiding name until I die."

Soon after her liberation, she commenced her traveling career as an abolitionist and developed into a noted Anti-Slavery lecturer. Side by side she stood with Frederick Douglas and in history they are the only two noted ex-slaves who were ardent workers for freedom and qualified public speakers. She was optimistic by nature and became prominent as a publicist and was readily received by Presidents and Statesmen. She became an orator of a superior type, enlisting the sympathies and effecting conviction wherever she spoke.

Few could match her earnest urgency or resist her persuasive plea. She was of that type of genius who knew without learning and understood with the certainty of instinct. She was blessed with a shrewd judgment and rare common sense. She was an ardent temperance and religious reformer and possessed a striking faith and simple piety. Many hearts which were never warmed by the eloquence of the learned were stirred by her homely renderings of the gospel.

She preached from one text as she told the renowned Dr. Beecher: "When I preaches I has jest one text to preach from and I always preaches from this one. My text is, '*When I found Jesus*'."

Nature seemed to have endowed her with the spirit of eloquence and poetry. She seemed to be clothed with a native nobility that broke down all barriers. Says Harriet Beecher Stowe: "I never knew a person who possessed so much of that subtle, controlling power called presence as Sojourner Truth." Wendell Phillips said that he has known a few words from her to electrify an audience and effect them as he never saw persons affected by another.

At a great, crowded public meeting in Faneuil Hall, Frederick Douglas was one of the chief speakers. He described the wrongs of his people, that they had no hope of justice from the white race, no possible hope except in their own right arms. They must fight for themselves and redeem themselves or it would never be done.

Sojourner was sitting there, tall and dark and in the

hush of deep feeling, after the eloquent speech of Mr. Douglas, she arose and spoke out in her deep, peculiar voice heard all over the house—"Frederick, is God dead?" The effect was electrical and thrilled through the house, changing, as by a flash, the whole feeling of that vast audience.

She made several visits to the White House to request and urge President Lincoln to enlist the free colored men of the north in defense of the Union. He gave her audience and promised to consider the matter. Shortly after, Mr. Lincoln and Congress gave consent; and Negro soldiers, north and south, were fighting for their freedom.

Sojourner continued in her work until the war of the Rebellion broke out in 1861 when she went to Washington to care for the wounded troops and to instruct and assist the newly emancipated slaves, who flocked to the Capitol, homeless, half-naked, half-starved, dirty and ragged. Through her exertions many were provided with comfortable lodgings, suitable employment and helped into a cleaner, better life.

After the close of the war, although nearly ninety years old, she continued traveling in behalf of her people, laboring in twenty-two states, speaking in Senate Chambers, halls, churches and at nearly every important convention and meeting where she endeavored to further their interest and always to large and appreciative audiences.

Presidents, Senators, Judges, Authors, Lecturers—all were proud to grasp her hand and bid her God Speed on her noble mission. By many of these her name has been made immortal. She is the Libyan Sibyl of Harriet Beecher Stowe and the ideal *Sibilla Libica* which the chisel of the eminent sculptor, Mr. Story, has given to the world.

She labored with William Lloyd Garrison, Wendell Phillips, Frederick Douglas, Harriet Beecher Stowe and other patriots in the cause of freedom. In her exhortations for the cause of truth in all things, pleading and demanding justice for her down-trodden race, she rose to the greatest heights of oratory. Her African dialect, quaint speeches and genial ways won for her an ever willing and interested audience. Her witty sayings would make a volume of themselves, had they been preserved. Her keen wit and repartee were strong weapons in debate or argument.

She was a zealous advocate for the enfranchisement of women and claimed warm friendship with many of the noted women of that cause. In the Suffrage Convention of Akron, Ohio, in 1851, it was Sojourner Truth who saved the day and won the victory for the women.

In her travels she carried a little book which she called the Book of Life. She could neither read nor write yet she had a large and varied correspondence. In this book were recorded the names, many extracts and testimonials of distinguished men and women. Among the first and most treasured name was that of the lamented President Lincoln who wrote, "For Aunty Sojourner Truth, A. Lincoln, October 9, 1864"; also these lines, "Sojourner Truth, U. S. Grant, March 31, 1870."

Sojourner had a remarkable memory. Though a child of about six years she remembered the "dark day" of New England in 1780. She says, "The candle was lit, the chickens went to roost and the roosters crowed." She distinctly remembered seeing the soldiers of the old Revolutionary War limping about with their bandaged wounds. She often spoke of seeing the *Ulster Gazette* brought in draped in mourning on the death of General George Washington which occurred December 14, 1799. At that time she was a full grown woman. She says she had reached her full height, which was nearly six feet, when the first steamboat moved up the Hudson River in 1809 and that the Dutchmen were very angry because it frightened away the fishes.

She sold her biography and photographs as a means of support. Many of her photographs bear one of her characteristic sayings: "I sell the shadder to support the substance." By her own industry and gifts from personal friends she obtained a modest little home in Battle Creek, Michigan, where she lived for more than a quarter of a

Sojourner Truth
and
Abraham Lincoln

century, esteemed by an intelligent community. Here she sought occasional repose from self-imposed and arduous labors.

The compiler of this sketch visited Sojourner Truth in this humble home a few months before her death. Seated in a large arm chair with an open Bible on her lap, her face wreathed in smiles, she recounted many thrilling events of her long and remarkable life. So far back in history had she led us that a little girl who had been an attentive listener innocently asked, 'Sojourner, did you see Adam and Eve?" As we left that heroic character she said "I isn't goin' to die, honey, Ise goin' home like a shootin' star."

Her eventful life closed November 26, 1883, and all that is mortal of Sojourner Truth rests in Oakhill Cemetery to await the return of the Giver of all life who rewards every one acording to the deeds done in the body.

ELIZABETH N. SMITH

(*A nineteenth century example, actual dates uncertain*)

Though an important division of the American people, in one phase we differ from most, if not all other divisions —we know so little about ourselves. We have neglected to preserve facts and incidents of those of us who have lived lives of strenuous endurance and unwavering self-sacrifice. Such had a lofty aim to sustain them, that of securing the unhampered enjoyment of life, liberty and property; and they could not be satisfied to plod along restricted paths marked out for them by certain self-styled superiors.

So the story still remains to be told in all its details how our forbears inaugurated a propaganda so insistent and forcible as to culminate in a train of events making emancipation both a political and a moral issue.

Regarded in the light of heroism, many Americans, bond and free, have passed on unhonored and unsung who yet were worthy of the olive crown and the victor's palm for their constancy, their courage and their firm belief in the ultimate triumph of justice.

Among this galaxy of heroes may be included a woman who, born in New England, well might a century ago have lived the restrained life of a gentle woman and left an illustrious example of culture, refinement and noble character.

Elizabeth Smith had wise, sagacious parents and enjoyed a material ease that seemed opulence in days of frugal habits and simple customs. This afforded her the opportunity to grow normally. With the advance of years she attained a fine physique, a trained intellect, a moral discernment acute and sensitive, all of which contributed to make her the exceptional woman she finally became.

Her earliest instruction was given her by private tutors belonging to the Quaker element of her home town, Providence, R. I. Studiously inclined, she was inducted into some branches then popularly deemed "too deep" for ordinary females. She also was at one time a pupil in the "Prudence Crandell" School. This was prior to 1832, for during the year the school building was dragged from its foundations and its brave principal was virtually driven into exile. In the prejudiced eyes of the Canterbury townspeople teaching of Negro and Indian youths was a misdemeanor. One year later the Connecticut legislature covered itself with ignominy by the passage of a law making the opening of a school for pupils of Negro descent a felony.

In Rhode Island, however, such an institution was tolerated. Just prior to the middle of the last century a "colored school" was established which was located within sight of the State House. There Mrs. Smith worked many years, first as a teacher, afterward a principal.

In 1865 the school law was so amended that children regardless of race, or color, were admitted into the schools of their respective districts. The only child of Mrs. Smith, a son, thus gained the right of attending the Boys' High School from which he graduated with honor.

This "opening" of Providence schools just at the close of the Civil War was indeed a notable event. Through the efforts of Albert Lyons and his intrepid wife, Mrs. Mary J. Lyons, a revival of a statute was secured making public school really not merely nominally free. The action was both warmly contested and as strenuously endorsed. The endorsers were most ably assisted by Mrs. Smith, Hon. George T. Downing, of Newport, and many of the influential men in Providence both white and colored. Despite the opposition of "Copperheads," fair play won in the contest. The third daughter in the Lyons family, after passing a grilling examination, written and oral, (for a certificate of graduation from Colored Grammer School 3, New York City, would not be accepted as qualifying for admission) entered the Girls' High School. This had been in existence only ten years and some of the "hayseeds" were still discussing the "pros and cons" of higher education for females. For females of African descent, such a departure in their undeveloped minds was equivalent to a revolution. And so it virtually proved to be, happily a bloodless one. Many of the graduates of her class became teachers but in a class reunion in 1892, it was stated that among those following the profession, Miss Lyons was the only one who had taken a rank above that of class teacher, and congratulations were gracefully accorded to her.

Many of our future women of mark attended this now venerable institution. Of these Amanda (Mattie) Bowen should be referred to for her successful work in Washington, D. C., as a teacher and her welfare work there where she literally spent and was spent in her voluntary sacrifices for her people.

Miss Lyons, writer of this sketch, has always kept in touch with some of her former classmates, with one, a member of the Tappen family, well-known in abolition days, she has maintained permanent close relations. Until the end of her fruitful busy life the renowned educator, Miss Sarah E. Doyle, remembered "her girls" in ways kindly and practical, and Miss Lyons as one of them had the high honor of assisting in the celebration of this noble woman's ninetieth birthday. The school taught by Mrs. Smith was never "opened" neither was it "closed" until she voluntarily ceased her connection with public education. She turned her attention to private tuition and soon found herself fully occupied in giving piano lessons and instruction in French. Her pupils being mainly children of her neighbors, as she resided on the aristocratic "East Side," were of the better class and she enjoyed her work with them.

Mrs. Smith was a pianist of high rank and a fine linguist. The writer is most happy to record her personal indebtedness to this woman who loved learning not only for learning's sake but for the privilege it gave her to aid in developing the mental growth and mental strength of the immature though aspiring.

In conversation Mrs. Smith was supreme. She lived when conversation was an art; her disciplined mind and varied reading, her choice of apposite quotations and illustrations, her animated graceful manners, charmed as well as her kind heart led her to intuitively adapt herself to her auditors. She had the faculty of drawing out the best in each and the good sense to avoid monologues. The secret of her popularity was that she was equally a good talker and a good listener.

Her endowments, her culture, her high ethical standard, her genuine charity gained for her in her maturity a more than local reputation. To the last she maintained a lively interest in all groups working for uplift recalling with satisfaction how she had helped him who became the "Grand Old Man" of our people, how she had fought and endured with the "real patriots who essayed such heroic service in stirring northerners' consciences just 'before the crisis'."

Her purity of intention, her faith, her fidelity mark her existence as noble for its endeavor and its fruition. Wonderful records are enshrined in the life stores of so many of our women of the past. We can but dimly realize what it was to do one's duty under the shade of a slavery-darkened country. All honor to our women who were faithful to ideals despite doubt, discouragement, disappointment, despair. The nimbus of serfdom weighted like a nightmare. With the conflict between the spirit of legality and the letter of the law they lay, as it were, between upper and nether millstones. Their joy was so commingled with sorrow, their place so harrowed by injusticed, their sense of justice so maltreated, that they were able to cultivate patience and keep the faith undimmed is an eloquent tribute to the nobleness of their humanity.

From the South have come many women who literally fought the stars in their course, to step out of the darkness of bondage into the light of personal liberty. Throughout the North and other sections our thoughtful women have lived clouded lives, made dim by the tales of the indescribable sufferings endured by their sisters by blood and lineage. Their tears have flowed in sympathy and their characters have been moulded by large sacrifices cheerfully made upon demand to aleviate distress which at best could only be surmised. An impregnable persistency, a luminous faith, combined to make both the bond and the free able to endure to the uttermost.

And they all have done their duty, much better than they knew. They have left a broad foundation upon which their successors are obligated to raise an enduring superstructure of character, one that will exhibit the progress of the much maligned "black woman of America," and so conserve the toils, vigils and prayers of the many whose lives have been lived in shade, who only in lives of others saw "the shine of distant suns."

MRS. SARAH H. FAYERWEATHER

MRS. DINAH COX

MRS. SARAH ELIZABETH TANNER

MRS. CHARLOTTA GORDON PYLES

SARAH HARRIS FAYERWEATHER

Born, Canterbury, Conn., 1802

Died, Kingston, R. I., 1868

The larger portion of the nineteenth century covered a period of great political activity in the United States, slavery being the foremost topic of discussion. Very much was then being said and written concerning the "peculiar" institution. Antagonists and apologists seized upon pulpit, press and forum to aid in moulding public sentiment to be utilized as barricades in defense of respective positions. From the earliest days there was launched and extended, a campaign for the emancipation of the slaves, the elevation of free colored people, and the practical application of the fundamental principles underlying humanity and justice in the administration of government. Naturally colored people in the free states had the condition of their brethren in bondage very near to their hearts and thought but little of the trouble and nothing at all of the risk and cost involved in making their oppressed fellow creatures objects of solicitude and devotion.

The record of the "Underground Railroad" disclose how the bondmen who were able to think at all regarded their anomalous state of existence. The creed and procedure of abolition and anti-slavery societies were in harmony with the sacred idea of human brotherhood. Tradition, which is verified through unwritten history, furnishes ample testimony to the race loyalty of the many who daily as it were had the fact forced into inner consciousness that they, too, suffered a thraldom none the less vicious because invisible. Any average man or woman living under such a disability might properly serve as a type to illustrate the self-abnegation displayed in an endeavor to minimize the nation's shameful traffic in human flesh. The selection of Mrs. Sarah Harris Fayerweather to exemplify a group of unhonored heroes is a happy one from more than one angle. All the circumstances of heredity and environment, save one only, combined to make her life honorable, responsible, care-free, and independent. The daughter of a New England farmer, she enjoyed all the advantages of the freedom and steadiness of existence in a rural community. She came from stock possessing elements of character essential to progress and contentment. All the then available opportunities for study open to girls were within her reach. Had she been an American by birth and descent, "only this and nothing more," her story would have been too commonplace to merit record or comment. But, she was in part, of African extraction; while this to an extent set her aside and apart, it also made her of importance because of the times during which she lived and of the part she played in the great drama of life.

At Canterbury a select school for girls was kept by a Quaker lady, Miss Prudence Crandell. The Harris sisters were entered there as pupils. This philanthropic high-minded woman who received them upon precisely the same terms as she did other village pupils, later became a victim to the meanest sort of persecution. Disgusted with a sporadic outburst of race prejudice in her native state, Miss Crandell tried for a while to maintain a school for colored girls exclusively. Finally she emigrated to Kansas toward which all eyes were then turned as a presumptive "free state."

In earliest youth Sarah Harris became the wife of George Fayerweather, who was descended from French West Indians named Monteflora. He was a blacksmith as was his father before him and one of his sons, C. Frederick Douglass succeeded him in the business. Their eldest daughter, another Sarah, was so deeply impressed by the Crandell episode that it influenced her entire life. She never married, but upon reaching majority devoted herself to the dissemination of literature upon anti-slavery, temperance and allied subjects. She even undertook the long and toilsome journey to Kansas to visit Miss Crandell whom she regarded with affection tinged with awe.

In the quiet precincts of a model New England village, Kingston, R. I., the Fayerweathers built a home and reared a family. After the formal, reserved habits of the day, they were trained in politeness and obedience. They were expected to study, to perform manual labor, keep early hours, and follow the strict practices of the Congregational Church.

Artisans, in days of yore could do well for and by their families, for the doubtful custom of living beyond or even up to one's means, had not as yet in rural localities become fashionable. Had this family been burdened only with the natural responsibilities attached to their position, affairs would have moved on easily and smoothly as in a groove. But they were "colored people" and that significant epithet embodies a "true tale" of sadness, sin, and sorrow.

The opponents of slavery have been divided into three classes, those who made appeals verbally and in writing to influence public sentiment, those who gave full financial support to aid in the propagation of the doctrine of personal liberty, and those who gave secret service of time, thought, and strength to make effective the attempted escapes of slaves. Almost without exception our men and women were numbered in at least two of these divisions. Douglas, Remond, Sojourner Truth, Sarah Lenox, Frances Harper, won world wide fame for their eloquence and aggressiveness. Countless obscure, though loyal adherents, worked differently but as effectively in a cause which to them had all the sacredness and importance of a latter day crusade. In many a household like that of Sarah Fayerweather, a portion of the income was duly set aside to be devoted to the forwarding of this work. The people responded to any call however sudden, cheerfully and with alacrity. Shelter, legal assistance, disguises, all necessary creature comforts, were forthcoming upon demand. The earnest helpers felt that the fugitives like the poor were always with them actually or in anticipation. They scrutinized the neighborhood to discern whom to trust in emergencies and to kindle and keep alive a healthy sentiment in the locality, was but one phase of the multifarious tasks undertaken. Safe housing, safe thoroughfare were prime essentials; to invariably secure these was a delicate dangerous mission.

Under such conditions, so continuous, so tense, the elders in a family could not fail in being thoughtful, cautious and full of rescources; the youthful members caught the reflected spirit and only awaited a signal to become participants as well as sympathizers in a work which they gradually began to know was being carried on. This missionary work as they understood it to be, was not disclosed to them in all its details until the age of discretion had been attained. Though no dawning intellect could be entirely oblivious of the sudden additions and as sudden subtractions to the household numbers, yet a premature reference to anything out of the ordinary was never hazarded.

Upon the passage of the Fugitive Slave Law there was a tacit understanding among the lovers of freedom, that the iniquitous statute was to be regarded in the letter only. The most sensitive New England conscience felt that in the spirit it ought to be violated with impunity. In a way, so far from being a hindrance, it gave fresh impetus to the effort of helping those who were encountering all sorts of risks to escape slavery.

In large cities like Boston where anti-slavery meetings were regularly held, they were not only attended by the townspeople, but by those living in outlying towns like Canterbury and Kinston. Persons traveled miles to hear the scathing indictments of a Garrison, the impassioned oratory of a Phillips, the pathetic pleadings of a Lucretia Mott, the dignified utterances and unassailable logic of a

Douglas. Having renewed their vows to continue steadfast in the fight to extirpate the nation's obliquity, having had explained and emphasized the part each individual had to perform in the premises, they returned to their respective homes fully imbued with the resolution to discharge to the utmost the "duty lying next." For women this involved the procuring of garments for change and disguise, the collection of extra food, the selection of places for hiding and security, last but not least, the proffer of first aid service to weary travelers long deprived of the barest opportunities for cleanliness either of persons or clothing.

For men it meant sudden, often dangerous trips, midnight watchings and waitings that sorely taxed body and mind. None knew until the very last moment when action would be required, but each one was aware that almost every day some would come seeking good offices. This was the responsibility undertaken by Sarah Fayerweather, and the discipline resultant made her alert, discreet, sympathetic, untiring. In addition to the ordinary wear and tear of family support and oversight, came the exigencies of this extraordinary current of under life.

Each family had silent advisers and informers in the guise of the newpapers of the times; the "Liberator," the "Anti-Slavery Standard," the "Colored American," and "New York Tribune," kept them in touch with the trend of affairs. No child old enough to have any measure of confidence reposed in him ever hesitated to take the usual lengthy walk to and from a village post office; to read any portion of a newspaper was ample reward. In such an atmosphere of unselfish service a spirit of race consciousness was developed. One daughter for many years a successful teacher in Wilmington, Del., transmitted to a second generation all that was valuable in the training she had received from her parents who upheld an ideal of self-respect and self-sacrifice. The eldest son, Prof. Geo. H. Fayerweather, was for a long time a member of the Board of Education at New Orleans, La. His assistance in the conduct of affairs in this department was greatly facilitated by the impressions he had received during the formative periods of childhood and youth.

Mrs. Fayerweather's sisters were fortunate in their children, who wherever they located, became valuable residents of their respective localities. The daughters of Mrs. Celinda Harris Anderson, were not only successful in teaching, but won reputations as devoted race women. As such they are still remembered in Washington and New York City.

Within the precincts of the Fayerweather homestead noted groups often assembled. Wm. Wells Brown and Wm. C. Neal enjoyed infrequent, brief vacations there. Leading anti-slavery women paid visits to Kingston exclusively to talk with "Friend Sarah." There the famous Hutchinson family sang their songs of freedom while all the neighborhood entered fully into the spirit of the occasion.

Personally, Mrs. Fayerweather presented a very distinguished appearance. She was tall, fine looking and had a voice of peculiar sweetness. Her favorite attitude was sitting erect with clasped hands (while her stead gaze seemed to pierce far below the surface of things. She made a beautiful picture with abundant gray hair framing an almost colorless ivory face, whose smile redeemed it from severity. She could listen as well as converse and had the happy faculty of eliciting confidences unasked.

This woman was representative; such were to be found everywhere. Their lives presented a grand illustration of faith reinforced by fidelity. This makes the memory of Sarah Fayerweather and her noble band of sisters a precious legacy to our women of today and should incite in them a spirit to do, to dare, and to suffer, and to become strong.

Our country has not yet attained the supreme position of a consistent republic. The "duty of the now" is the teaching of an axiomatic doctrine. "So long as one chained and oppressed man in any part of the world remains bound and unredeemed, no army is invincible against him and no cause is just but his own." All women who are lovers of fair play should teach and preach this: white women from a patriotic desire for the permanent establishment of civic justice; colored women for their self-preservation and the moral safety of their men fresh from the struggle to keep inviolate in foreign climes that very consistent democracy so conspicuous by its absence at home. Women at large ought to help to justify their contention to be accorded places side by side with men in administering the affairs of government.

DINAH COX

1804—1909

Dinah Cox was born in Roanoke, Virginia. She was the slave of John Randolph, and was freed by the terms of his will when he died in 1833. The first item of that famous document reads as follows:

> "I give and bequeath to all my slaves their freedom, heartily regretting that I have ever been the owner of one."

He also provided that a portion of his wealth be given to them namely:

> "Forty acres of land and to each slave a portion of the sum of two hundred and fifty thousand dollars."

After fourteen years of litigation caused by relatives who sought to break the will, the Executors purchased a tract of land in Mercer County, Ohio, and the slaves prepared to start for their future home.

Aunt Dinah, as she was called by every one, was a fearless leader among the people. She was also famous for her knitting and quilting. An incident occurred which showed her spirit. She was told that she would have to go out to work to help herself and family get ready to move. She said, "Oh, no, John Randolph left enough for me, and besides, I must get my children's clothes ready. I won't have time to work." There were more than three hundred in the party, men, women and children.

As they started from the old plantation, sorrowful at leaving the only home they knew, they sang:

> "Don't weep, don't cry,
> I shall never turn back any more."

The poor whites who came to jeer and ridicule broke into tears so great was the effect of that song.

They traveled on foot and by wagons, the latter being for the old people and children. They went by river to Cincinnati and from there by canal boats to New Mremen. Here they met great hostility. The old Dutch settlers of Mercer County came out in force, with their muskets patroled the banks of the canal and refused to let them settle on their own purchased land. The weary travelers' dismay and disappointement can never be told.

They finally settled in Miami County near Piqua, Ohio. The Mercer County land was sold and resold and is now said to be the finest farm land in that county and all that the slaves, now free-men, received was their fare from Roanoke, Virginia, to Piqua, Ohio.

In 1917 an effort was made by the descendants to recover their possessions. It was carried to the Supreme Court and decided in favor of the present owners, the verdict being that the time was so long that it was *outlawed.* Dinah Cox had carefully preserved her "Free Papers" which played an interesting and important part in the "Famous Randolph Will Case." This document is in the possession of her great grand-daughter, Mrs. Amy Logan, in Springfield, Ohio.

Aunt Dinah was the mother of fourteen children. Only three, however, lived to come to Ohio with her. She had an interesting personality, ready in conversation and possessed a remarkable memory. She distinctly remembered when the soldiers of the War of 1812 halted at the Randolph plantation. She was a devout Christian and a member of the Park Baptist Church. She lived to see her fifth generation, passing away at the great age of 105 years.

SARAH ELIZABETH TANNER

1804—1914

Sarah E. Miller was born in Winchester, Virginia. She was one of six children. In 1843 the family moved to Pittsburgh, Pennsylvania. She attended the day school and latter Avery College. When she was sixteen years of age her father, Jefferson Miller, died. Sarah was compelled to stop school and became a teacher.

In 1858 she was united in marriage to a promising young minister, Benjamin Tucker Tanner who later became a successful pastor, Editor of the Christian Recorder, The Church Review and finally a Bishop of the A. M. E. Church. For some years they lived in the cities of his pastorate and in 1872 made a permanent home in Philadelphia remaining there till death.

Mrs. Tanner was the mother of nine children, two of whom died in infancy. She was in the truest sense of the term a home-maker, devoting her whole time to the welfare of her family. The residence, 2908 Diamond Street, Philadelphia, was for over a quarter of a century a haven of rest to the traveler and a solace to the family. She was tutelar angel of inspiration and light to that hearth-stone. Her cheerful, unselfish spirit was manifest at all times. Her high ideals, her lofty concept of life, her refined and elegant manner made lasting impression upon all who came within her charmed circle.

She also possessed great business ability which exceeded that of her learned husband and he, realizing this, relinquished the family finances to her which she so ably managed, and demonstrated her all-around domestic capacities.

She devoted herself almost exclusively to her domestic affairs.

Her one sole exception was the church to which her consecrated service was unreservedly given. As a teacher in the Sabbath School she taught many little lips to lisp the name of the Redeemer of the world.

In the church was the Parent Mite Missionary Society, in which she held offices for years, first as president and then as treasurer. Her children remember the quarterly occasion which called their mother to the missionary meetings. Such outings were events of great moment in the family history.

When her children were grown she felt that she could devote more time to the cause of missions and travel in its interest. Accordingly she redoubled her efforts. As the years sped by she gave her whole time and full energy to the work. Like the Psalmist, she could say, "The zeal of thine house hath eaten me up." With her husband, Bishop B. T. Tanner, she traveled extensively carrying the gospel to missions throughout the country to the women who sat in darkness, thus she claimed "His promised blessing the brightening little while."

She lived to see her children reach manhood and womanhood. Lived to see three of them attain more than ordinary distinction. Her eldest daughter, Dr. Halle Tanner Johnson, became a physician; Reverend Carl Tanner a minister of his mother's church and her eldest son, famous on two continents, Henry O. Tanner, the gifted artist.

Her children rise up and call her blessed.

CHARLOTTA GORDON MacHENRY PYLES

1806—1880

Down below the Mason and Dixon's Line, near Bardstown, in the good old state of Kentucky, among the various Negro families, who lived on the plantations, was one named Pyles. This family of father, mother and twelve children was one of those favored families before the war. I say favored because they did not have to suffer many of the hardships of slavery. The father, whose name was Harry MacHenry (Pyles) happened to be the offspring of his master, who was William MacHenry and hailed from Scotland, while his mother was a light colored maid, who worked in the home. Is it any wonder then, that the son had blue eyes, fair complexion and all the ear marks of his white ancestry, and his father, in order to atone for his sin, declared him free and allowed him to roam where he would? The father not only did this for him, but saw that his son had good training in the harness and shoe mending industries and gave him a shop where he worked for the plantations, far and near, and thus supported his family in a comfortable way.

Tall and majestic as a straight pine was his good wife, Charlotta Gordon, with the high cheek bones, the copper colored hue and straight, glossy black hair, which denoted Indian extraction. Her parentage, while different in some respects, was similar in others to that of her husband; for her father was a mixture of German and Negro, while her mother had been a full blooded squaw of the famous Seminole tribe of Indians. Coming from such parentage it was not surprising that later in life, she displayed such courage and endurance in the face of difficulties, as would have defeated other hearts less brave than hers. She received the name of Gordon from the white family that owned her. The Gordons were Wesleyan Methodists and the father of this splendid old family was as fine a Christian man as you would meet anywhere. It was because of his great faith in humanity that when he died he left Charlotta Pyles and her family as a heritage to his only daughter rather than to two sons, and as the daughter's heritage she and her little family were blessed. They attended the same church with Miss Gordon, enjoyed many privileges and were never made to feel that they were slaves.

Miss Gordon was a very conscientious young woman and promised her father on his death bed that she would free this family according to the Wesleyan Methodist Manumittant Law for slaves a few years after his death.

Charlotta had married a John McElroy before she met Harry MacHenry; and had one daughter by this union. The girl's name was Julian.

The ten children who blessed the union of Charlotta Gordon and Harry MacHenry were as follows: Emily, the eldest, Barney, Benjamin, Pauline, Sarah Ann, Mary Ellen, Henry, Charlotta, Elizabeth and Mary Agnes.

In the year 1853, Miss Gordon decided to give them their Manumittant papers. In order to do this, it was necessary for her to move the entire family North.

In those days when pro-slavery sentiments were at fever-heat, on account of the activities of the Abolitionists and the Underground Railway, it was very dangerous for colored people, and especially free ones, to move about from place to place without a pass.

Miss Gordon happened to have several brothers who did not share her religious opinion and who had always coveted the MacHenry family as a fine possession. One of the sons of the family, Benjamin, who was a tall, light complexioned man with blue eyes, straight brown hair and fine physique was caught one evening by some of the brothers and sold to a slave driver in Mississippi. This cowardly act of her own relatives caused Miss Gordon to take action promptly, for she began a lawsuit shortly afterwards to have her possession of the entire Pyles family established by law. To keep them safe, she accompanied them to jail in Springfield, Kentucky, and there had the entire family incarcerated for a couple of days and remained with them to protect them from the kidnapping tactics of her brothers.

Harry MacHenry Pyles was not allowed, as yet, to have charge of his family, though permitted by his father to go and come as he pleased and no one dared to molest him.

Miss Gordon finally won the lawsuit and began preparations to take the family North. The laxness of the laws concerning slaves at that time, and the fear of her brothers caused Miss Gordon to send to Ohio and have a white minister, Rev. Claycome, come to Kentucky and start with her family northward. Before starting, Grandma Pyles, who was one of the famous old Southern cooks, had prepared meats, ginger bread, cakes and food of every description, enough to last the family on their trip; so it would only be necessary to cook a few corn pones and make coffee from time to time to supply the travelers. Occasionally, when their paths happened to cross that of a deer, they would have an addition of venison to their store of food.

You can here, perhaps, let your imagination supply the details of this wonderful trip, beset on every side by the dangers and treachery of the old slave law, the wild animals lurking in the forests; and the lawless renegades who often roamed about at will. Yet who would exchange even this apparent wild flight for freedom for the hideous nightmare of unending slavery and degradation which remained behind? Many at this time had lost their lives in a similar flight for freedom. To go or to die a moral death was the question before them. And they determined to go, because they felt that God was with them.

The most noted of this party was the noble hearted white woman, who was willing to brave the scorn of her relatives, the criticism and reproach of neighbors, and to sacrifice friends, all for the sake of giving this Negro family the heritage, which was theirs by right. Then there was the minister, reverend in appearance, who was also impelled by a bond of sympathy for the unfortunate, to leave his home and come to Kentucky and travel thence through the dangers and wilds of an unknown land in order to perform this heroic deed.

The family consisted of the father, mother, the eleven children, and one small daughter and son, Thermon and Louanne belonging to the older daughter, Julian; and three small boys, John Wesley, Daniel and James T., sons of Emily. Both of these daughters had married, but their husbands were slaves belonging to other masters and therefore could not accompany them.

In one of the old time-worn schooner wagons drawn by six of the best blooded horses that Kentucky could afford with four in the rear as a supply for the others when they became tired, with all their household goods neatly packed in the wagon, the women and children were crowded in and started off on their journey to the Land of Promise.

It was in the early fall of the year 1853 that the family started out on their eventful trip.

I have often heard my mother, whose name was Mary Ellen, say that when they arrived at Louisville, she thought it was as near like the "Torment" as any place she had ever seen, because of the smoke and fire she saw belching from the chimneys of the factories and distilleries, and she told how none of the children strayed far from the wagon because they were too afraid they would be burned up.

As they proceeded on their journey Miss Gordon discovered that she had forgotten her register and they turned back to secure it. When they arrived at Bardstown, she was told she could not get it, so incensed were the officials in the court-house over what they considered a very foolish act—that of giving her property away. She therefore proceeded without it. The party traveled overland to Louisville, Kentucky, the people of their neighborhood all regretted their going bcause they had filled such a useful place. Aunt Charlotta, as she was commonly called, made the best ginger bread of any one round about and at all the basket meetings, protracted meetings and other gatherings, both white and black, she was always there to sell her famous ginger bread cookies and other delicacies. Uncle Harry was missed for his tradesmanship, too, for it would take a long time for the white people of the plantations to find some one to make harness or half sole shoes as neatly as he had done it.

At Louisville, after they had finished all negotiations with the state officers as to their right to leave the place, they boarded one of the old sidewheel boats, so common on the Ohio in those days, and traveled to Cincinnati, thence to St. Louis.

When they finally reached St. Louis, they met a white man by the name of Nat. Stone, who promised to pilot them all the way to Minnesota for the sum of $100, which Miss Gordon agreed to pay. Later on in the journey, he attempted to be treacherous and held that unless they gave him $50 more, he would turn them over to some slave holders in Missouri. So afraid was Miss Gordon that her plans would be frustrated, that she paid the extra $50 and they continued their journey. After leaving St. Louis, they again started overland in their schooner wagon traveling in Woodford County, Saline County, across the Missouri River on the ferry to Howard County, then Shelby, then Monroe. This was a very tiresome and difficult journey and ofttimes, it was necessary for them to throw out some meat and use powder as well, to keep the bears and wolves away from the wagon, but after many trials and difficulties, such as are encountered by all pioneers, going into a new and sparsely settled country, without any of the conveniences of this progressive age, they finally crossed the Des Moines River and arrived at Keokuk, Iowa. Many times they were stopped in Missouri because it was a slave state, but when they saw the two white men and the white woman with these colored people, they were permitted to go on grudgingly but unmolested.

It had been their aim to go on to Minnesota, but when they arrived at Keokuk, which was then a mere trading post with one small tavern on the river bank, the winter had set in with all its severity for it had taken them many months to come so far.

Any one who has taken a trip in a schooner wagon with only canvas covering for its protection and encountered the blizzards of the northwest, which almost cover the wagon with snow and ice, will realize that such weather must be considered before it is encountered. The older boy, Barney Pyles, was the main driver all the way from Kentucky and he it was who looked after the women and children and assisted the father with the chores and work on the trip. After arriving in Keokuk, the father being somewhat of a carpenter, as well as having a very thorough knowledge of some of the other trades, proceeded at once in the spring to build a substantial little brick house on Johnson Street for Miss Gordon and the family.

During the next year, he found it an ever increasing burden to take care of, not only his own family, but that of the two daughters and their children as well, even though the oldest son, Barney, had a very lucrative position of hauling all the freight overland from Keokuk to Des Moines, because there were no railroads through at that time.

The mother finally devised a plan whereby the burdens of the two oldest daughters' families could be shifted to those who should really care for them. She had letters written to the owners of Catiline Walker, the husband of her daughter Emily and Joseph Kendricks, husband of

Julian and found that these two men could be bought for $1500.00 each.

Meanwhile she received a letter from her long lost son, Benjamin, who had been sold into Mississippi and who in some way or other found out that she was making plans to buy the sons-in-law and decided that if this were true, surely she would be willing to buy her own son. He therefore wrote her that he could be bought for $1500.00 also and suggested that only one of the sons-in-law be purchased together with himself, leaving the other man to trust his fate. Grandma Pyles, however, felt that as her son Benjamin was not married and had not little ones to care for it would be easier for him to liberate himself than for the others to do so. Hence, she wrote him that if he would only trust in God, a way would be provided. This irritated Benjamin and they never received any direct communication from him again. They did hear, indirectly, that he was sold into Fayette County, Missouri, and known as Benjamin Moore and from that all trace of him was lost; and while inquiries made through various channels to determine his whereabouts, no word has ever been received from him.

Charlotta Gordon Pyles in her plan to go out and raise the money to buy the sons-in-law had secured good letters of recommendation from Major Kilbourne, Gen. Scoeffield and other prominent white citizens, and armed with these good letters, she started out on a trip to the East, traveling through Pennsylvania, where in the city of Philadelphia, she was hailed with delight by the Quaker families, residing there at the time, many of whom threw open their doors and entertained her. She also had the pleasure, though a poor slave, of speaking in Old Penn Hall in which hangs the famous Liberty Bell. The good people of Philadelphia not only entertained her, but allowed her to speak in church, hall and home against the wrongs of slavery and provided her with means to go on and tell her story to others as she traveled. And ofttimes in her travels, she met and exchanged confidences with that fearless and dauntless advocate of liberty, Frederick Douglas. Night after night, I have listened to my mother, as we sat around her knee and heard her tell how kind friends used to have grandma take off her black bonnet, which she invariably wore, and how they stroked her glossy black hair, while she told of her travels and the distance that separated part of her family from her and how she was trying with might and main, though ignorant, to unite that family again. Through all the state of New York and through the New England states, made famous at that time by such strong characters as William Lloyd Garrison, Harriet Beecher Stowe and others, who spoke out in all the intensity of their souls against slavery, this good woman traveled. She numbered as her personal friends, John B. Gough, Lucretia Mott, Frederick Douglas and Susan B. Anthony. These knew her, and admired her, and made her way easier by preparing and arranging various audiences to hear her and today we, as her offsprings, have as our most precious heirlooms the photos and recommendations of these beloved men and women, given to her as a personal reminder of their association and contact with her in her noble cause.

It was a difficult task for a poor ignorant woman, who had never had a day's schooling in her life, to travel thousands of miles in a strange country and stand up night after night, day after day before crowds of men and women, pleading for those men back in slavery and for the union of their wives and children. So well did she plead, however, that in about six months, she had raised the $3000.00, retraced her way to Iowa and then to Kentucky and there she bought the two men from their owners and reunited their families.

Her activities in this holy cause did not stop here, but many a slave, coming from Kentucky, Tennessee, and Missouri, found at the gateway into Iowa an enthusiastic member of their own race in the person of Grandma Pyles who received them into her own home and in connection with the many white friends whom she had made in the East, enabled them to secretly make their way into Canada. It seems to me that I can now hear ringing in my ears the song which my mother said the slaves would sing when they were enroute through this channel. The lines were:

"O, fare-you-well Kentucky,
  You are not the place for me,
I am on my way to Canada,
  Where colored men are free."

It would be impossible to tell you the many good deeds which Grandma Pyles performed for her own people for she was a quiet, home-loving body and modest in all of her good deeds and no record of them has been preserved.

Among her daughters was one, who had the same indomitable spirit which characterized her mother. Her name was Mary Ellen. She was seventh in age of the sons and daughters and had always been a great favorite with Miss Gordon.

It was she who was chosen to live in the Big House with Miss Gordon and whenever the latter went to church or visiting, she always took Mary Ellen with her, for she was so fair with her gray eyes and light hair that she could easily pass for a white child. I have heard my mother tell how, after Miss Gordon's father died and she lived in the house with Miss Gordon, often in her childish fancy she would imagine she heard a heavy step like that of Mr. Gordon coming down the steps and the latch of the stair door raised and she would expect to see his ghostly self finish his nightly vigil, but nothing would happen, and then she would steal to Miss Gordon's side to receive her kindly embrace and be assured that it was nothing but her childish imagination, which ofttimes comes when a death has occurred in the family.

Again, mother would tell the children of a famous old

wizard who lived not far from Miss Gordon's and whose name was Rhinehearson. She was mortally afraid of him because he walked on both his hands and feet with his body and head turned upwards and back turned to the ground. He was a white man and whenever anything was lost, stolen or killed, both white and black would consult Rhinehearson and he would stop them a long way off before they arrived and tell them why they came. He was the authority on all mysteries and it is said that he never laughed until after he was seven years old. The incident which provoked his laughter was that of his father attempting to climb over a stake and rider fence with a small barrel of whiskey, when the latter fell out of his grasp, rolled down the hill and spilled its contents and left his father in great confusion.

Miss Gordon thought so much of Mary Ellen that she never allowed her to be punished, and even one time when she failed to get the water from the spring, which was her daily task, and it had been reported to her mother and Grandma Pyles was about to give her what she needed, Miss Gordon intervened and said, "Let her go this time, Charlotta, and next time she must be attended to."

When her mother brought her from the South, Mary Ellen was about seventeen years old and had never attended school, but she had a great thirst for knowledge and a determination to get an education at any cost. She finally heard of a Quaker family in Salem, Iowa, who needed a girl to help with their housework and they also offered the extraordinary inducement of a school education. Mary Ellen immediately had a letter written to them offering her services and was accepted. Thus, the dream of her life began to materialize and after she had been there awhile, she pleaded for her younger sister, Mary Agnes by name, that she might also come. This was finally allowed and she redoubled her efforts by working both for her own and her sister's board. The two sisters attended four terms of school in this way, but the younger sister became homesick and returned home. Mary Ellen remained until she had secured a good education such as was to be had in those days, for schools were few and far between for colored people; and so Mary Ellen's gaining an education was looked upon as a great achievement.

The Pyles family not only fraternized with the Indians, farmed and worked for their right as pioneers of industry, but they were also pioneers for the cause of education. Small wonder again that in the year 1876 Charlotta, the namesake of Grandma, who had sent her oldest boy to the very inadequate colored grade school in Keokuk and after he had finished the eighth grade of this school, as they had no colored high school, she appealed to the white high school for admittance of her son, Geroid Smith. When she found the doors of this institution securely closed against him because of his color, in the same business-like manner that had characterized her mother's spirit she took the matter to the courts of Iowa and secured the decision of opening the Keokuk high school to white and black alike; and thus her son became one of the first colored high school graduates in the state of Iowa in the year of 1880.

Let us now for a few minutes go back to the history of the noble soul, Miss Gordon, who brought the family North and after reaching Keokuk gave each his freedom. The family kept these Manumittant papers till after the colored people were free, but so great was their abhorrence of the idea that they had ever been considered slaves, that these papers were destroyed and thus only the tradition remained. Miss Gordon, however, continued to live with the Pyles family, visiting her rich relatives in Kewanee, Illinois, at stated periods, and died in the early '70's in the home of the family she loved so well. Both she and Grandma Pyles, belonged to the First Baptist Church of Keokuk, for at that time there was no other church there. And the same pallbearers, who carried the remains of Miss Gordon to their last resting place, also did this same service for

Grandma Pyles at her death in the year 1880 at the advanced age of seventy-four.

The spirit of Grandma Charlotta Pyles still goes marching onward in that of her grand children who are engaged in the work of educating the Negro race in the Piney Woods School, Mississippi.

MRS. JANE ROBERTS

1809—(?)

"The Love of Liberty Brought Us Here."

Mrs. Roberts was the wife of the first African President of Liberia. She was an American as was also her distinguished husband, Joseph Jenkin Roberts, a Mulatto born in Virginia in 1809. He went to Liberia in 1829 and engaged in trade. At the death of Thomas H. Buchanan, as Governor of the Commonwealth of Liberia, Mr. Roberts was appointed Governor by the Colonization Society of America and held the office for six years. He was at the head of the Liberian force in its war against the Golah Chief, Gatumba.

During his governorship Mr. Roberts visited the United States and made a good impression and met the lady who later became his wife. As a result of his visit an American squadron visited the Coast of West Africa. Governor Roberts found the English and other foreigners unwilling to pay customs duties, on the ground that Liberia was not an actual government and had no right to levy duties on shipping and foreign trade.

A crisis was reached. In 1846 the Colonization Society resolved that it was expedient for the people to take into their own hands the management of their affairs and severed relations which had bound Liberia to it.

The Liberians themselves called for a Constitutional Convention which began its sessions June 25, 1847.

On July twenty-sixth the Declaration of Independence was made and the Constitution of the Liberian Republic was adopted.

J R Roberts

with loves for Miss Brown

MRS. JANE ROBERTS

Wife of the First President of Africa

"The flag consisted of eleven stripes alternately red and white; the field, blue, bore a single white star. It is suggested that the meaning of the flag is this: The three colors indicate the three counties into which the Republic is divided. The eleven stripes represent the eleven signers of the Declaration and the Constitution; the lone star indicated the uniqueness of the African Republic."

The election was held in October and Joseph Jenkin Roberts, the governor of the Commonwealth was elected to the new office of President of the Republic. One of his earliest acts was to visit Europe in order to ask the recognition of the new nation by European countries. The first to recognize the Republic was Great Britain in 1848; the second, France in 1852; the United States in 1862. In 1858 Mr. Roberts was appointed president of Liberia College. In 1862 was sent to Europe and appointed Belgian Consul.

In 1872 he was re-elected president for the fifth time. President Roberts was a superior man in intelligence and moral integrity. His excellence in conversation and elegance of manners rendered him popular in the Courts of France and England.

During his long and eventful public life, he was ably assisted by his excellent wife, the subject of this sketch.

Mrs. Roberts graced the Executive Mansion with ease and dignity. She spoke English and French fluently and in all respects was well-bred and refined. She accompanied her husband on many of his visits and was the recipient of great attention wherever she appeared. She had the distinction of being twice presented to her Majesty Queen Victoria, once with her husband on the Queen's royal yacht. At the conclusion of that visit to England, the President and Mrs. Roberts were courteously returned to Monrovia on the British war-ship Amazon.

Her second appearance before the British Queen was no less interesting. An African woman by the name of Martha Ricks, famous for her patch work quilts, had for twenty-five years been piecing an intricate pattern, which she declared when completed was to be a gift to Queen Victoria. The good woman grew old as she pieced and stitched and quilted, never wavering nor doubting. It became a standing joke—*Aunt Martha's quilt*—"Is Aunt Martha still quilting?" "When will Aunt Martha finish her quilt?" were questions often heard.

Thus a generation passed until at last it was finished and Aunt Martha unfolded a most beautiful creation. A quilt which showed a complete coffee tree all in green and yellow on white ground—its branches and leaves perfectly formed, the flowers at the root of the leaves and its berries—exquisite in tracery and workmanship.

The design was so unique and true to nature that it was admired by all who saw it.

The laugh was turned, but how was the Queen to get it? "I shall take it to the Queen myself," said Aunt Martha. Again the joke went around—"Aunt Martha's going to take her quilt to England," they laughed and joked. Mrs. Roberts saw and admired the quilt, heard the story and the way was found. She and Aunt Martha embarked for England carrying the much prized quilt. On reaching London a meeting was arranged and Aunt Martha stood in a palace and had the joy, after years of patience and perseverance, to present in person her quilt which was graciously accepted by that noblest of sovereigns, the Queen of Great Britain and Empress of all India, Victoria Regina. Today the workmanship of this humble African woman adorns a niche in the art collections of Windsor Castle. Mrs. Roberts and Aunt Martha, the latter laden with gifts from the royal household, were returned to Monrovia, by her majesty's command, on a special ship with royal escort.

On reaching her home, Clay-Ashland, a great concourse of people, men, women and children were at the wharf to greet Aunt Martha, while Sunday school scholars sang a song of welcome.

The writer during a visit to London in 1910 met Mrs. Roberts at the home of Mr. William Archer the first colored man to become Mayor of Battersea, a district of the Metropolis.

Mrs. Roberts, notwithstanding the weight of ninety-one years, was clear in mind and wonderfully active. She related the story of Aunt Martha among other incidents of interest. She was in England on official business.

In previous years she had secured considerable money to erect a hospital in Monrovia and was endeavoring to enlist the support of English friends to supplement the same through generous gifts.

Whenever Mrs. Roberts went abroad she was spoken of as "the sweet old lady who looked so much like the Queen."

She passed away in London, never returning to the land of perpetual verdure, the country she loved so well and to which she had given the best years of her life to redeem.

AUNT MAC

A LIFE IN THREE CHAPTERS

CHAPTER I.

It was about the 1st of April, in the year 1820, that an emigrating party started from Green Springs, Virginia, to the State of Kentucky. It consisted of Col. Richard Morris, his six children and their mother. There were twenty other families, making a total of 100 persons. Their route was overland, being undertaken in wagons and carriages. The spring season being unusually early the journey was a very pleasant one. Their way lay through the charming, rolling land of Virginia, now fording a muddy, dashing brook, and again riding over some mountain spur.

When eventide began to settle heavily around them, they halted amid a thickly sheltered wood, near some friendly, gushing spring, and when the eastern sky was crimsoned by the blush of the coming morn, the party resumed its journey. How eagerly they drank in the balmy spring air, and how they admired the beauteous scenes as they arose, one after another, like some grand panorama. The Cumberland Mountains loomed up before them with its shaggy brows, and vehicle after vehicle rolled through its noted gap.

One month was thus spent, the party reaching its destination the first of May. They settled on a farm consisting of three thousand acres, which was situated six miles below the city of Louisville.

The parents of the Morris children died shortly after their arrival, leaving them under an executor's care, who was to educate them and see that the estate was equally divided among them. The agreement was not kept. The children received no education at his hands and were defrauded of thirty thousand dollars. They were thus thrown upon their own responsibilities, and let it be known that each attained honorable manhood and womanhood.

Our sketch has to do principally with the second child, Hannah. She was born in the year, 1810, and consequently was ten years old when the family removed to Kentucky. Her home was with her eldest brother, Shelton Morris, until her marriage to Mr. McDonald, which occurred in the year 1833. Albany, Indiana, was chosen as their future place of abode, and here seven years—golden years of joy and happiness—sped swiftly by, when her companion was called from labor to reward. The desolated home was abandoned and Mrs. McDonald removed to Cincinnati, where she became an inmate of her younger sister's house.

Here she began living only for others and wholly forgetting self—one of her loveliest traits that shone out in every action. How weak are the words employed and how short the space allotted to tell the half of this dear saint.

CHAPTER II.

Several years have elapsed since the closing events of chapter one. We find ourselves standing in a large grove where tall symmetrical trees nod and wave to each passing breeze. Nicely-kept paths intersect each other, winding here and there and leading to the neat cottages that stand in orderly rows on either side of the campus. Before us, some distance back, a large brick building—a central one flanked on each side by a wing—raises itself even beyond the tallest forest tree.

A wide carriage drive rolls from the road to the building and the whole is surrounded by a white, paling fence with its neat stiles and wicket gates. The dew trembles on every leaflet and blade of grass; the day king mounts higher and higher, while the feathery songsters warble their most tuneful lays. What an enchanted spot is this! Can you not recognize the place, dear friend? Ah! yes, you say, 'tis the name so dear to many, the oft-repeated name of Wilberforce. It is here we find Mrs. McDonald in the home of her sister, Mrs. D. A. Payne.

Mrs. McDonald, did we say? How strangely that sounds. Scarcely one in a score knew that she had any other name save Aunt Mac. She was everybody's Aunt Mac, from the hoary-headed man to the prattling babe. But the pleasant sitting-room is before us now, and the low rocking chair in which she used to sit and knit. How the needle would click and fly. The stockings and mittens piled on each other, came as if by magic. Everywhere and always could be heard her firm elastic step going on some errand of mercy, to relieve some heavy heart by her deeds of kindness and by that sweet happy face over which no shade of sorrow ever seemed to pass. All the little ones for miles around knew and loved her. She had a kind word for Willie and a caress for Jennie, and when in the height of their childish sports her laugh would ring out and mingle with theirs in innocent glee. And such a laugh! I wish you might have heard it! It was like the rippling of some happy stream, so cheery its sound and so full of hearty good will. She was the very providence, too, of the whole neighborhood. Her clear head and peace-loving spirit has helped overcome many straits and brought about numerous reconciliations. She—our dear Aunt Mac—loved us all and wished there were more to love. A great expansive heart was hers beneath that stately black, or the folds of that plainer Quaker dress. We can see her today, those soft brown eyes with more beauty in them than time could touch, those eyes that had both smiles and tears within the faintest call of every one she loved. Her charity was even more beautiful than her patience or kindness. There was no hut so mean, or its occupants so poor, that had not a claim upon her. It was at such doors that her faded and tremulous hands tapped the oftener for admission.

From her capacious pocket and basket that dear hand

was ever withdrawn closed, only to be opened in some little toddler's with nuts, the little egg she had found, or the cakes she had baked. And how the mother's eyes would shine with gratitude as she received the warm shawl or frock that Aunt Mac had brought. This, dear reader, is no fiction, but a glimpse only of one of the most beautiful, Christian characters that was ever perfected for immortality.

CHAPTER III.

A pretty home with many a cluster of shrubs and cedars. May flowers fill the air with fragrance. 'Tis Evergreen Cottage—Aunt Mac's home. But why are the shutters closed, and what means that bow of heavy crape? We enter—a death-like stillness pervades. Then we learn that she has flown—that our dear Aunt Mac is with us no more. "It was only this morning she went," says one. A loving hand penned a letter she dictated, and then—a look of recognition, a smile and that sweet spirit took its gentle flight into the fullness of life. Her work was done and nobly done. She was not left to suffer, but while fond hearts would detain her and loving hands were clinging to her to keep her from dying, she silently vanished from our sight, and we can hardly see to write for the memory of her, though it is an arm's length till sunset. It is only a short time since we folded her in the soft gray robe—a short time since we placed her within the casket and gazed affectionately upon the serene face whose youth and freshness seemed to return and made her even more beautiful in death than in life.

So vivid is it all before us, that we are again in the past and beside her. The white hands are so meekly folded upon the still bosom that there seems to be prayer in them there. All lips are mute and all hearts are touched. Even merry, rollicking Dash quits his sports and whines piteously. The pet canary has ceased its song, while the lofty pines outside sing a sad refrain as we bear the dear form from the home she has gladdened for forty long years. The college bell sends out its solemn toll, as the casket is rested near the alter, and that good man the preacher, repeats words of consolation that fall like balm upon our wounded hearts. Then the funeral train moves slowly to the cemetery, that peaceful city of the dead, where the tall grass bends in sadness and the willows sob and sigh; there we laid her. No, no; not *her,* only the tenement. "That home above; that scene of love"—is thine, forever, Aunt Mac. Thou art "robed in whiteness, clad in brightness, sweeping through the gates." No memorial services were held over her, no resolutions printed, but she was "one of them"—the blood-washed, whose works do follow after them.

Aunt Mac is no more and we shall miss her forever, but each of her loved ones can set up a tablet in the heart and write upon it simply this:

Sacred to the Memory

of

OUR DEAR AUNT MAC

HARRIET TUBMAN

HARRIET—THE MOSES

1821—March 10, 1913

When America writes her history without hatred and prejudice she will place high in the galaxy of fame the name of a woman as remarkable as the French heroine, Joan of Arc, a woman who had not even the poor advantages of the peasant maid of Domremy, but was born under the galling yoke of slavery with a long score of cruelty.

Her service to her race and country are without parallel in like achievements by any member of her sex in the history of the world.

Harriet Tubman may be justly styled a Homespun Heroine.

This historic character is in a class to herself. She had the skill and boldness of a commander,—the courage and strategy of a general. A picturesque figure standing boldly against the commonplace, dark background of a generation in which her lot was cast.

Stranger than fiction have been her escapes and exploits in slavery.

She was called "Moses" because of her success in guiding her brethren out of their land of Egypt.

She was also called "General Moses"—an Amazon in strength and endurance and is described as a woman of no pretensions, a most ordinary specimen of humanity. Yet in point of courage, shrewdness and disinterested exertions to rescue her fellow men she had no equal.

Harriet appears to have been a strange compound of practical shrewdness and of a visionary enthusiasm. She believed in dreams and omens warning and instructing her in her enterprises. At times she would break forth into wild and strange rhapsodies which to her ignorant hearers seemed the work of inspiration, to others a power of insight beyond what is called natural, to excel in the difficult work she had chosen for herself. The first twenty-five years of her life were spent as a slave on a Maryland plantation.

She worked beside oxen and horses as a field hand and developed a strong muscular body and at the same time an unconquerable spiritual force which was regarded as dogged stubbornness in not submitting to the lords of the lash. One fair morning Harriet left for freedom. She managed it so easily that she began planning to help others. She worked in Northern hotels till she saved enough money to pay the expenses of a trip to her old neighborhood.

The first to be rescued were her own family at different times. Her three brothers left under her direction hiding for days in their father's corn crib, among the ears of corn. The father was in the secret but they feared to trust their mother's excitable nature lest it betray them.

The boys could see their mother come out shading her eyes and gazing down the long road, in the fond hope of seeing her boys coming home to spend the Christmas with her.

The father pushed food through the chinks but took care not to set eyes on them, that he might be able to swear when the time came for questions. At night they started looking through the cabin window at the poor old mother crooning over the fire, pipe in her mouth, rocking her head on her hand mourning that the boys did not come.

The father went some miles blindfolded, the sons holding his arms and when they took leave of each other he could still say he had not seen them.

Notwithstanding all this precaution the old man came under suspicion and was to be tried for helping fugitives slaves. At this juncture Harriet came to settle the matter by "removing the case to a higher court." In an old broken down sort of a wagon she quietly drove off with her parents and seemed to have met no trouble in reaching free soil.

For two decades, prior to the Civil war, Harriet made many journeys to the South and brought four hundred slaves to the North and Canada not one of whom was caught nor did she ever fall into the hands of the enemy, though at one time twelve thousand dollars reward was offered for this mysterious "black ghost." Along the route this modern Joan of Arc marched without an army or panoply of war; with niether shield nor spear, but many lurking foes and hidden perils to be met and overcome.

Swamps and tangled brush their bed at night, preferring the company of the wild things of the forest, even venomous reptiles to the infuriated slave catcher. Foot sore and weary with her scared and hunted followers, she forged ahead with an unconquerable spirit truly heroic in her sacrifice for her fellow creatures.

Harriet was employed in the Underground Rail Road service. William Still in his records regards her as a highly trusted ally. On this work in the late forties she would be absent for weeks at a time dropping completely out of sight, running daily risks making preparations for herself and passengers, but she seemed wholly devoid of personal fear, and seemed proof against all adversaries. While she manifested such utter personal indifference she was most watchful with regard to those she was piloting.

Half of her time she appeared to be asleep and would actually sit down by the roadside and go fast asleep, yet she would not suffer one of her party to whimper once about "givin' out and goin' back," however wearied they might be from hard travel. She had one short, pointed law of her own which implied death to any one who talked of 'givin' out or goin' back." Her followers had full fatih in her and would back up any words she uttered. So, when she said to them that a live runaway could do a great harm by going back, but a dead one could tell no secrets, she was sure to have strict obedience.

She was the friend and counselor of John Brown, who spoke of her with enthusiasm as the "Most of a man," he had ever met with. In his hut at North Elba in the Adirondacks—"Today a worthier goal or pilgrimage than any medieval shrine"—they drew plans for his attack on Harpers Ferry.

During the Civil War, Harriet served with distinction as a scout for Governor Andrews with his Massachusetts troops and guided Colonel Montgomery of the Union forces in his memorable expedition in South Carolina. She had many narrow escapes but succeeded in out-witting the Confederates and avoided capture as well.

She was introduced to Boston's cultured audience by noted Abolitionists as "Our foster sister Moses."

Her courage and deeds of self-sacrifice should be a lasting inspiration to the youth of the race.

Harriet's proceedings and her peculiar methods of escape are not related in detail. Only one complete story of any length is presented.

The Story of Joe

A slave named Joe fell into the hands of a new master whose first order to him was to strip and take a whipping as a reminder to better behave himself. Joe, seeing no present help submitted to the lash, but thought to himself, "This is the first time—and the last!" That night he went to the cabin of Harriet's father and said, "Next time Moses comes let me know." In a few weeks Harriet came, then as usual men, women and children began to disappear from the plantations. Joe, his brother and two others went with the party. Hunting and hiding,—separated and brought together again by roundabout ways, passed on through the aid of secret friends they got at last opposite Wilmington, Delaware. The pursuers were hot after them and large rewards offered for the arrest of each member of the party.

It was Harriet's method, we are told, to leave on a Saturday night, since no advertisements could be issued on Sunday, thus giving the fugitives a day's start of publicity. They found the bridge at Wilmington closely guarded by police officers on the lookout for them. It seemed impossible to cross in safety. But in that city lived Thomas Garrett a great lover of humanity through whose hands two thousand slaves are said to have passed on their way to liberty. His home was the North Star to many a fainting heart.

This century has grand scenes to show and boast of among its fellows. But few transcend that auction-block where the sheriff was selling all Garrett's goods for the crime (?) of giving a breakfast to a family of fugitive slaves. As the sale closed the officer turns to Garrett saying: "Thomas, I hope you'll never be caught at this again." "Friend," was the reply, "I haven't a dollar in the world, but if thee knows a fugitive who needs a breakfast, send him to me." Harriet had secret news sent to this good Quaker. He was equal to the emergency. He engaged two wagons and filled them with brick-layers, Irishmen and Germans. They drove over the bridge, shouting and singing as if for a frolic in the country. The guards let them pass and naturally expected to see them return. As night fell the merry party came back making as much noise as before and again passed without suspicion, but this time the runaways were concealed at the bottom of the wagons and soon hidden away in the home of Mr. Garrett. So far so good, but Joe could not feel at ease until he was safe in Canada.

As the train in which they were approached the suspension bridge below Niagara Falls, the rest of the excited party burst into singing even before they were out of danger, but Joe was too oppressed to join in their joy.

When the cars began to cross the bridge Harriet, anxious to have her companions see the Falls, called eagerly for them to look at the wonderful sight, but still Joe sat with his head upon his hand.

"Joe, look at de Falls!" "Joe, you fool you—come see de Falls! It's your last chance." But Joe sat still and never raised his head. At length Harriet knew by the rise in the center of the bridge and the descent on the other side that they had crossed the line. She sprang across to Joe's seat, shook him with all her might and shouted, "Joe, you've shook de lion's paw." Joe did not know what she meant. "Joe, you are free."

Then the strong man who could stand under the master's whip without a groan, burst into a hysterical passion of weeping and singing, so that his fellow passengers thought he had gone crazy. But all rejoiced and gave him sympathy when they knew the cause of his emotions.

HARRIET TUBMAN

In 1441 Negro slaves were introduced into Portugal; in 1474,Seville, Spain, had Negroes in abundance and their welfare was the special care of the joint sovereigns. A letter is extant signed by Ferdinand and Isabella describing a certain Negro as of noble birth, investing him with the title of Mayoral of the Negroes and giving him credit for 'sufficed ability and good disposition." This proves that all African slaves were not debased savages, that under human treatment they displayed the better phases of human nature, that not innate depravity but inhuman depression tended to lower them into a submerged stratum of sordid existence.

The entrance of the African into what is now the United States is at once a tale of glory and of shame. His presence remains a monument to the cupidity of those who abrogated to themselves inherent superiority. His survival and steady numerical increase despite oppression strongly confirms the facts of his innate power of endurance and of his power of recuperation. Generations of slavery failed to blot out entirely all vestiges of manliness from this maltreated African and his descendants. The stories of thousands of self-emancipated slaves are recitals of deeds of daring, determination, and decision that favorably compare with the far-famel exploits of universally acknowledged heroes. Again and again men and women voluntarily exposed themselves to the miseries of stealthy journeys involving hunger, thirst and fatigue with perils by land and by water. Sustained by a burning desire to be free they risked discovery which meant virtual death by torture. Nor have the qualities which proved their manhood in days of bondage lessened in either force or character during the days of nominal freedom that have followed formal emancipation. Despite a pernicious "custom of the country," the contingent of American citizens of African descent is steadily forging ahead with a growing consciousness of both the duties and prerogatives attached to unshackled manhood. Our country's history is replete with instances of Negro patriotism. Unlike the Indian, the American Negro will continue to live. His future is inextricably bound up with the fate of the land where his loyalty has been repeatedly tested and never found wanting.

In the Negro are fundamental traits which have insured his practical salvation. Negro faith, fidelity, patience, patriotism, have passed into proverbs. Negro imagination, optimism, appreciation of the artistic sense of humor, are the occasional stars illumining the habitual gloom of surrounding mists of insensate race prejudice. Therefore there is a broader than individual application implied in the forceful tribute written many years ago by Miss Pauline Hopkins in honor of Harriet Tubman. Of this grand women she speaks with rare delicacy, accuracy and appreciation: "Harriet Tubman, though one of earth's lowliest ones, displayed an amount of heroism in her character rarely possessed by those of any station of life. Her name deserves to be handed down to posterity side by side with those of Grace Darling, Joan of Arc, and Florence Nightingale; no one of them has showed more courage and power of endurance in facing danger and death to relieve human suffering than did this woman in her successful and heroic endeavors to reach and to save all whom she might of her oppressed people."

Harriet was born a slave; at the immature age of six years hired out by a cruel master and mistress who surpassed him in fiendish ingenuity, she had literally no childhood. In her early teens she was put to work in the fields. There she followed the oxen, loaded and carried wood, for the work of a full grown man was expected of her. The hard work she performed and the heavy burdens she carried developed her physically until her feats of strength and muscular agility made her a wonder. Yet she suffered under the strokes of the lash as if she were one of the least willing or efficient. Till the day of her death her scarred shoulders and bruised back bore mute though eloquent testimony to the inhumanity of the customary plantation discipline. A blow on the head with a weight from the scales inflicted permanent injury. She had in consequence irregular fits of apparent insensibility. Her lucid moments were nevertheless frequent enough and lasted long enough for her to do some thinking and to the purpose. She at last decided she could no longer exist in the miasmatic atmosphere of thraldom; the propect of being sold brought the matter to a crisis. Late one afternoon she set off singing, but with painful step and slow. Though her body was weak from deprivation, her spirit was brave and steadfast. She thought "there's two things I've got a right to—'Death or Liberty'—one or t'other I mean to have." That such a woman inspired by such a resolve should succeed is more a matter of admiration than of astonishment; that such a woman could be satisfied to become free while so many dear to her were still in bondage would have been indeed a surprise. A person of her broad sympathies could find permanent happiness only in concentrating her energies outside and beyond herself upon finding there was now but little comparatively speaking to call for strenuous action on her own behalf. Not only did this intrepid woman essay but she succeeded in leading ten of her immediate family and many friends to attain the boon she had so assiduously sought. Nineteen times she essayed the hazardous journeys covering and recovering the trackless waste stretching between the desert of bondage and the promising fields of freedom. She began this crucial traverse of a "via dolorosa" in her prime and continued it through her mature years until the need for such sacrifice no longer existed. Not once did she fail in her attempts to discharge what she considered her duty; during the interim she was never one hour free from the handicap of broken health. A reward of forty thousand dollars was at one time offered for the head of this woman whose only crime was that she loved liberty more than life. She traveled where posters advertising her were read by others in her hearing—"being unable to read herself, she went on trusting in the Lord." By her people she was known as "Moses" and they too believed: "De Lord he gave Moses the power." In underground circles she was called "Moll Pitcher" because of her energy and determination.

The struggles of the pioneer mothers of this great republic supply themes for many an absorbing romance, many a glowing verse of poetry; the equally unique tales of the self-abnegation of the black woman of the South are largely as yet traditional. Some day they will be enshrined in permanent form and the world will learn in detail what they effected by their exercise of indomitable will, enduring fidelity and unsullied faith. In no other way can the meed of simple justice be accorded a host of noble souls of whom Harriet Tubman was a distinguished representative.

When in the march of affairs Harriet found no further need for continuing her mission of mercy she transferred her activities from her people to her country. During the earlier stages of the Civil War, "Moses" hung upon the skirts of the Union Army, helping the "contrabands" who sought refuge within its lines. When the freedmen became soldiers she went from camp to camp nursing the sick and succoring the wounded. To the ordinary pursuits she added another, one none the less important because carried on in secret; she became virtually a volunteer spy and penetrating the lines of the enemy, gained valuable information as to the strength of armies and batteries. Illiterate as she was her mental alertness and spiritual development were extraordinary. Shrewed, loyal, God fearing, "Moses" was in her glory while she still found she could be of service. To do for others was more than a principle with her, it was a passion.

In personal appearance Harriet was ordinary almost to repulsiveness; at most times she had a half vacant stare, and rarely when quiet seemed more than half awake. Yet her lack of education did not prevent the most cultured persons from listening absorbed to her strange eventful tales, told with the pathos and simplicity that bore conviction with their recital. She knew all the leaders in the abolition movement and had in her possession letters sent to her by patriots like Gov. Andrews of Massachusetts, William H. Seward, and other prominent persons. At Concord, a welcome was always in waiting for her ,for Lowell, Emerson, Alcott, and Mrs. Horace Mann all respected, admired and placed implicit confidence in and reliance upon her truthfulness. She was practically purely true African, but her patience, foresight, devotion and sagacity put her apart and above the rank and file of those who have passed meritorious careers under ordinary conditions, and elevated her to that high citienship in the realm of genius where race nor sex, extraneous circumstances nor color are given even passing consideration.

When the "cruel war" was over, on the way to a northern home with a soul overflowing with rejoicing, an unfeeling conductor forcibly ejected her from a car. From the injury resulting she was a life long victim.

Through the good offices of Hon. William H. Seward, Harriet was enabled to procure a tract of land in Auburn, N. Y. Upon this she built a cabin and there placed her parents whom she had rescued during her last journey south. She also erected a home for aged and indigent colored people upon the same tract. Compelled later to relinquish the charge of this, she surrendered all her interest in the same to a religious organization. Constantly soliciting from others for others, for a long time she helped to support two schools for freedmen.

At length the combined disabilities of permanent ill health and advancing age overcame her and she was found to be in an enfeebled, destitute condition. A philanthropic woman, Mrs. Sarah H. Bradford of Geneva, wrote her story; a generous citizen of Auburn gave it to the world, having had it published by subscription, so that the gross receipts could be devoted to her needs, and the Empire State Federation sent its president, Mrs. Mary B. Talbert of Buffalo to pay her an official visit. From thenceforth the comfort of this veteran was assured. The thoughtful ministration of the Federation did not cease with her life, but continued until her final resting place was fittingly marked with a simple, but appropriate shaft of stone. Harriet deeply appreciated the practical sympathy of those good women, her sisters by ties of lineage and race extraction. The last message she sent was this: "Tell the women to stick together. God is fighting for them and all will be well!"

Upon her decease the city of Auburn erected a tablet to her memory. This adorns one of the public buildings and upon it is inscribed the outlines of the life story of this woman whose charity was unbounded, whose wisdom, integrity, and patriotism enabled her to perform wonders in the cause of freedom.

"Harriet Tubman" uplift and betterment clubs are

maintained by our women in Boston, Philadelphia and Greater New York. These are devoted to the laudable intention of keeping alive the influence of her perservering endeavor to incite to noble action, the friends of liberty, humanity and justice.

HARRIET TUBMAN

(From the "American Review," August, 1912)

No one knows exactly when Harriet Ross was born, but it was on the eastern shore of Maryland and not much less than a hundred years ago. She knows that her mother's mother was brought in a slave-ship from Africa, that her mother was the daughter of a white man, an American, and her father a full-blooded Negro.

Harriet was not large but she was very strong. The most strenuous slave-labor was demanded of her—summer and winter she drove ox-carts—she plowed—with her father she cut timber and drew heavy logs like a patient mule. About the year 1884 she was married to a freedman named Tubman. He proved unworthy of her and deserted her. She determined to try and escape from slavery and induced her two brothers to go with her. The three started together, but the brothers soon became frightened and turned back. Harriet went on alone. When she reached a place of safety it was morning. She says, "I looked at my hands to see if I was the same person, now I was free—there was such glory over everything, the sun came like gold through the trees and over the fields and I felt like I was in Heaven." Not one to enjoy Heaven alone was that generous heart. Nineteen times did she return to the land of slavery; and each time brought away to Canada groups of men, women, and children, her parents and brothers among them, about three hundred in all. A prize of $40,000 was offered for her capture, but Harriet was never caught. She delights to recall the fact that on all these long perilous journeys on the "Underground Railroad" she never lost a passenger! Her belief that she was and is sustained and guided by "de sperit of de Lord"—is absolute. Governor Andrew of Massachusetts appointed her scout and nurse during the war. She is now receiving a pension.

One of the most important episodes in which Harriet took a leading part and proved the saving factor was Colonel Montgomery's exploit on the Combahee River. General Hunter secured Harriet's assistance for the great undertaking. The plan was to send several gunboats and a few men up the river, in an attempt to collect slaves living near the shores—and carry them down to Beaufort within the Union lines. It is worth a day's journey to hear Harriet herself describe the vivid scene. Throngs of hesitating refugees, a motley crowd, men, women, children, babies—"Peers like I nebber see so many twins in my life"—and pigs, and chickens and such domestic necessities as could be "toted" along. The slave-drivers had used their whips in vain to get the poor refugees back to their quarters; and yet the blacks were almost as much in dread of the stranger soldiers. How to deal with this turbulent mass of humanity? The colonel realized the danger of delay, and calling Harriet to the upper deck, in voice of command said: "Moses you'll have to give 'em a song!" Then the power of the woman poured forth—Harriet lifted up a voice full of emotional fervor in verse after verse of prophetic promise. She improvised both words and melody:

Of all the whole creation in the East or in the West,
The glorious Yankee nation is the greatest and the best!
Come along! Come along! Don't be alarm,
Uncle Sam's rich enough to give us all a farm!
Come along! Come along! Don't be a fool,
Uncle Sam's rich enough to send us all to school! (etc.)

As she chanted the refrain "come along!" she raised her long arms with an imperious gesture impossible to resist. The crowd responded with shouts of "glory, glory." The victory was won—about eight hundred souls eagerly scrambled on board the ships and were transported to freedom.

Among the many men of note who trusted and encouraged the intrepid little woman were Wendell Phillips, William Lloyd Garrison, Thomas Garrett, William H. Seward, Emerson, Alcott, Dr. Howard Brown. Frederick Douglas wrote to her—"Excepting John Brown, I know of no one who has encountered more perils and hardships to save our people." John Brown said, "Mr. Phillips, I bring you one of the best and bravest persons of this continent, General Tubman, as we call her." He also said, "She is the most of a man I ever met with." This war-time general now speaks with tender reverence—"John Brown my dearest friend" —and she whom he called "the most of a man" IS also more of a mother than most women. She founded and maintained a home for colored men and women. She "dwells in the midst of them singing."

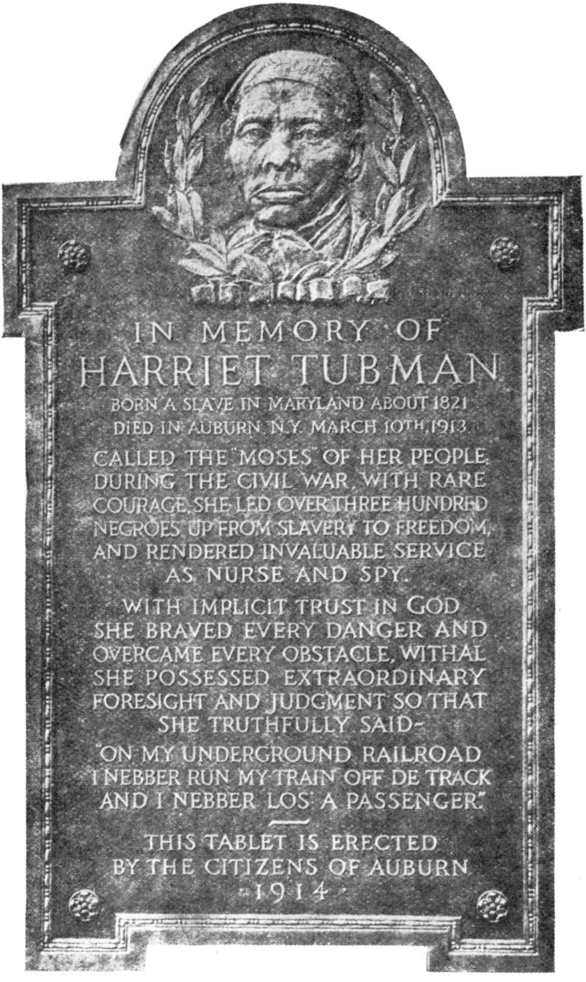
IN MEMORY OF
HARRIET TUBMAN
BORN A SLAVE IN MARYLAND ABOUT 1821
DIED IN AUBURN N.Y. MARCH 10TH, 1913
CALLED THE "MOSES" OF HER PEOPLE
DURING THE CIVIL WAR, WITH RARE
COURAGE, SHE LED OVER THREE HUNDRED
NEGROES UP FROM SLAVERY TO FREEDOM,
AND RENDERED INVALUABLE SERVICE
AS NURSE AND SPY.
WITH IMPLICIT TRUST IN GOD
SHE BRAVED EVERY DANGER AND
OVERCAME EVERY OBSTACLE, WITHAL
SHE POSSESSED EXTRAORDINARY
FORESIGHT AND JUDGMENT SO THAT
SHE TRUTHFULLY SAID-
"ON MY UNDERGROUND RAILROAD
I NEBBER RUN MY TRAIN OFF DE TRACK
AND I NEBBER LOS' A PASSENGER."
THIS TABLET IS ERECTED
BY THE CITIZENS OF AUBURN
1914

GRANDMOTHER GROSS

1817—(?)

The subject of this sketch is a picturesque and interesting personage of 108 years of age.

Elizabeth West Gross, familiarly and affectionately known as "Grandmother Gross" was born in New Liberty, Owen County, Kentucky, October 7, 1817.

When three years of age, her mother was sold for debt to Dr. Gayle, New Liberty. There she lived until she was twenty-one, when she married Peter Herndon Gross.

"Granny Gross" is the mother of five children, has fourteen grandchildren, and seventeen great-grandchildren. Her youngest son and last child, nearing seventy years of age, died recently in Pittsburgh, Pa.

During all of her years before the Civil War, "Granny Gross" never left the old plantation, and when freedom came she lived with the daughter of her former mistress, Mrs. Hallum, who lives with her daughter, Mrs. Russell Reville.

Grandmother Gross has been and is yet a great traveler. She has made ten visits to Washington, D. C., some of which were to inaugurations. She has seen many notable persons among whom were Abraham Lincoln and James Buchannon.

She tells of the Indians who often passed her home in great numbers, going to school which was taught by old Col. Dick Jackson. Ofttimes they would stop and she gave them food.

She remembers clearly the night of November 13, 1833, when the stars fell as thick as hail.

Sometimes when "Granny Gross" is in a reminiscent mood she will sing snatches of old campaign songs, popular during the Harrison and Tyler and Polk campaigns, to the great delight to her listeners and her own enjoyment.

Grandmother Gross possesses few characteristics peculiar to old persons. She has not taken any medicine in ten years, has recently completed three beautiful silk quilts and crocheted several sets of mats. She seldom uses glasses.

On the occasion of her 106th birthday, October 7, 1923, a noted local baker made and presented to her a handsomely decorated cake mounted by 106 candles.

There was never a more faithful follower of Isaak Walton than is "Granny Gross." Only last September she spent an afternoon fishing at her favorite spot.

A few years ago, she made a visit to the home of her former owner's daughter who is past seventy. Upon her arrival there she found a very sick member of the family. The trained nurse in charge proved incompetent and was forthwith discharged. Then "Granny Gross," at the age of 96, was given the case and the patient recovered. In her prime, she was unsurpassed as a nurse.

Even now at her advanced age, she is wonderfully active and requires the aid of neither crutch nor cane to climb a long stairway to her bedroom.

The Sunshine Club, a charitable club of Urbana, has for several years made Grandmother Gross the guest of honor at its annual dinner given for the elderly women of the city. She looks forward to this event with the delight and happiness of a child.

She makes her home with a grand daughter, Mrs. John Kennedy, of Urbana, Ohio.

MRS. FRANCES JANE BROWN

At the Age of 70 Years

At the Age of 94 Years

HOMEWOOD COTTAGE

Wilberforce, Ohio

FRANCES JANE BROWN

April 15, 1819—April 16, 1914

Frances Jane Scroggins first saw the light of day in Winchester, Virginia. Her mother, Ellen Anne Scroggins, with three other small girls formed the household. Their names were Harriet, Eliza Anne and Martha Ellen. Their father died leaving them alone and unprotected.

The grandfather of these children was an officer in the Revolutionary War. He did the honorable thing by emancipating the mother and the four little girls. But they were left destitute and were bound out until a few years later when their mother married a free man, William Tocus, and the children were brought under the shelter of a home.

Frances Jane, the subject of this sketch, often related the cruel treatment at the hands of her "bound mistress," lack of food, clothes and sharp reproof; often stripes from leather tawse upon her bare shoulders. She was frequently mistaken for the daughter of her mistress which so enraged that lady that Frances' long, black hair was cut zigzag that it might grow curly, but it only grew out the straighter. She was made to stand in the sun to tan her, but her complexion was as soft and beautiful as a rose petal. The rigid laws of Virginia prohibited her from ever learning to read or write.

Other children came to the Tocus family increasing the number to seven. It was then that the father, with rare courage and faith determined to migrate to a free state. Frances relates the journey. "We were placed in a big old fashioned covered wagon drawn by four large, black horses which were Daddy's pride. There was plenty of room for us all with feather beds and patch work quilts. We were often frightened going over the mountains and dangerous roads. As night came on we halted, built a fire and ate from the well filled hamper mammy prepared. Several times we were held for hours by the patrol to see if our free papers were correct or valid. Our joy knew no bounds when we sighted and finally crossed the Ohio river and reached free soil."

Slavery

Frances never forgot her first impression of slavery. One bright spring morning, as a little girl, her mother sent her to the nearby town pump for water. Hanging her new tinpail on the spout and swinging onto the huge wooden handle, she was startled by a great cloud of dust which seemed to be coming up the road toward her. Greatly frightened, she left her pail and hid herself behind a clump of bushes by the roadside. She had scarcely concealed herself when a man, with black whiskers and a big straw hat, seated on horseback, brandishing a big, black whip rounded up a long line of naked slaves two by two, chained to each other, calling sharply on them to drink in a hurry. She saw them lap the water from the horse trough under the pump as the soul-driver drank from the pail. Then with the crack of the whip, he dashed down the road, the slaves running at full speed to keep pace with the horse and its rider. For days together, she could not lose sight of those poor creatures with wild staring eyes and tongues lolled out lapping the water like dumb, thirsty animals.

Crazy Jane

There was not much in those early days to interest a little girl like Frances and so minor incidents loomed great in her childish mind.

A strong impression was made upon her by a poor old white woman known as "Crazy Jane" who roamed the streets and lanes repeating snatches of poetry and verses from the Bible, telling the people God was angry with them for holding slaves. As night came on she would sit on some friendly door-step or by the way-side, crooning and singing her favorite bits. One couplet never left Frances.

Seated in the quiet of Homewood Cottage at twilight in the evening of her long life—memories of her childhood came as the plaintive notes of the woodland dove were heard and the couplet heard so often would be given in the drawl of "Crazy Jane"—

"O, don't you hear the mournful dove
Token of Redeeming Love."

For several years after reaching Ohio, Frances made her home with the family of Major W—in Cincinnati. She became deeply interested in the cause of the slaves and joined the Abolitionists. She had several narrow escapes from being arrested.

Walking down the street one day, she came face to face, with a beautiful, young colored woman who was running and looking back. "What is the matter," said Frances. "I just got of'n the boat," she exclaimed breathlessly, "I'm a slave an' runnin' away. They are after me. Won't you hide me?" Frances took her hand, turned about and the two girls ran as fast as they could and had barely got inside of a friend's house before loud knocks were heard. When the door was opened an irate man demanded his slave whom he said he had seen enter the house. Frances stood trembling. The slave-holder declared she was his property. "O, no," said the friends."we know this girl but you are at liberty to look further." In the meantime the slave girl Caroline, had been passed over back-gates and fences and was several doors away. With mutterings of wrath, the man hurried back to the boat which had whistled a warning to depart. Caroline was kept in hiding for some time and finally sent to Canada, where after forty years, she and Frances met on English soil to recount that narrow escape from slavery.

Marriage

At the age of twenty-two, Frances was married to

Thomas Arthur Brown of Frederick, Maryland.

He was held in slavery by his own relatives. By industry he purchased his freedom, that of his only sister, Ann, his brother and his aged father. He was a man of remarkable character and intellect. The full account of his eventful life cannot now be given.

The young couple made their home in the city of Pittsburgh, Pennsylvania. Six children were born to them; all save one reaching womanhood and manhood; Jere A.; Belle J.; Anne E.; Mary F.; Hallie Q. and John G. who was born in Salem, Ohio, the others in Pittsburgh in the homestead on Hazel Street.

Mr. and Mrs. Brown were industrious and accumulated considerable property. Their greatest ambition was to give their children useful education. The older ones attended private school at Avery College under such renowned instructors as Miss Amanda Wier, Prof. J. B. Vashon, Professors Freeman and Samuel Neal. Having seen the horrors of slavery together they espoused the cause of the slave and fought his battle.

Their home became a Station of the *Underground Railroad.* Many a hunted slave found food, shelter and encouragement while waiting to be sent to Canada. At one time a mother and her five children remained one cold winter hidden by Mrs. Brown even from the rest of the family and the knowledge of the neighobrs. At another time, a family, well-known today, escaped from Texas and were cared for in their home for weeks. A remarkable incident occurred when the slave-holder came demanding his property. The children of this family were so fair with blue eyes and golden hair, that none believed they were former slaves. Mr. and Mrs. Brown had their pictures taken, with the American flag wrapped about them, which were sold to help finance the family.

A Haven of Rest

Their home became a haven of rest for the weary, traveling ministry, while one room was set aside and known as "The Bishop's Room." The eldest son was christened by the first Bishop Brown, the youngest daughter was given the name of Bishop Quinn. From this home, while the A. M. E. General Conference was in session in Pittsburgh, Daniel A. Payne was elected Bishop. That home was one of plenty and comfort and for that day and time of elegance and refinement.

Mr. Brown traveled through the states of Pennsylvania, Ohio and Kentucky collecting funds to build Old Wylie Avenue A. M. E. Church while Mrs. Brown with the women of the church raised great sums at home.

Mrs. Brown was the guiding star of the home. Quiet, unobtrusive, she ruled her household by love and gentleness. A model housekeeper, a worker in the church and a neighbor beloved. Mr. Brown was a steward on a Mississippi steamboat making the run from St. Louis to New Orleans. The eldest son, a lad of 16, was allowed to accompany his father on one of his trips on the steamboat, "The Pennsylvania." The crew was composed of colored men and women. That was a fatal trip. The boiler burst, the boat was destroyed and 600 souls were lost. For days no tidings came to Mrs. Brown of her husband and son. With a calm, hopeful manner, she went about her daily task ministering unto and consoling her children and showing only a cheerful face when the report came that Captain Clinefelter and his entire crew were lost. Early one morning, father and son returned, empty handed, dressed in old clothes given them by strangers, but unharmed. It was the occasion for great rejoicing in that home which had been cheered by the faith and trust of a devoted wife and mother.

Failing Health

Mrs. Brown's health became greatly impaired and the family removed to Chatham, Ontario, remaining in that city a year, then went to the farm purchased by Mr. Brown on the 9th Concession, County of Kent, four miles away; well stocked and with a modern and commodious house, well constructed barn and out buildings. Mrs. Brown gained in health and strength and prosperity seemed to wait on the inmates. This, however, was not to last.

Early one Sabbath morning in June that home was destroyed by fire and the fairest of the family, pretty little Mary, with her winning ways, soft black curls and large dark eyes was burned to death. The house had fallen in before she was missed. When the cry came—"Where is Mary?" frantic screams from women and children were heard, terrified men ran here and there seeking the child. Mr. Brown, the father, lost his mind and was restrained by kindly hands from leaping into the flames. Again that quiet, little mother went from one to the other comforting, consoling and during that ordeal—for weeks when the father's mind was a blank—hers was the strong arm upon which the family leaned. Friends by the score came to their relief and through their aid a five-room cottage was built. Here the mother found herself—stripped of all material wealth—no fine furniture or polished mirrors; no rich carpets or silverware; no instruments of music or costly pictures; only plain deal tables and bare floors.

Soon flowers and vines bloomed and clung outside that cottage door, muslin curtains draped the windows and homemade carpets covered the floor. The mother was teaching her children how to be frugal and content. She was Mary and Martha in one. "Homewood Cottage" became a beauty spot on the 9th Concession.

Mr. Brown still plied the river for a livelihood. It was during the Civil War. One day as the boat lay in port at St. Louis, Mo., two men came aboard and asked the porter, Mr. Brown, to take charge of two large carpet bags until they had finished their shopping, taking note of the boat's departure. Always courteous and obliging, Mr. Brown readily consented. The boat left without the two men appearing. At Memphis, Tenn., officers came aboard searching for contraband goods. The carpet bags were seized. The porter could give no other account than that two men in St. Louis left them in his care until their return. The carpet bags contained percussion caps sent to the rebel army. The porter was returned to St. Louis in irons and imprisoned.

It was early autumn when Mrs. Brown learned of her husband's imprisonment. Not knowing how long he would be detained, she began with that calm, quiet spirit, full of determination and action, together with the help of the older children and one hired man to plan for the comfort of her family. It proved to be a most severe winter but there was plenty of meat in the smoke-house, canned and dried fruit, with jellies and pickles on the pantry shelves. The apples and vegetables were stored away; grists of flour and meal were brought from the mills; cords of wood stacked near the cottage door; the cattle were well housed with corn and fodder in crib and barn. Well, could the inmates smile at the great snow drifts that blocked the highways and piled in fantastic heaps about the cottage? All that was missing was the father far away. Words of sorrow and grief came from the helpless, imprisoned one but letters of cheer and happiness were sent to him from Homewood Cottage to brighten the gloomy cell.

Four books adorned the little center table in the home, the Bible, Pilgrim's Progress, Jane Porter's Scottish Heroes, and Spurgeon's Sermons. Each Sabbath, the children gathered around the family altar, passages from the Bible were read and then a sermon from the collection of Charles Spurgeon, the noted English preacher. During the week tales from Jane Porter's Scottish Heroes were read by a member of the family. Every evening after the milking and the chores were done, as twilight approached, a huge back log was rolled into the wide fire-place and soon warmth radiated cheer through the big living room.

The frugal meal of milk and mush was over the dishes tidied, then each would take her task. The wool would be carded by one, another would be at the spinning wheel and the yarn reeled into hanks by the mother.

Deprived of the music of former years, the children sang without accompaniment making melody in their hearts.

During the short winter days there would be an occasional wood chopping bee for the boys and a quilting party for the girls. Again on the moonlight nights a sleigh ride party when several wagon beds, placed on bob-sleds, filled with soft clean hay and merry boys and girls covered with buffalo robes skimmed over miles of road while gay, happy laughter rang out on the frost-laden air.

One day in late spring when the snow had gone and the ice had melted in the nearby streams the father, emaciated and pale came home. It was a season of rejoicing in that happy re-united family. He told them how he had prayed until some one said he not only shook the jail but all St. Louis and as nothing was found against him, he was liberated. "Yes," said Mrs. Brown, "and we prayed too."

One by one the older children left the home to make nests for themselves. Two remained with the mother.

After a few years Mrs. Brown concluded to rent the farm and move to the United States, which she did taking her two youngest children Hallie Q. and John G. to Wilberforce, Ohio, where they could obtain an education at Wilberforce University. Shortly afterward a residence was purchased and the name of the Canadian abode was transferred to the Ohio one. Here in the new "Homewood Cottage" she was permitted to spend in quietude and comfort her declining years. She entered heartily into the spirit of college life and placed her children under the tutelage and training of that master instructor, President Daniel A. Payne. She befriended scores of poor, worthy students and for thirty years brought into her home young men and women to "work for their board" but treated as members of the family, many of whom are today of sterling character and worth in the arena of life.

Mrs. Brown was an active worker in the Holy Trinity Church and one of the first members of the College Aid Society, an organization formed to assist indigent students. She saw borne from the cottage door to peaceful Massie's Creek Cemetery three children and her faithful husband and companion who with her had trod the path of life together for fifty years. Two devoted daughters were left to minister to her declining years. Her influence for good was felt by student body and community while little children loved to lisp the name of "Ma" Brown, the pretty old lady.

Her gentle life and gracious presence fell as a benediction upon that home. A visiting friend remarked that it was worth a trip across the Atlantic to see her. Trained by long schooling and patient labor, possessed by great social timidity and extreme shyness, the writer often gazed on her placid face and wished that hers might grow so fair and pure. She was ninety-five years and a day when silence came to that clear voice, "Thou shall come to thy grave in a full age, like as a shock of corn cometh in His season."

A tribute to Mrs. Frances J. Brown on her 91st birthday, April 15, 1909, by Mrs. B. F. Lee, Sr.:

With glad and reverent hearts we come
Our high esteem to prove,
To bring the lady of this home
Some token of our love.
This lady fair, this mother queen,
With eyes serene and bright,
(Upon whose brow no scowl is seen)
Is ninety-one tonight.

But she is young in heart and soul,
For years have never aged
A heart so warm, with love its goal;
Nor gloom her spirit caged.
What sphere or what position high

Does our sweet lady fill?
With no ambition did she try
To gain fame's shining hill.

But hers was highest of them all
And hallowed most of heaven.
Her children do arise and call
Her blest. To her is given
A calm and ripened womanhood,
Noble type of mother;
And all that's gentle, pure and good
In her has come together.

The secret of endurance long,
By love and duty bound,
She learned and in her task grew strong
And true contentment found.
We thank you for the life you live
Of labor, peace and love;
For sure the creed which you believe
Was handed from above.

The Lord bless thee and keep thee still,
O mother true and dear;
His loving grace thy cup o'erfill,
His presence be thy cheer;
His smiling countenance ne'er cease
To shield thee from all fear
And give thee everlasting peace
O mother true and dear.

Mrs. Eliza Anna Clark
(Eliza Anna Scroggins)

Mrs. Lucretia Simpson

Mrs. Catherine A. Delany

Mrs. Mary Ann Shadd Cary

ELIZA ANNA SCROGGINS

1820-1912

Eliza Anna Scroggins was born March 12, 1820, at Newtown, Virginia, a small town not far from Winchester which is now called Union City. At an early age her mother moved to Winchester where she lived for some years. When a young girl, being born free, she was bound out as a nurse. During the day she looked after the children and after they retired she was made to knit stockings. This knitting was always done standing until nine p. m. Her employers were hard task-masters. Several times she ran away but was always pursued and taken back. As a punishment an extra task was added to her daily duties and always a threat accompanied to cut off her beautiful curls. To have curls was the greatest desire of her employer's children, but their hair was very straight; hence, arose a spirit of jealousy. Mrs. Scroggins went to see Eliza. Eliza told her mother all of her sorrows and few joys and of the threat to cut her hair. The mother protested and said that under no circumstances must this be done. With Eliza's feeling of discontent and the continuous running away it was decided to have her return to her home. Some time afterward she left Winchester for Wheeling, W. Va. She became a member of the Presbyterian Church (white) of that city and was an acceptable member during her stay. Among her employers of Wheeling was the family of a Presbyterian minister, Wade by name. The Wades were very fond of her and treated her more like one of the family, permitting her to sit in the living room with them evenings to sew or knit. She often related how Mrs. Wade would leave the house by the back gate every Sunday after dinner, clad in clothes very different from the ones she wore to church in the morning. It was whispered that she went to teach colored children to read the Bible. Several years were spent in Wheeling when she decided to go to Pittsburgh. One of her first acts after arriving in that city was to join the A. M. E. Church which was then located in Miltenburger's Alley. She made her home with her sister Mrs. F. J. Brown until she was married to William B. Austin in 1844. The ceremony was performed by Rev. Frederick Davis pastor of the A. M. E. Church. After the minister was paid the bridegroom had twelve cents in his pockets. The newly-married began house keeping on a small scale, having one thought, 'Marry for love and work for riches." It was through her Christian character and influence that the husbang joined the church. Their interest and activities knew no bounds and when it was decided to buy land and build a church on Wylie Avenue corner of Elm Street Mr. Austin gave the last five dollars he had to aid in the establishment of the new church. This zeal never abated. In 1857 the husband was called from labor to reward. In the early morning (Friday) of November 13, 1857, the boiler of the steamer *Commonwealth* which was plying in the Missouri river north of St. Louis exploded. Mr. Austin's quarters being near the boiler room, he was scalded so badly that his condition was considered serious. Being taken to a hospital in St. Louis he lingered ten days and passed into the great beyond, leaving a young widow and two small children. At 7 p. m. of November 12th the second child was born to the subject of this sketch. It was Thursday, a damp dreary night and a drizzling rain had set in. The baby sneezed three times when being dressed, some considered it a singular coincidence, others an omen. However, kind friends watched over the widow while others sped to St. Louis with all possible haste to bring the remains of the husband to Pittsburgh where he was laid to rest by the worthy order of Masons of which he was a member. After the husband's death the widow could always be found in her pew in the "Amen Corner" giving voice and aid for every uplift. She was four years on the stewardess board and always showed an interest in every good work. After six years the older child, a boy of ten years was killed by the cars on Easter Saturday while he was trying to sell papers to help his mother. The abounding faith in God only made this Christian woman work for the advancement of Christ and His Kingdom.

At the age of 92 years she fell asleep in Jesus leaving a shining example of Christian fortitude for loved ones and friends to follow.

LUCRETIA HARPER SIMPSON

1820—(?)

Lucretia H. Simpson, now 105 years old (December, 1925) was born in Lafayette, Woodford County, Kentucky, in the blue grass country.

Her master, Edward Darneal, was a planter. He was kind to his slaves. Her father, Reuben Ford, was a free man. His master liberated his slaves and left his estate to them. The will was broken by relatives of the master and all the younger slaves, including her father and his three brothers were sold down in New Orleans. This happened three weeks before Lucretia was born. She never knew her mother for she too was sold soon after Lucretia's birth. When she reached womanhood she was married. Her husband was a free man, but all too soon died, at Lafayette, Kentucky.

She and three other young women decided to go to Maysville and cross the river into Ohio. This they did taking "French leave." Although the war had begun, they were in fear of being caught and returned to slavery but by traveling at night and hiding by day they soon were safe on Ohio soil. Friends came to their relief and Lucretia was sent to Toledo where she soon found employment. She vividly recalls the day when the first colored soldiers came to her home in Kentucky—the praying in secret for *Freedom.*

When she reached Ohio she heard the open unafraid petition. It was most interesting to hear her relate the news that spread that glad hour. It was on one night. They were on their knees singing, praying when excited voices in the street were crying what all thought to be fire, fire, fire. Hurrying out they found the cry was freedom, freedom, freedom. The streets soon were thronged with men and women, white and colored alike crying, clasping hands, praising God, shouting for joy that freedom had come. And not until the sun arose next day did the multitude disperse to their homes.

After Emancipation, "Granny" as she is called, went to Adrian, Michigan, where she now lives with her son, Mr. William Simpson. She goes up and down stairs unaided. Stands and walks erect without the use of cane or support. She loves flowers and may be seen during the summer in the midst of blooms by the cottage side.

She is a member of the Presbyterian Church and has an abiding faith in God's mercies.

SARAH GOULD LEE

1821—1905

In Cumberland County, New Jersey, there is a unique settlement known as Gouldtown. Unique because it represents two hundred years of Negro rural development. The original Goulds held over five thousand acres of rich, Jersey land. A thrifty, sturdy race, they left their impression upon generations of the community. Of the fifth generation was born to Benjamin F. and Phoebe Gould, Sarah, the subject of this sketch.

There were nine children in this family, all noted for their physical comeliness, but Sarah was considered the handsomest of the daughters. With the other children she daily walked three miles to the district school where instruction was given in the three R's. There she gained also some knowledge of history and geography.

But the "readers" of those days were filled with cultural material, veritable anthologies of prose and verse. Sarah early developed a love for books and formed a devotion to literature that remained a characteristic of her life.

There was no need for manual instruction in those schools of yesterday. The home was the vocational school for the little Goulds. Sarah proved as conscientious about the home duties as she was diligent in school, and with her sister, Prudence, had quite a reputation as a needlewoman.

At sixteen, Sarah was teaching in the Gouldtown school, an eager, earnest young "school marm." She held this position for two years, then Abel Lee, a young farmer from near-by Salem, persuaded her to leave the school room and become his wife. An old daguerreotype still preserved gives a dim idea of the young bride's beauty, as she stood in her bridal dress of fine cotton fashioned stitch by stitch by her own clever fingers. Her heavy hair is worn in coronet, and her thoughtful eyes show a confidence seldom found in so youthful a bride.

Abel Lee and his wife set up their home in a little four-roomed house built on his ten acres of land. Six children were born to them. Sarah's was the busy life of the pioneer during the summer. In the winter her cares were additional, for that was the time that the husband joined others of the community for the annual wood-cutting. Early in the fall the men set out for the pine forests, taking provisions to last for weeks. This was the time they chose to lay in fire woods and logs for lumber. During these weeks, crowded with cares as they were, Sarah still found opportunity to read to herself and children. Her reading material was limited to few books; the Bible, a few poems, Pilgrim's Progress, two or three novels, and such current papers and periodicals as she could find.

The wood cutters often found the life of exposure hard on them. But the winter of '52 was marked by a record snowfall preventing them from leaving their shanties and also closing them in from outside relief. Finally a succoring party cut their way through the drifts to the wood-cutters. All of the men showed the effects of the extreme cold, but Abel Lee had suffered most. Double pneumonia had gripped him so strongly that there was no hope of recovery. He reached his home and lingered with the beloved wife and little ones for a few days. The eldest son, Bishop Benjamin F. Lee, who passed March 12, 1926, at the age of eighty-four, recalled the last moments when the father summoned the stricken family to him and gave them his parting message to try to be good and strong.

What a change in the life of Sarah Lee, a widow, with six little children! Elizabeth, the eldest, twelve on the day her father died!

Her indomitable spirit gave her such self-reliance that

she determined to pay off the debt remaining on their property. The creditors thought so highly of the integrity of Abel Lee, that they assured her there would be no need to hurry. However, Sarah was not content to owe anyone a debt, and, as she said, "I have nothing so long as I owe on my possessions."

This brave woman then decided to rent out her home and take a room in town in her brother's home. Here she kept the three youngest children putting the two older boys with relatives to work for their board, clothes and schooling privileges. The eldest daughter was placed with an aunt.

There was almost no opportunity for women to earn money in this rural district, other than to work "at service," for meagre wages. This was no light ordeal for one who, though always poor, had never before labored "for hire." Then, worst of all was the separation from her fatherless children, her beloved circle so broken! Many a bitter tear she shed through the long, weary years of widowhood. Nevertheless she struggled on, trusting in the Lord. Her great solace was the weekly visit to her three absent children. What lessons of probity, endurance and perseverance they received at her knee! Even now, she clung to her reading, inculcating in her boys and girls a love for education and some idea of what was going on in the outside world.

After her debts were all settled and her boys were old enough to work for wages, she moved back to her little home, with her children around her again.

When the eldest son was about twenty years old, he became eager for a better education and decided to go away to school. In this day of opportunity it is hard to picture just what such a decision meant to the entire family. It took a strong woman to be willing to give up the help of her son after waiting so many years for the time to come when he could help bear the burden. Again her Spartan-like qualities asserted themselves. Not only did she consent to his going, but urged him to follow this leading out that he felt. Never, in the lean years that followed did she call him from his purpose.

In spite of her many anxieties she kept cheery and helpful. Her widowhood left but little leisure from its burdens and responsibilities for her to take part in the social life about her. In this way she formed the habit of retirement. But everyone knew that Sarah Lee was a "friend in need," and that what she said was worthy of consideration. She held her place in the community by her solidity, integrity and her endurance through years of hardship.

Her eighty-third birthday found her less rugged in body, but satisfied in the blessed assurance she had redemption through Jesus Christ. Still clear in mind and spirit, she passed on before her eighty-fourth year was completed, leaving the memory of her sterling qualities to her descendants.

MRS. CATHERINE A. DELANY

1822—1894

Mrs. Catherine A. Delany was born in Pittsburgh, Pennsylvania. She was the daughter of Felicia Fitzgerald, a native of Cork, Ireland, and Charles Richards a man of financial standing. His father, familiarly known as "Daddy Ben," was a man of considerable influence and wealth, for many years being the leading butcher of Pittsburgh. He is said to have erected and owned the first brick building in Pittsburgh. In this building for some years the Court held its sessions.

Catherine was united in marriage to a rising young physician, Dr. Martin R. Delany. His parents were pure Africans, coming directly from the South Coast to the state of Pennsylvania.

Catherine linked her life with a man who was destined to be a noted character in race history. During the great epidemic of black, Asiatic Cholera in Pittsburgh, while hundreds died from the scourge, Dr. Delany did not lose a single patient.

As a physician and ethnologist he spent a year on an exploring expedition in the interior of Africa with Mr. Robert Douglas and Prof. Robert Campbell of Philadelphia, Pennsylvania. On his return to England he was accorded high honor by Lord Brougham and other noted men and women of the nobility.

As a tribute and token of esteem, a social organization, composed of English and Scotch members, and an adjunct of the Royal Geographical Society, presented Dr. Delany with a handsome jeweled sword and a Field Marshal's uniform for his activities and research in Central Africa.

At the close of the Civil War he was made a Major, the first Negro to be thus breveted.

The couple lived in Pittsburgh until after the Fugitive Slave Act was passed and was actuated by the infamous Dred Scott decision which followed in its wake to leave this place. Hence in 1856 they moved to Chatham, Ontario. Again in 1864 they moved to Wilberforce University, Ohio, where they could educate their children and where they spent the remaining years of their lives.

Mrs. Delany was a woman of sterling character and marked attainments, an intense reader of history, the highest type of current and standard literature and the Holy Bible. To her children she was a heroine, the strong, self-reliant, faithful mother; their friend and confidante, sharing their joys and sorrows. She willingly sacrificed for the good of her family as well as for the community in which she lived. Her interest in and sympathy for the needy or suffering was untiring. At all times and seasons she heard the call of the distressed and ministered to their wants. Mrs. Delany was a faithful and devoted wife. During her husband's long career and varied activities she kept the home and reared their children to man's and woman's estate. Eleven children were born to this couple. Four died in infancy. Major and Mrs. Delany decided that the children should be named for illustrious members of their own race, and these are the seven who reached their majority. Toussaint L'Ouverture, Charles Lenox Remond, Alexandre Dumas, Saint Cyprian, Faustin Soulouque, Placido Rameses, Hallie Amelia, Ethiopia. And they arose and called her blessed!

MRS. MARY ANN SHADD CARY

1823—1893

THE FOREMOST COLORED CANADIAN PIONEER IN 1850

"Only the actions of the just,
Smell sweet and blossom in the dust."

Among the women of the colored race who rendered signal service in the cause of freedom, the subject of this sketch by reason of the great energy displayed and sincere devotion to the cause, joined to remarkable intellectual power, is entitled to stand in the front rank of that noble band whose virtues and services are the priceless heritage of the colored race.

Few women of any race have left their impression more indelibly stamped upon the age in which they lived, or wrought more beneficially than Mrs. Cary.

Mary Ann Shadd was born October 9, 1823, in Wilmington, Delaware. It being a slave state she was deprived of obtaining the education of which her early development gave promise. At the age of ten years she was taken by her parents to West Chester, Pennsylvania, and placed in an educational institution carried on by Miss Phoebe Darlington under the supervision of the Society of Friends. At the completion of a six-year course she returned to Wilmington, opened a school and taught colored children. Some years after, when public school took the place of private tuition, Miss Shadd taught first in West Chester, New York City, and Norristown, Pennsylvania. While teaching in this state in 1850, the infamous Fugitive Slave Act was passed whereupon she determined to go to Canada and ascertain what opportunities the country offered favorable to the settlement of emigrants of colored people from the north and west. She had seen the effects of slavery on the runaway slaves who found shelter in her father's home, as they fled to a free state. Her young soul burned with indignation as she realized the breadth and depth of this moral malaria, this putrid plague spot—slavery.

At first the law—this latest outrage on suffering humanity—was derided and condemned by liberty loving citizens and fugitives did not fear, asserting that they could protect themselves. This fatal dream was of short duration. Men were arrested and when they resisted or refused to surrender, were shot dead. Many who had been free for twenty years or more, and had in many instances acquired considerable property found themselves only nominally free. Whole families who had lived for years in freedom were pounced upon at mid-night, beaten and dragged back to slavery. A growing feeling of humanity stirred the north—a creative force that produced strong men and women as the result of its awakening force. Colored and white citizens met in private and public meetings, sermons were preached from the pulpits—discussions and resolutions were not unlike the sentiments and expressions of the patriotic outbursts of the American Revolution. As an act of precaution to preserve their freedom, thousands of men, women and children fled to Canada for safety. Many had only sufficient means to enable them to reach the land of freedom, and, until they could get employment, would be wholly dependent upon charity. Miss Shadd located at Windsor, Canada, opposite Detroit, Michigan. She at once began a vigorous and active campaign by publishing a pamphlet which was widely circulated in the United States, setting forth in plain language the opportunities for emigrants in Canada.

To make her work more effective she returned to the United States and for several years delivered lectures throughout the middle, eastern and western states. At that time Abbey Kelley, Lucretia Mott and Lucy Stone, anti-slavery lecturers, took their lives in their hands each time they attempted to urge freedom for the slave. How much greater danger threatened a young colored woman, who publicly sought to aid fugitive slaves to seek a home in Canada and offered the means to carry them there.

So successful was her mission that in 1854 a number of colored men in Toronto assisted her in establishing a weekly paper called "The Provincial Freeman," which was devoted to the interest of the colored people generally, but especially to the fugitives from slavery. Owing to the vigor and relentless war with which Miss Shadd through her columns attacked the slave interest, the sympathizers of slavery located in Windsor, St. Catherines and on the American border made every effort to suppress the sheet; but for three years she fearlessly braved the storm and thus rendered heroic service, and established her record as the first woman editor of the race, as well as the first *educated* race woman as lecturer, Sojourner Truth having begun her work as early as 1843.

In 1856 Mary Ann Shadd was united in marriage to Mr. Thomas F. Cary of Toronto.

After marriage she and her husband resided in Chatham, Canada West. But her public career was by no means ended. Stirring times for the nation and the race were just ahead. She continued to be friend and helper to the refugees.

One Sunday a slave boy without hat, coat, or shoes who had thus far eluded his pursuers, was overtaken in Chatham and about to be carried off. Mrs. Cary tore the boy from the slave hunters, ran to the court-house and had the bell rung so violently that the whole town was soon aroused. Mrs. Cary with her commanding form, piercing eyes, and stirring voice soon had the people as indignant as herself—denouncing in no uncertain terms the outrage perpetrated under the British flag and demanded that these man-hunters be driven from their midst. The result was that the pursuers fled before the infuriated people, happy to get away without bodily harm; and so this insolent slave-power, this monster of hideous mein, was rebuked as he sought to pass the bounds of the prison house and darken the realm of light—even the free air and soil of Canada.

In 1858 John Brown and his companions went to Chatham where on the 8th of May they held a Convention and adopted a "Provisional Constitution,"—John Brown the brave and heroic who went to seek those who were lost that he might save them. He found many who aided him in his daring project. And when the great blow for freedom had been struck and the tragic end had come in 1861, the subject of this sketch compiled the notes of Osborn P. Anderson, sole survivor of the Raid, entitled a "Voice from Harper's Ferry."

At the beginning of the Civil War, Mrs. Cary was teaching school in the State of Michigan. In 1863 a call for 500,000 men was issued by the government. Mrs. Cary with true patriotic fervor, which had always characterized her actions, was on August 15th appointed by special order, *Recruiting Army Officer,* to enlist Colored Volunteers in the Union Army. She accepted the commission from Governor Levi P. Morton of Indiana and actually assisted in recruiting a regiment of soldiers for service at the front. At the close of the war Mrs. Cary moved to Washington, D. C., where she served as teacher under the direction of Howard University. Later she was appointed in the public school system of Washington, D. C., and for seventeen years served as principal of three large schools.

At the same time she was a regular contributor to newspapers: *The New National Era,* edited by Frederick Douglas, and *The Advocate,* edited by John Wesley Cromwell. In 1881 she became an active member of the National Woman's Suffrage Association. Being progressive and energetic Mrs. Cary entered the Law Department of Howard University and was graduated in 1884. She resigned from her school activities to devote her time to the profession of law, in which profession she met with notable success to the end of her life.

Mrs. Cary died in Washington, D. C., June 5, 1893, sincerely mourned by all who knew her and her sterling worth.

Mrs. F. E. W. Harper

Mrs. Caroline S. A. Hill

Mrs. Sarah J. S. Garnet

Mrs. Fannie Jackson Coppin

FRANCES ELLEN WATKINS HARPER

1825—1900

"One of the ablest advocates of the Underground Railroad and of the Slave."

Frances Ellen Watkins was born in the city of Baltimore, Maryland, in 1825, not of slave parentage but subjected to the oppressive influence which bond and free alike endured under slave laws. Her childhood days were desolate. Sentences from her own pen express the loneliness of those days. "Have I yearned for a mother's love? The grave was my robber. Before three years had scattered their blight around my path death had won my mother from me. Would the strong arm of a brother have been welcome? I was my mother's only child."

She fell into the hands of an aunt who watched over her during those early helpless years. Rev. William Watkins, an uncle taught a school in Baltimore for free colored children to which she was sent until she was thirteen years of age.

After this period she was put out to work to earn her own living. She had many trials to endure, but she evinced an ardent thirst for knowledge and a remarkable talent for composition. This talent was recognized through an article which she wrote, at fourteen years of age, and which attracted the attention of the lady in whose family she was employed. In this situation she was taught sewing, took care of the children, and at the same time, through the kindness of her employer, her thirst for books was satisfied from occasional half hours of leisure. She was noted for her industry and in a few years had written a number of prose and poetic selections which were deemed of sufficient merit to be published in a small volume called "Autumn Leaves."

Some of her productions found their way into the newspapers and evoked considerable comment. The ability exhibited in some of her productions was so remarkable that some doubted and others denied their originality. Happily many are extant and may be read by all. Her mind was of a strictly religious cast, the effusions from her pen are of a high moral and elevating tone.

About the year 1850 she left Baltimore to seek a home in a free state and resided in Ohio. Here she was called to teach domestic science, being the first colored woman to do vocational work in Columbus, at Union Seminary, with Rev. John M. Brown (late Bishop) as principal. It may be interesting to note here that Union Seminary with its location changed to near Xenia became Wilberforce University. We next find her teaching in Little York, Pennsylvania, but she was sorely oppressed with the thought of conditions of her people in Maryland.

Not infrequently she gave utterances to such expressions as the following: "Not that we have not a right to breathe the air as freely as anybody else in Baltimore, but we are treated worse than aliens among a people whose language we speak, whose religion we profess and whose blood flows and mingles in our veins. Homeless in the land of our birth and worse off than strangers in the home of our nativity."

During her stay in Little York she had frequent opportunities of seeing the fleeing slaves on the Underground Railroad. Alluding to a traveler she wrote—"I saw a passenger by the Underground Railroad. Notwithstanding that abomination of the nineteenth century, the Fugitive Slave Law, men still determine to be free. Notwithstanding all the darkness in which they keep slaves, it seems that somehow light is dawning upon their minds. These poor fugitives are a property that can walk. Just to think that from the rainbow crowned Niagara to the swollen waters of the Mexican Gulf, from the restless murmur of the Atlantic to the ceaseless roar of the Pacific, the poor, half-starved, flying fugitive has no resting place for the sole of his foot."

While plying her vocation as a teacher in Little York, she was deeply engrossed in thought as to how she could best promote the welfare of her race. It happened that just about this time she was moved to enter the Anti-Slavery field as a lecturer, substantially by the following circumstances: About the year 1853 Maryland, her native state, had enacted a law forbidding free people of color from the north to come into the state on pain of being imprisoned and sold into slavery. A free man who had unwittingly violated this infamous statute, had recently been sold into Georgia and had escaped thence by secreting himself behind the wheel house of a boat bound northward; but before he reached the desired haven he was discovered and remanded to slavery. It was reported that he died soon after from the effects of exposure and suffering. Referring to this outrage, Mrs. Harper thus wrote: "Upon that grave I pledged myself to the Anti-Slavery cause. It may be that God Himself has written upon both my heart and brain a commission to use time, talent and energy in the cause of freedom."

She visited Philadelphia, New Bedford and Boston. She won her way to a favorable position as a lecturer and on September 28, 1854, was engaged by the Anti-Slavery Society of Maine as a permanent lecturer. Every door was opened before her and her gifts were universally recognized as a valuable acquisition to the cause.

For nearly two years she traveled almost continuously in the eastern states, speaking in them with marked success. The following extract clipped from the *Portland* (Maine) *Daily Press* respecting the lecture she was invited to deliver after the War by the Mayor, Mr. Washburn, is a fair sample of the many notices from this section of the country.

"She spoke for nearly an hour and a half, her subject being 'The Mission of the War and the Demands of the Colored Race in the Work of Reconstruction' and we have seldom seen an audience more attentive, better pleased, or more enthusiastic. Mrs. Harper has a splendid articulation, uses chaste, pure language, has a pleasant voice and allows no one to tire of hearing her. We shall attempt no abstract of her address. None that we could make would do her justice. It was one of which any lecturer might feel proud and her reception by a Portland audience was all that could be desired. We have seen no praises of her that were overdrawn. We have heard Miss Anna Dickinson and do not hesitate to award the palm to her darker colored sister."

From Lewis Centre, Ohio, comes this message from her pen—"You have probably heard of the shameful outrage upon a colored boy named Wagner, who was kidnapped in Ohio and carried across the river and sold for a slave. Ohio has become a kind of Negro hunting ground, a new Congo's coast and Guinea's shore. A man was kidnapped almost under the shadow of our capital. Oh, was it not dreadful? Oh, may the living God prepare me for an earnest and faithful advocacy of the cause of justice and right."

In those days the blows struck by the hero John Brown were agitating the nation. Scarcely was it possible for a living soul to be more deeply affected than Mrs. Harper. She gave material aid as well as heartfelt commiseration. She wrote words of sympathy to John Brown's wife and Brown's comrades who lay in prison under sentence of death. "May God, our own God, sustain you in your hour of trial," she wrote. Later she passed two weeks with Mrs. Brown while she was awaiting the execution of her husband and sympathized with her most deeply. An extract from one of her letters shows her great interest in Brown and his comrades: "Poor, doomed and fated men! Has not this suffering been overshadowed by the glory that gathered around the brave old man. Oh, is it not a privilege if you are sisterless and lonely, to be a sister to the human race and to place your heart where it may throb close to down-trodden humanity"?

About this time her health failed and she yearned for

the home of her childhood days, but she did not desire to die and be buried in a slave state. She says: "I have lived in the midst of oppression and wrong and I am saddened by every captured fugitive in the North; a blow has been struck at my freedom, in every hunted and down-trodden slave in the South. North and South have both been guilty and they that sin must suffer." Again we find the Muse evoked to voice her sentiments:

"Make me a grave where'er you will,
In a lowly plain, or a lofty hill,
Make it among earth's humblest graves,
But not in a land where men are slaves."

The tragic and bloody deed which terminated in the capture and death of Margaret Garner in Ohio called forth the following from her pen: "Rome had her altars where the trembling criminal and the worn and weary slave might fly for an asylum; Judea her cities of refuge; but Ohio with her Bibles and churches, her baptisms and prayers, had not one temple so dedicated to human rights, one altar so consecrated to human liberty, that trampled upon and down-trodden innocence knew that it could find protection for a night, or shelter for a day."

In 1860, in the city of Cincinnati, Mrs. Harper was married to Fenton Harper, a widower, and resident of Ohio. As a home maker she was compelled to give up her travels but did not cease from literary and Anti-Slavery labors. Her retirement was of short duration for on May 23, 1864, death deprived her of her husband.

She entered heartily into the cause of freedom being waged in the Civil War and lost no opportunity to speak, write or serve the cause of freedom. She writes: "We may look upon it as God's controversy with the nation, His arising to plead by fire and blood the cause of His poor and needy people." When the long looked for Emancipation Proclamation came Mrs. Harper was in great demand as a platform speaker. In the days of reconstruction she began her battle for equality before the law, for education and manhood rights. She traveled through the Southern States under trying and hazardous circumstances; going on plantations into the lowly cabins of the freed men, into cities, churches, meetings in court houses and legislative halls. In this labor of love, unsustained by any society, she came in contact with all classes, going through the southern states alone and unafraid, upheld by a courageous faith and the noble impulses of her own heart.

"You would be amused,' she wrote a friend, "to hear some of the remarks which my lectures call forth. 'She is a man,' again 'She is not colored, she is white. She is painted.' I am constantly talking and how tired I am some of the time. Still I am standing with my race on the threshold of a new era and though some may be far past me in the learning of the schools, yet today, with my limited and fragmentary knowledge, I may help the race forward a little. Some of our people remind me of sheep without a shepherd. I am going to have a private meeting with the women. I am going to talk with them about their daughters and about things connected with the welfare of the race. Now is the time for our women to begin to try to lift up their heads and plant the roots of progress under the hearthstone."

Grace Greenwood in the *New York Independent* commenting on a Course of Lectures in which Mrs. Harper spoke in Philadelphia pays tribute to her:

"Next of the course was Mrs. Harper, a colored woman, about as colored as some of the Cuban belles I have met with at Saratoga. She has a noble head, this bronze muse; a strong face, with a shadowed glow upon it indicative of thought and of a nature most femininely sensitive, but not in the least morbid. Her form is delicate, her hands daintily small. She stands quietly beside her desk and speaks without notes, with gestures few and fitting. Her manner is marked by dignity and composure. She is never assuming, never theatrical. In the first part of her lecture she was most impressive in her pleading for the race with whom her lot is cast. There was something touching in her attitude as their representative. The woe of two hundred years sighed through her tones. Every glance of her sad eyes was a mournful remonstrance against injustice and wrong. Feeling on her soul as she must have felt it, the chilling weight of caste, she seemed to say: 'I lift my heavy heart up solemnly, as once Electra her sepulchral urn.' As I listened to her, there swept over me in a chill wave of horror, the realization that this noble woman had she not been rescued from her mother's condition, might have been sold on the auction-block to the highest bidder—her intellect, fancy, eloquence, the flashing wit that might make the delight of a Parisian salon, and her pure christian character all thrown in—the recollection that women like her could be dragged out of public conveyances in our own city, or frowned out of fashionable churches by Anglo-Saxon Saints."

Her prose and poetry are extant and attest her literary skill. Among the best known productions are "Moses." A Story of the Nile," "The Dying Bondsman," "Eliza Harris Crossing the Ice." Mrs. Harper was the first woman of the race to write a novel, entitled, "Iola Leroy. The Shadows Uplifted."

After peace was established and for many years prior to her death Mrs. Harper devoted her entire time to the work of temperance. Her grasp and mastery of the subject—her forensic ability and devotion to the cause made her the peer of effective orators of her day. At the World's W. C. T. U. held in Philadelphia, November, 1922, although long since dead, she was accorded a signal honor, when her life-long services were recognized and her name placed on the Red Letter Calendar so that wherever, around the world, the name of Frances E. Willard, the Lady Henry Somerset, with other staunch supporters of temperance are spoken, there too, will be heard the name of *Frances Ellen Watkins Harper.*

CAROLINE SHERMAN ANDREWS-HILL

1829—1914

Mrs. Caroline Sherman Andrews-Hill was born in "middle Tennessee," Columbia County, September 16, 1829, of slave parents.

Her father was a man of great strength of character and, as often was the case in what is called "slavery days," was foreman of his master's plantation. Her mother was also a favored and highly esteemed member of her owner's household, having under her training many younger women and girls of her people.

The young Caroline early gave evidence of unusual intelligence and aptness to learn both her duties as a little nurse-maid about the house, and also of letters, for it was found that at a very tender age she was learning "by heart" the lessons she heard conned by her white charges. Prompt measures were taken to prevent her progress in book learning by removing her from the proximity of the schoolroom when her nurselings were reciting their lessons.

In 1843 the Sherman family—the masters—moved from Mississippi to Arkansas bringing the subject of our sketch with them. The family "settled" on a large plantation some eight or nine miles east of Little Rock then but a village, though styled the "Capital" of the state.

Here the young Caroline grew into young womanhood, and in 1848 was married to Rev. William Wallace Andrews, who, though a slave, had the unusual advantages of a good education and great freedom of personal self-direction for the day and times. Upon his marriage, Mr. Andrews was allotted a comfortable dwelling through the liberal kindness of his owners, and, by their aid in his application to his wife's owners, who were not his owners, his wife was allowed to "hire" her time, that is to become her own employer, and, by paying her owners the same wages per month which they could have gotten by hiring her to some white person, she was allowed to live in the home provided by her husband.

So energetic, shrewd and prudent in industry and management was this remarkable young woman, that for fifteen years she earned and paid the greater part of her wages monthly, clothed and fed a family of growing children, furnishing all medical attendance needed from time to time at her own expense, and in the last few years of this period paying house rent besides.

Her husband was able to lend but little financial assistance at this time to his wife and family, on account of the close confinement to his home duties of chief steward and butler in his owner's household.

This noble-spirited couple did not allow the strenuous task of their own family life to render them narrow and selfish, but both united in striving to brighten the lives of their fellows in bondage by inviting the less fortunate to come to their freer home and there hold prayer meetings, class-service and Sunday school.

In the last named service Mr. Andrews used every opportunity possible to teach not only the word of God by hearing but taught many eager friends to actually read the printed page. While his devoted wife comforted and aided the young mothers in the care of their little ones by both word and deed.

The glorious Emancipation Proclamation of the immortal Lincoln freed this noble couple from the shackles of slavery which, resting never so lightly, are yet insupportable to the free exalted spirit of a man or a woman.

Immediately Mr. and Mrs. Andrews set the good example to the newly liberated people about them to "own a piece of land." This was her earnest and constant exhortation to friends and neighbors—"Go down into the soil."

The Rev. Andrews, immediately upon freedom's coming to the people of Little Rock, opened a school in the Methodist Church of which he was in charge. To this school Mrs. Andrews went along with her children as did many other grown-ups. Her burning desire was to learn to read and write fluently, for the pressing needs of her situation had not allowed her to make much use of her husband's desire and willingness to teach her.

She persevered at home and at school (by long intervals in the latter) until she could read fluently and could write her name.

In 1866 she was bereft of her noble and devoted husband who died at his post while holding his presiding elder's quarterly meeting in Pine Bluff, Ark.

This sad blow was followed seven weeks later by the loss of her only son, a promising youth of sixteen years of age.

From the almost utter prostration of grief and desolation into which these unspeakable losses plunged her, Mrs. Andrews arose in the strength given her by her heavenly Father in whom she implicitly trusted and by dint of industry, thrift and resolute effort succeeded in finishing the purchase of the home which she and her husband had contracted to buy.

She believed in "Schooling," and always urged parents to send their children to school regularly and as long as possible. She lived to see her daughter teach in her (the daughter's) native city for more than thirty-five years.

Mrs. Andrews became Mrs. Ohmer Hill in 1867, and she with her husband continued to wield a wide influence for good in their community by lives of earnest, honest industry, their example of thrift, and their earnest christian spirit and deeds of benevolence to all about them.

Mrs. Hill was especially esteemed for her great-hearted warmth of love for all who came to her. She was indeed a child of God and an heir of salvation. Her grandchildren, six of whom she helped to bring up to young manhood and womanhood, all loved her devotedly and considered her a fount of love and comfort in time of stress and of wisdom and counsel in every dilemma.

She passed peacefully and triumphantly into the Mansions Above, Sunday, November 25, 1914, full of days, honor and blessings.

MARY CATHERINE WINDSOR

1830—1914

Mary Catherine Windsor was born in Newtown, Virginia, March 17, 1830. When a girl she was taken by her parents, William and Ellen Tocus to Pittsburgh, Pennsylvania. Here she attended school under a famous teacher named John Templeton and acquired a fair education. She became a Christian early in life, was a member of Wylie Avenue A. M. E. Church, living an exemplary life until her death.

When a young woman she was united in marriage to Mr. Henry Williams, who was engaged in the coal business on the Bingham Estate, Coal Hill, Pittsburgh, Pennsylvania. Their wedded life was of short duration. Mr. Williams died and the young widow lived with her relatives. Shortly after the Civil War began she made a trip by vessel to New Orleans, La., with her brother-in-law, Mr. Thomas A. Brown who at that time was in the mail service.

The vessel ran the blockade under heavy fire and later became a war transport for the Union Army.

On the return trip as the vessel was cautiously creeping up the Mississippi river late one afternoon and about to weigh anchor, "Aunt Kitty" as she was familiarly called sitting in her state room, discovered rebel forces cautiously crawling through the under brush and about to open fire upon the transport.

Rushing out of her state room she gave the alarm, crying, "The rebels are coming. The rebels are coming!"

The guns were trained on the enemy and they were soon put to rout. Aunt Kitty had saved their lives and prevented the destruction of the vessel. She became the heroine of the hour. After this event she was made a regular spy. Quick witted, alert, with keen black eyes and diminutive form, not quite four feet in height, and less than one hundred pounds in weight she ventured on deck when no one else dared; reconnoitered without fear of being seen and thus rendered valuable service. On several occasions she touched off the guns that stopped rebel advancement, and thus did her humble part in the Civil War even as Molly Pitcher did hers in the Revolutionary War.

At the close of the Civil War she was married to William Windsor and for many years lived on a farm near Naples and Hull, Illinois.

At Hull, their home on the farm was destroyed by fire. Friends and neighbors gave lumber and built a new house for this aged, worthy couple. The following incident will show the high esteem in which they were held by the citizens of the community. The school children for several miles around brought to the school house fruits, vegetables and clothing. It required a two horse wagon to convey the children's gift to Aunt Kitty's door.

Shortly after this event, Mr. Windsor, advanced in years, dropped dead while ploughing in a nearby field.

Aunt Kitty, now a lone widow but greatly beloved by all who knew her in her Illinois home, was taken to Wilberforce to spend her remaining years with relatives.

She was cheerful and bright, but infirmities of old age caused her to live a retired life.

Her constant companion was her Bible and at any time during the day she could be seen pouring over its sacred page.

One day, without warning, Aunt Kitty slipped away as quietly and unobtrusively as she had lived. Thus closed a long, eventful life and full of good deeds. He giveth His beloved sleep.

SARAH J. S. (TOMPKINS) GARNET

Born 1831, in Brooklyn, N. Y.

Died October, 1911 in Brooklyn, N. Y.

Mrs. Garnet (nee Smith) a retired school teacher, well known in New York educational circles, suddenly terminated October, 1911, a career of unusual length and usefulness. Her demise at her residence in Brooklyn followed almost directly a welcome home reception tendered to her by an Equal Suffrage Club of which she was the moving spirit. She had just returned from a trip abroad, having gone to London to be present at the first Universal Race Congress. The journey, the sessions, the visit to the continent, gave unalloyed gratification to this grand old woman whose birthday was celebrated for the eightieth time while she was sojourning in foreign lands.

So thoroughly did she appear in touch with things vital and progressive, her friends in the warmth of greetings barely remembered her recent passage through the "eight-boned" gate. Delighted to have her in their midst again, they naturally inferred the indefinite enjoyment of her association with them. Her multiplied acts of kindness and unselfish devotion, her rare sympathy and exquisite tact were profoundly appreciated. As a champion of equal rights, a club woman, an ardent pleader for fair play for women; as an illustrious example of a developed American woman of African descent—in these various phases she attracted an attention at once respectful and permanent. Her single mindedness, persistence, self-abnegation; her faith, loyalty and reverence for humanity, gained for her an enviable reputation which she maintained with a modest dignity and becoming seriousness.

Her parents were Sylvanus Smith and Annie Springstead; both were partly and directly descendants of aboriginal Indians of Long Island. Mr. Smith was a large land owner and a successful farmer. His eleven children of which Sarah was the oldest, were strictly trained in habits of regularity, industry and thrift. The Smiths proudly boasted that they were "Americans of the Americans." Prior to the advent of Europeans, many members of the family had placed their names and records of their deeds upon the unwritten annals of Indian story. These were faithfully rehearsed from misty times until the era when Sylvanus came under the influence of these traditions, always stirring, often pathetic.

A line of exceptional women were the progenitors of the subject of this sketch. The records of the town of Southhampton state that in the early sixteen hundreds, Quashawan, a direct descendant of Massasoit, had her royal wigwam upon the hills of Shinney-cock, where in the early morning one can catch a glimpse of the sea through the mist as through a bridal veil. A century later, the traditions of the Indian Reservation refer to a Queen Betty who dwelt on Mastic Creek where the tide-water and the Forge River unite.

With the progress of time came the forcing of resistless changes upon the Indians. They were no longer able to roam and could with difficulty claim and hold meagre portions of the territory once theirs to an unlimited extent. Harsh laws and oppressive acts compelled a vast majority to become tenants where their forefathers had been owners. On the records of Queens County for 1808 is written that Sylvia Hobbs purchased of Cornelius VanWyck, a few acres on Hempstead Plain for an abiding place. This "Granny Sylvy" as she is still affectionately recalled, was great grandmother to Sarah Smith. In Sylvia's home, Sylvanus, Sarah's father, learned to work and to think, and catching the impetus of his grandmother's indomitable courage, became cautious yet intrepid, reserved but unsubdued. No opportunity was laid at hand for an Indian child to get the "larnin" so prized by the settlers, so the farsighted "Granny Sylvy" expended part of her restricted means to maintain a school in her homestead attic. Imbued with the spirit to achieve, the desire to make something of himself and for himself, from this lowly estate Sylvanus went forth to try his fate in the arena of existence.

Sarah inherited much from her father and vied with him in resourcefulness and persistency. At the age of fourteen she began teaching, the compensation for which was twenty-dollars per annum, a rate of pay considered quite adequate. At the time of her retirement from active professional labor she was receiving twenty-five hundred dollars yearly and women of her grade were waging a fight to secure "equal pay for equal work." The appointment she held calls for today, thirty-five hundred dollars, but the high cost of living and the many legitimate demands connected with the position make even this sum no extravagant remuneration.

The period of her service covering fifty-six years was coincident with the time of the elevation of teaching from a haphazard occupation to a plane of systematic efficiency. Its gradual rise from a trade to a profession made possible the foundation of a science of education, made necessary the evolution of methods in teaching, resulting in gradation of both work and the workers. All of Sarah Smith's contemporaries in the work of teaching and including herself, had to learn what their work really comprised and how it was to be done, had to become learners while continuing to instruct. Those alert enough to discern the signs of the times and aspiring enough to undertake the onerous task of keeping abreast with new conditions and their demands, found their services not only retained but required. Those who failed to comprehend the evolution in school room activities sooner or later sought more congenial pursuits.

During her five decades of service, Mrs. Garnet, as Sarah finally became, worked diligently from pride, a sense of duty and deepening apprehension of the vital importance of her work. She took stock of her resources and resolved to sail, not to sink in the tide of progress. This entailed severe and exhausting hours of study and reflection. She perceived in her advance toward broader views and a more discerning outlook, much that fully compensated her for her assiduity. She learned that much book knowledge, more culture and most executive ability should be included among the assets of the successful teacher. She never faltered in her resolve to evolve from her own inner consciousness exhaustive and intelligent replies to the most important questions within the range of her professional experience. "What is teaching? What is a teacher?" This she believed and rightly so, was the only way to do justice to herself and her pupils. And truly the meritorious end did indeed crown the laudable work. From the position of under teacher in one of the caste schools of former Williamsburg, she came at last to the exceptional dignity of a principal in a grammar school in Manhattan Borough of Greater New York. This distinction has until now been attained by no other of "our women" in the metropolis where there is no race or color discrimination in public education.

Though she found the position not an easy one to fill, her reasonableness, her serene temper, her combination of affability and dignity, her patience and her tact, insured her success. She secured the regard of patrons, the fidelity of teachers, the obedience of pupils and the deference of supervisors, and she maintained the reputation she so honorably gained with an unconscious grace and dignity peculiarly her own.

Among her pupils are many whose after careers redound to her credit. Among these are Walter F. Craig, violinist, Richard Robinson, music director in public schools, Ferdinand L. Washington, well known in financial circles and Harry A. Williamson, a podiatrist, and an author of monographs on Free-masonry of international renown. Her prolonged life brought her into association with more than one generation of teachers. Some of these pre-eminently successful are Catherine Thompson, Mary E. Eato, Rosetta Wright, J. Imogen Howard, Florence T. Ray, Fanny Murray, S. Elizabeth Frazier and Maritcha R. Lyons.

As a young woman she could be met in one or more of the circles founded for social relaxation and intercourse, though in those days no very hard and fast lines were drawn for New Yorkers. Among our people who were comparatively few in number, all lived as close neighbors. Strangers with proper introductions were always extended a welcome that was sincere, if sober.

In the first flush of womanhood Sarah Smith married an Episcopal priest, by the name of Tompkins, who died young leaving two children. Later she contracted a second marriage with Rev. Henry Highland Garnett, who died after a few years while Resident Minister at Liberia. A widow again in her maturity as she had been in her youth and having survived her children, she returned to her father's home, undertaking the role of mother's helper and "big sister," she became for an indefinite period a valuable acquisition to the household.

Marriages, deaths, and separations for various natural causes, at last depleted the family circle. Mrs. Garnet finally set up her own establishment on Hancock Street, Brooklyn, where with always one or more of the younger generation for company, she spent her last days in a refined leisure that gave her ample opportunity of doing much for uplift and betterment. In such a congenial atmosphere she remained active yet calm until almost instantly her "energy was transmuted into repose."

MRS. S. J. S. GARNETT

An Appreciation

At her home in Brooklyn, N. Y., there passed from labor to reward, Mrs. S. J. S. Garnett, one of our most remarkable women. The subject of our sketch was the widow of the famous Henry Highland Garnett, clergyman and diplomat, and as distinguished as her renowned husband, having served in the highest degree, her day and generation. She was a member of an old and highly honored family of Brooklyn. She attended school, was an apt scholar and at an early age became a teacher, being one of the first of the race to adopt that profession. Her energy and ability were soon recognized. From the grades she was elected principal of a large number of teachers and pupils. She was always frail of body, never self-assertive, but possessed with a supreme faith and confidence in God and a dauntless courage in the face of the evil-doer. She belonged to that old school of heroines which crossed cudgels with the enemy and battled unceasingly for the full manhood rights of the Negro. When certain discriminations were made against colored teachers of New York, Mrs. Garnett, Bishop W. B. Derrick and Lawyer T. McCants Stewart, went to Albany, confronted the legislature with indisputable facts and won the contest.

After a long career in the schoolroom Mrs. Garnett retired on a handsome pension. She could have withdrawn from life's busy throng and lived in ease and comfort, but her zeal was not one whit abated for the great principles she had espoused. The cry of humanity and its needs rang clearer and stronger than a life of self-ease and inactivity. Duty called; she must obey! Her intellectual ability and nobility of character made her the center of attraction in any circle. Mrs. Garnett was founder of the Equal Suffrage League, the only colored organization in Brooklyn representing the cause of Equal Rights. She was superintendent of the Suffrage Department of the National Association of Colored Women and the most noted suffragist of our race. She was tendered a reception on her return from London, England, where she attended the first Universal Races Congress. The spacious parlors of her residence presented a brilliant scene. An assemblage of one hundred guests greeted her home coming. Among the distinguished guests were Dr. W. E. B. DuBois and Mrs. Garnett's sister, Dr. S. Maria Stewart, resident physician at Wilberforce University, also a delegate to the Races Congress. While in London, Mrs. Garnett celebrated her seventy-ninth natal day. Always magnetic, she drew about her the young who kept her heart youthful.

Mrs. Garnett literally died in harness. While in London she gathered suffrage literature and twenty-four hours before her promotion to her Heavenly Home, was distributing the same among her club in Broklyn. She fell asleep without serious illness or a struggle.

What is the summary of this beautiful character? Mrs. Garnett's life has been as a bright shaft of light let down into the darkness round about her, which illuminated the furthest corner. A career full of good deeds and noble endeavor. Her example has been inspiring alike to the youth and the aged. She was a friend whose purse and door were open to the distressed and her hospitality was as boundless as the ocean itself. Her deep piety, her thorough learning and achievements, her great will-power, her high courage, with such frailty of body make her one of the remarkable women of the age. Her family lost a beloved companion and counselor, her friends, a confidante and sympathizer. The race, one of its foremost educators, a pioneer of the school room. The community in which she lived, a noble, inspiring God-fearing citizen, the world a benefactor, a valuable contributor to literary, domestic and State affairs. Women of the world, let us emulate the virtues of this mother in Israel.

ELIZA ANN GARDNER

1831—1922

"None knew her but to love her
None named her but to praise."

Eliza Ann Gardner was born in New York City, May 28, 1831. Being the daughter of an enterprising contractor for sailing vessels, her family was always comfortably situated. In 1845, when Eliza was fourteen years old, her family took up residence in Boston, at West End on North Grove Street, which section of the city was then largely populated by colored families. Eliza's early schooling was acquired in the only public school for colored children that Boston ever had, and at the feet of anti-slavery leaders. As a student she excelled, being an extremely apt pupil. The keenness of her mind and the retentiveness of her memory were marvelous. Because of her scholastic brilliancy, in the course of her education she won several scholarships.

As a young woman, Eliza learned the trade of dressmaking, and did needle work on the first banner made for the Plymouth Rock Lodge of Odd Fellows. After the death of her parents she inherited the homestead located at 20 North Anderson Street, Boston, where she continued to work at her trade. She devoted practically all of her time to church work and to the cause of anti-slavery. For this reason her home was a veritable "Bethel," being one of the stations of the famous "Underground Railroad,"—in the days of William Lloyd Garrison, John Brown, Wendel Phillips, Charles Sumner, Lewis Hayden, Frederick Douglass, Harriet Tubman, Sojourner Truth, and countless others with whom Miss Gardner was personally acquainted. She was associated with these great people as a guardian of the liberties of the oppressed. One of Miss Gardner's hobbies was to acquire positions for our girls in the business places of the white race. In this particular she was very successful.

Eliza Ann Gardner was known as the "Julia Ward Howe" of the Negro race, and as such they paid her annually an unfailing tribute upon her birthday. She was connected with various temperance organizations, and with the first Colored Women's Club of Boston—"The Women's Era." Her influence was strong in all the branches of the A. M. E. Zion Church, local, national and international. Bishops and general officers, as well as pastors, held her in high esteem. In 1909 Miss Gardner organized "The Butler Club of Zion Church," and was president until her death. The celebration under the auspices of this club brought together in immense concourse of her large circle of friends.

After reaching the age of ninety, Miss Gardner died in Boston January 4, 1922.

FANNIE JACKSON COPPIN

1835—1912

Teacher and Moulder of Character

On the fly leaf of "Hints on Teaching," by the subject of this sketch is the following dedication: "This book is inscribed to my beloved Aunt Sarah Orr Clark, who, working at six dollars a month saved one hundred and twenty-five dollars and bought my freedom."

The woman thus redeemed rose from the depth of slavery and became one of the most eminent educators of this country. The hardships of her childhood, the struggles for an education are sad to contemplate but a ray of sunshine here and there brighten the path and lighten the burden. In her short biography, for she was too busy teaching the race to write at length concerning herself, she tells us somewhat of herself. Fanny Jackson was born in Washington, D. C. The children called their grandmother "Mammy." One of Fanny's earliest recollections was when about three years old, she was sent to keep Mammy's company. It was in a little one-room cabin. They used to go up a ladder to the loft where they slept. Mammy was accustomed to make long prayers in which she asked God to bless her "offspring." Only one word was remembered by Fanny and that was offspring, for she wondered what offspring meant. Mammy had six children, three boys and three girls. The father bought his own freedom and then that of four of his children, her Aunt Sarah being one, but Lucy, her mother, remained in slavery.

Sarah went to work at six dollars a month, saved one hundred and twenty-five dollars and bought little Frances.

During her babyhood she had two severe burnings. At her christening, a party was given and while the company made merry, she was tied in a chair and left near a stove. At night when they took off her stocking, they found the whole skin from the side of the leg next to the stove peeled off. At another time when her mother was out at work for the day mammy had charge of the baby. When the mother returned mammy exclaimed, "Here, Lucy, take your child, it's the crossest baby I ever saw." When she was undressed at night it was found that a coal of fire from mammy's pipe had fallen into the baby's bosom and burned itself deep into the flesh.

After the aunt saved the one hundred and twenty-five dollars and bought her, she was sent to live with another aunt at New Bedford, Massachusetts. She was put to work at a place where she was allowed to go to school, when not at work. But she could not go on wash days, ironing days, nor cleaning days, which interfered with her progress.

When fourteen years old she decided that she ought to take care of herself. She soon found a permanent place at Newport, Rhode Island, in the family of Mr. George H. Calvert, a great grandson of Lord Baltimore who settled in Baltimore, Maryland. His wife was Elizabeth Stuart, a descendant of Mary, Queen of Scotland. Every other afternoon in the week Fanny was given one hour to take private lessons. Mrs. Calvert taught her many useful things, how to darn, to take care of laces and to sew beautifully. At the end of several years she was prepared to enter the examination for Rhode Island State Normal School, located at Bristol, Rhode Island, under Dana P. Colburn. Here her eyes were opened to the subject of teaching.

Having finished the course of study there she felt she had just begun to learn. She heard of Oberlin College and made up her mind to try to get there. She had learned a little music while at Newport and had mastered the elementary studies of the piano and guitar.

With the assistance of her aunt she found herself at

Oberlin College, which was at that time the only college in the United States where colored students were permitted to study. The course of study then was the same as that at Harvard College. The faculty did not forbid a woman to take the gentleman's course, but they did not advise it. There was plenty of Latin and Greek in it and as much mathematics as one could shoulder. Our student took a long breath and prepared for a delightful contest. All went smoothly until she was in her junior year in college. Then one day she was summoned before the faculty. The call seemed ominous! It was a custom in Oberlin that forty students from the junior and senior classes were employed to teach the preparatory classes. It was now time, so the faculty informed her, for the juniors to begin their work and that it was their purpose to give her a class; but if students rebelled against her teaching, they did not intend to force it. Fortunately her training at the Normal School coupled with her own dear love for teaching sustained her; there was a little surprise on the faces of some, but there were no signs of rebellion. The class increased in numbers until it had to be divided and she was given both divisions.

Miss Jackson, speaking of her college life, expressed her lasting gratitude to Bishop Daniel A. Payne, of the African Methodist Church, who gave her a scholarship of nine dollars a year upon her entering Oberlin. She further states that her obligations to the dear people of Oberlin can never be measured in words. When she first went to Oberlin she boarded in the Ladies' Hall. She began to run down in health and was invited to spend a few weeks in the family of Professor H. E. Peck which ended in her staying several years until independence of the Republic of Haiti was recognized under President Lincoln and Professor Peck was sent as first United States Minister to that interesting country; then the family was broken up and she was invited to spend the remainder of the school year in the home of Professor and Mrs. Charles H. Churchill. These two christian homes, where she was regarded as an honored member of the family circle had a great influence upon her life and was a potent factor in forming her character, which was to stand the test of new and strange conditions in her future life. Her life at Oberlin was varied and interesting; at one time at Mrs. Peck's when the girls were sitting on the floor getting out their Greek, Miss Sutherland from Maine suddenly stopped and looking at her said, "Fanny Jackson, were you ever a slave?" "Yes," replied Fanny. The girl from Maine burst into tears. Not another word was spoken, but those tears seemed to wipe out a little that was wrong.

She tells us that she never rose to recite in her classes, but that she felt she had the honor of the whole African race upon her shoulders. At one time when she had won a signal honor in Greek, the Professor in Greek decided to visit the class in Mathematics and see how they were getting along. She had heard it said that the race was good in languages, but stumbled when they came to mathematics. Being always fond of demonstration she was given the very proposition she was well acquainted with and so "went that day with flying colors." French was not in the Oberlin Curriculum, but under private tutelage, she completed a course and graduated with a French essay. She went to Oberlin 1860 and was graduated in August, 1865, after having spent five and a half years. She was elected Class Poet for the Class Day exercises and carried away the kindest remembrances of the dear ones who were her classmates.

When Miss Jackson was within a year of graduation an application came from a Friend's School in Philadelphia, Pennsylvania, for a colored woman who could teach Greek and Latin and higher Mathematics. The answer returned was: "We have the woman but you must wait a year for her." The years 1860 and 1865 were of unusual historic importance and activity. In 1860 the immortal Lincoln was elected, and in 1865 the Civil War came to a close but not until freedom for all the slaves in America had been proclaimed and that proclamation made valid by the victorious arm of the Union forces. In September, 1865, Miss Jackson began her work in Philadelphia.

In the year of 1837 the Friends of Philadelphia established a school for the education of colored youth in higher learning, to make a test whether or not the Negro was capable of acquiring any considerable degree of education. For it was one of the strongest arguments in the defense of slavery that the Negro was an inferior creation; formed by the Almighty for just the work he was doing. No doubt they had in mind the remark made by John C. Calhoun, that if there could be found a Negro that could conjugate a Greek verb, he would give up all his preconceived ideas of the inferiority of the Negro. "Well, let's try him and see," said the fair minded Quaker people and for years this institution, known as the Institution for Colored Youth was visited by interested persons from different parts of the United States and Europe.

It was here that Miss Jackson was given the delightful task of teaching her own people and rejoiced to see them mastering Caesar, Virgil, Cicero, Horace, Xenophon's Anabasis, and also taught the New Testament Greek. At one of her examinations, when she asked a titled Englishman to take the class and examine it, he said, "They are more capable of examining me, their proficiency is wonderful." When she began her work at the Institute, Ebenezer Bassett had been Principal for fourteen years. In 1869 Mr. Bassett was appointed United States Minister to Haiti by President U. S. Grant, at which time Miss Jackson was elected Principal and held that important office for nearly forty years. During that long period she wrought many changes to better the condition of the school and pupils.

She instituted normal training with a Preparatory Department to give ample practice in teaching and governing under daily direction and correction. The Academic Department of the Institute had been so splendidly successful in proving that the Negro youth was equally capable with others in mastering a higher education, that no argument was necessary to establish its need, but the broad ground of education by which masses must become self supporting was to this broad minded educator, a matter of painful anxiety.

At the Centennial in 1876, the foreign exhibits of work done in trade schools of Europe, opened the eyes of the directors of public education in America as to the great lack existing in our own system of education. If this deficiency was apparent as it related to the white youth of the country, it was far more so as it related to the colored. Richard Humphrey, the Quaker, who gave the first endowment to found this school stipulated that it should not only teach literary studies, but that a mechanical and industrial department, including agriculture should come within its scope.

Miss Jackson now began an eager and intensively earnest crusade to supply the deficiency in the work of the Institute. With the great thought of bettering the condition of her people she spoke before literary societies, churches in Philadelphia, New York, Washington, anywhere, everywhere the opportunity presented. The minds of the colored people needed enlightment upon the necessity of Industrial Education. The money was forthcoming, the work advanced and finally in 1879 the Industrial Department was fully established and the following trades were being taught to boys; brick laying, plastering, carpentry, shoemaking, printing, and tailoring. For girls; dressmaking, millinery, typewriting, stenography and classes in cooking, including both boys and girls. Stenography and typewriting were also taught the boys as well as the girls. As a means of preparation for this work, which she called an Industrial Crusade she studied Political Economy for two years under Dr. William Elder, who was a disciple of Mr. Henry C. Carey, the eminent writer on the doctrine of Protective Tariff. In the year 1878 the Board of Education of Philadelphia began to consider what they were doing to train their young people in the industrial arts and trades. Before the directors and heads of some of the educational institutions, Miss Jackson was asked to tell what was being done in Philadelphia for the industrial education of the colored youth. She said: "You may well understand that I had a tale to tell." She told them that the only place in the city where a colored boy could learn a trade was in the House of Refuge or the Penitentiary, and the sooner he became incorrigible and got into the Refuge, or committed a crime and got into the Penitentiary, the more promising it would be for his industrial training.

Such was the argument used in her appeal to the public for funds to start the wheels of industry in Philadelphia. Having taught the trades it now became necessary to find work for those who had learned them which was no easy task. She saw building after building going up and not a single colored hand employed in the construction. Nor was she comforted by what the Irishman said, that all he had to do was to put some brick in a hod and carry them upon the building and there sat a gentleman who did all the work. She said she was determined to know whether this industrial and business ostracism was "in ourselves or in our stars" so from time to time she knocked, shook, and kicked at those closed doors of industry. A cold metallic voice from within replied, "We do not employ colored people." "Ours not to make reply, ours not to question why." "Thank heaven," she said, "we are not obliged to do and die, we naturally prefer to do"—with this heroic motive she established the Woman's Industrial Exchange, where the work of various departments could be exhibited. In 1881 Miss Jackson was married to Reverend Levi J. Coppin, who in 1900, was elected one of the Bishops of the African Methodist Episcopal Church and assigned to South Africa. This was most fortunate and came as a culmination to a long and useful life to finish her active life in Africa, the home of the ancestors of those whose lives she endeavored to direct.

In 1888 as president of the Woman's Home and Foreign Missionary Society of the A. M. E. Church, she was elected delegate to the Centenary of Mission held in London, England. And so, this woman born in slavery and poverty became the polished, masterful exponent of higher education, and the pioneer of industrial education, antedating Tuskegee, and other institutions in training the head, the hand and the heart. The message she leaves to those who contend today is to go forward to teach, to uplift, to co-operate for the millions of our fellow beings with a faith firmly fixed in that "Eternal Providence" that in its own good time will "Justify the ways of God to man."

(*Compiled from "Reminiscences of School Life"*)

ANNE E. BALTIMORE

August 6, 1836—Januuary 11, 1922

Mrs. Anna E. Baltimore was the daughter of John and Susan Tinsley. She received her preliminary education at Gilmore School, Cincinnati, Ohio. Afterward she attended and graduated from Oberlin College, Oberlin, Ohio. She studied music under both Italian and French Vocal teachers and the piano under Miss Julia Coburn.

She traveled extensively with her own concert Troupe, composed of Margaret Shelton, Margaret Butler, Julius Wade, William Dunlap and William Boone. Known as the Annie E. Tinsley Concert Troupe.

She died January 1, 1922, at the age of 85 years. A daughter and son are still living in Cincinnati, Ohio.

AMANDA SMITH

1837—1915

"O, woman, great is thy faith; be it unto thee even as thou wilt."

Amanda Smith was born at Long Green, Maryland, January 23, 1837. She was the daughter of Samuel Berry who, though a slave, was far above the average in intelligence. By working nights, holidays and extra hours, he earned enough money to buy his own freedom and afterwards that of his wife and five children.

He removed his family to the state of Pennsylvania where Amanda grew to womanhood. She had only three months' schooling, but this gave her a start and she improved every opportunity to gain knowledge. On March 17, 1856, while living at Columbia, Pa., she was converted; but it was on the first Sunday in 1860 that God wonderfully blessed her soul with the fullness of his love. Her work for the Lord took shape from that time and His leadings were marvelous. She became known as one of the most remarkable preachers of any race or of any age. At the time of her conversion she was a poor widow, taking in washing to support herself and a little daughter. She tells us that she was called upon to surrender all and follow Christ. This she did placing her little girl and her earthly possessions, which consisted of her washing outfit, on the altar.

The following Sunday found her in a fashionable Church in New York City. The spirit was poured upon her to such an extent that she gave God the praise, shouting "Amen"

MRS. AMANDA SMITH

MRS. SUSAN PAUL SMITH VASHON

HER MOTHER. ANNE PAUL SMITH
From An Old Painting

several times to the complete consternation of the aristocratic congregation gathered there. She began her evangelistic work at once. Calls for services in camp meetings, churches, in city and country were many and urgent and for several years she responded to them all until she found herself in the complete nervous prostration which inevitably follows such exhaustive labor that the body had means to make its rights respected, or at least to make the violator of those rights severely suffer.

At this time Mrs. Eli Johnson of Brooklyn, a Quaker lady of wealth connected with the Gurney family of England, proposed that she go across the waters and offered to provide the funds. This was a startling idea, a trip to Europe for a poor, uneducated colored washer woman—and at first she merely laughed at it. But it gradually became evident that it was a pointing of Providence. The door opened more and more widely and so finally she went. She attended the Keswick conference for the promotion of higher life, presided over by Canon Battersy and participated in by Dr. Mahan, Mr. and Mrs. Boardman, Miss Smiley and many prominent members of the Church of England.

Thus she became well known among these people, many of them moving in high circles, and at once had all the invitations she could accept, and more, to hold meetings.

She spent a year in Great Britain visiting the large centers of England, Scotland and Ireland.

In the summer of 1879 she was invited by Rev. W. B. Osborne to visit India which she treated at first as an altogether ridiculous idea. However, her friends urged and interested themselves in the matter. Money of course was needed for the journey and she had none. But this difficulty was quickly removed by unsolicited gifts till an abundance was provided. So, needing a warmer climate in which to spend the winter and provisions having been duly made also for her daughter in America, the way was clear and after three weeks' passage she stood on the soil of India.

She gave her first Gospel Address in Falkland Road Hall, Bombay, November 9, 1879. During the two years spent in that far off country she visited Poona, Calcutta, Cawnpore, Allahabad, Jubbalpore, Lanorvli and Lucknow. She went northward to Bareilly and Naini Tal at which mountain retreat she spent the hot season getting rested and strengthened for a more extended campaign.

Her labor in India was an unqualified success, even beyond the expectations of her friends.

Dr. (later Bishop) Thoburn of Calcutta, where her largest meetings were held and the vast community deeply stirred, wrote—"I have heard speakers of her race who were much more eloquent, but never any of her race or, for that matter, of any other race to whom I have listened with such delight and profit." He testified also, that while the attendance on the services of other evangelists that had visited Calcutta had almost always fallen off, hers steadily increased to the last. In portraying the secret of her power, he ascribed her success to the thorough understanding of God's method with sinners and with every object bearing the impress of our common humanity. "She knows the 'way of the Lord'." She has a keen insight into character, she talks with God as with a familiar friend; and her kindly heart burns at the sight of every human sorrow or want."

Great numbers were saved and scores quickened in the divine life.

It was something entirely new in India for a woman to mount the pulpit and when to this element of startling novelty was added the fact that she was a colored woman, once a slave, come from America and gifted with a marvelous sweet power of song the excitement awakened in any community by her advent may easily be imagined.

Multitudes not at all church-going people and scarcely coming within the range of an ordinary preacher, crowded the places of worship. Drawn by the power of curiosity they heard the gospel most plainly and faithfully set forth and they came again.

Wherever she went there always sprang up an eager discussion on the subject of woman's right to preach.

A great deal of prejudice was swept away and the true position on this matter was fully explained, finding its way into many minds and hearts as they perceived how God used this humble, uneducated woman as one of his choice instrumentalities. Furthermore she impressed with much power the educated non-christian natives who understood English and in the large stations assembled in great numbers to hear her relate her glowing experience in God's love.

For the most part she spoke through an interpreter, but did not feel at home in it.

She gave India Mission a decided impetus. Wherever she went she made a mark. The toilworn workers were cheered, their experience took on a new glow caught from the burning love that filled her heart, and their numbers were increased. In private intercourse too, her influence was admirable and the many homes she visited will cherish very pleasant and profitable reminiscences of her stay. She returned to America much improved physically and better fitted in every way to do many years more of faithful service for the Lord. One writer from Lucknow said—"India has had many visitors of rank and wealth, but we are sure that very few of them have contributed as much to her real advantage as this obscure colored woman, poor in this world's riches and unschooled in earthly learning, but very rich toward God and well instructed in the school of Christ. How earnestly this land and every other, cries out for more such."

A year later she went to Africa where she labored for eight years among the benighted people on the West Coast. Arriving at Monrovia she was compelled to remain a year suffering for the most part of that time, with the African fever. While in that country she was a co-laborer with Bishop Taylor, although on the field as a missionary two years prior to his coming. Bishop Taylor often remarked that Amanda Smith had done more for the cause of missions and temperance in Africa than the combined efforts of all the missionaries before her.

Having lost all her own children except a daughter, Mrs. Smith adopted a native boy and girl whom she intended to educate and return to Africa to labor among their own people. On the eve of leaving for England the girl, Frances, was taken ill and Mrs. Smith was forced to leave her with friends. She brought the boy, Robert, as far as England where he was educated and afterward returned to his native country as a missionary. While in London, England, in the spring of 1894, attending the W. C. T. U. Convention the Lord spoke to her and said, "What have you done to help your own people in a permanent way that will live after you are gone"? "Nothing, Lord." Then the thought came to her, "Why not start an Industrial Home for Colored Children"? She began to work to that end. She wrote her autobiography and the profits on the sale of the books were used for the purpose of founding this home. A twelve room brick house was purchased at a cost of six thousand dollars and in this way, "The Amanda Smith Industrial Home" was inaugurated. She counted her friends of both races by the thousands. A cottage fitted up with comforts and all her wants supplied by loving hands at Seabright, Florida, made her last days on earth a haven of rest to enter into that fuller, eternal rest prepared for the faithful of the Lord. Amanda Smith lived on earth, but her conversation was in heaven.

Being dead she yet speaketh.

SUSAN PAUL VASHON

September 19, 1838—November 27, 1912

Mrs. Susan Paul Vashon was born in Boston, Massachusetts, September, 19, 1838, and passed away in St. Louis, November 27, 1912.

Her father Elijah W. Smith was famed in *ante-bellum* days as a musical composer and cornetist and played in 1850 at Windsor Castle at the "Command of Queen Victoria."

Her mother, Anne Paul Smith, was a daughter of the Rev. Thomas Paul who was founder and pastor of the old Joy Street Church, Boston, in which the American Anti-Slavery Society found the only available refuge in which to organize. Mrs. Vashon lost her mother at an early age and was reared by her maternal grandmother, Katherine Paul. At the age of sixteen she graduated from Miss O'Mears' Seminary, Somerville, Mass., with valedictorian honor, and as the only colored girl in her class. Her grandmother having died she went to live with her father in Pittsburgh, Pa., where she was appointed teacher in the one colored school of that city.

Of that school Prof. George B. Vashon was principal, whose remarkable pedagogic career had already comprehended a four years' tenor at College Faustin, Port-au-Prince, Haiti, and one of three years at New York Central College, McGrawville, N. Y.

She was married to Prof. Vashon February 17, 1857, and seven children were born of the union. She was widowed October 5, 1878. Mrs. Vashon taught in the public schools of Washington, D. C., from 1872 until 1880, being principal of the Thaddeus Stevens School.

In the fall of 1882 she removed with her family to St. Louis, Missouri, where she resided until her death.

Her earlier environments gave to her character a puritanic cast, and all through her life she held close to the undeviating line.

She was a mother, profoundly so, and directed the lives of her children with the personal guidance and watchful care of tenderest love and wisest admonition.

She blended domestic excellence with a decided and active interest in all movements for the moral and social uplift of her people.

The home, the church, and the community were the work shops in which she wrought. The mother's club to guide young girls aright, the Book Lovers' club to develop literary taste, the Women's Federation to accomplish a loftier womanhood and the church were the fields in which she led and molded thought and proved herself to be one of the most useful and cultured women of her day. Possibly the most far-reaching of Mrs. Vashon's public services was the direction of several sanitary relief bazars that netted thousands of dollars for the care of sick and wounded soldiers of the Civil War, and for the housing of colored refugees at Pittsburgh, in the years 1864-65—the aftermath of the Rebellion.

Mrs. Vashon lived to a ripe old age and passed on fully ready for the Master's use.

We present her character as a model, believing it will shine brighter and brighter until the perfect day.

GEORGIANA FRANCES PUTNAM

Born 1839, Salem, Massachusetts

Died 1914, Worcester, Massachusetts

Miss Putnam was a daughter of George Putnam of Boston and Jane Clark of Hubbardstown, Mass. Her girlhood was passed in Salem where she enjoyed all the educational advantages available to the youth of her generation. Also, she grew up under marked salutary home influences. In that home plain living and high thinking were conspicuous. There the formative hand of an intellectual mother laid an indelible impress upon a family who responded to her touch almost automatically. They adored her, reverenced her; she moulded and manipulated them wisely and with a view to making them self-reliant, persistent and able to discriminate between filmy illusions and laudable ambitions. The children early arrived at a realization of life's responsibilities, becoming practical without being made sordid or narrow. They were a serious family but never dull or pessimistic. While the girls of their set who were entering womanhood were inclined to the notion that labor outside the pale of home was degrading, the Putnam sisters anticipated with enthusiasm a near future when they could attempt to be self-sustaining with the ultimate end of arriving at positions of confidence affording both dignity and competence. Animated by this spirit of independence each girl who reached maturity made her mark and became a vitalizing factor in the community where she settled.

Georgiana became a superior woman, physically and mentally. Though not a beauty she had a distinguished personal presence, was tall, finely formed and moved with grace and ease. She had a clear modulated voice whose tones were free from the nasal twang typical of the New Englander. Her poise was accentuated by her pride, and her air of self-control invested her with a dignity as unique as unusual in so youthful an aspirant.

Upon attaining her majority, Miss Putnam left Salem for New York, resolved to take up teaching, a pursuit she had decided upon as most agreeable to her. At that time no special hard or fast restrictions impeded anyone who fancied the routine work of the "little red school house." Between that wooden edifice and the massive structure housing a common school of today lies a long, long distance, stretching far out of sight on one hand and farther out of sight on the other. This lengthened way is outlined not only by the lapse of time but by an evolution from arbitrary rote and unscientific practice to normal rational procedure having for its aim the judicious guidance of a pupil while directing that pupil's own efforts toward self-education.

At the start of her professional career, Miss Putnam was like Mrs. Tompkins-Garnet, an assistant in the old Williamsburg caste school. A friendship sprang up between these two women which lasted from prior to the opening of the Civil War till the demise of the latter in 1911. The points of likeness between the two were few, the points of contrast, many; some things and thought they had in common however, which appreciably affected their respective futures. Each had a deep interest in the general well being of a child; believed that a normal child should develop normally, and that the days of youth and adolescence should be the habit forming period and that it was the special duty of a teacher to supplement the parent's effort to see that a child acquired those habits recognized by all as forming the base of a life of usefulness and contentment. So, though neither was a trained instructor in the formal sense of the term, each from the beginning was of far different sort than pedagogues of the Ichabod Crane variety. The flowering years brought to them the heritage of diligent observation and extended experience. They gradually arose to the consciousness that problems in teaching existed, were to be studied, and had to be solved; in proportion as these were discovered and solved, their work with children grew in importance and efficiency. Aided by increasing familiarity with child nature and its needs, they began to formulate and carry out plans in teaching founded upon common sense, and do original work for children, if without precedent, certainly unhampered by the trammels of a convention whose only merit was that it was time honored.

Like Mrs. Garnet, in the fullness of time, Mrs. Putnam "arrived." From assistant she became a "head of department" and later a principal of an independent primary school. In this highest position she was a model supervisor. She learned to understand and respect the relation between chief and subordinate; to see that at one and the same time, they are conservative yet elastic, formal though confidential. When race and color discrimination became a thing of the past in matters of public education, and colored schools were merged into public schools, a final promotion to an assistant principalship in a large Broklyn grammar school found Miss Putnam both waiting and ready. In this extended sphere of activity she knew just what to do and how to perform the responsible task of assimilating the diverse nationalities that comprise the rank and file in a cosmopolitan school. She was well prepared to help her teachers to help themselves to become familiarized with school routine and to catch the spirit underlying the effort; making it fruitful and vigorous. To the last day of her active service Miss Putnam kept in close touch with the multiplied affairs, administrative and executive, attached to the satisfactory oversight of hundreds of pupils. She particularly and practically demonstrated that scientific teaching discriminates between unity and uniformity; that a teacher should possess something above and beyond book learning and a minimum of culture. Of a speculative, philosophic turn of mind, she weighed and tested all new departures in the work before indorsing them. So in an endeavor to shun the Scylla of rote and mechanical precedent, she never fell a victim to the Charybdis of vague unsupported generalities. With her the result of education was the emphasis of progress in physical and mental alertness, in moral clarity of insight. Her directions to her teachers were: "Keep the end in view always; note your aims and your resources, see if they will make it possible to transmute theories into practices that are seasonable and reasonable. Scrutinize all means to fully establish to the extent they will further what they are designed to accomplish."

The period of Miss Putnam's coming to New York and settling in Brooklyn, just acrosos the river was prior to 1865. The number of colored people in the locality was then comparatively small. Slavery in the state had long been abolished and none living there had any practical knowledge of it, nor were any of its after effects especially apparent. Being an epoch before the large influx of immigrants, the strenuous life was unknown, habits were simple and restrained, desires were limited and there was work enough for every worker. Tasks were undertaken leisurely and all were contended with small gains. Gradually as the population increased, the era of hustling and competition was launched, an economic revolution ensued in which old ways were swamped and the weaker worker as usual went to the wall. The radical changes so affected all sorts of business that the days for making money with a limited capital ceased to be. While it lasted many colored men and women acquired property in lands and houses, were able to accumulate savings and invest them judiciously. Their material prosperity was genuine if not extensive. A competence brought luxury and reasonably availed afforded comfort and satisfaction. Our women in New York included not a few engaged in widely differing trades and professions, each of whom was an ornament to her sex. With many of these, Georgiana Putnam come more or less in contact. Sarah Ennalls, Fanny Tompkins and Eliza Richards deserve special mention. They were the heralds of that corps of our teachers who have so signally left their impress upon the important work of public education. Teaching was then not only done by rote, a method long since abandoned but also by example, a method always commendable. These women by restrained, industrious and unselfish living, exerted a marked influence for good over the young who literally sat at their feet.

When the Emancipation Proclamation went into effect, Miss Putnam was young, yet mature enough to understand the delirium of joy that seized her people. It was like what the Israelites felt when they started out to leave Egypt all unconscious of what was awaiting farther on. Till 1863, colored people in the free states toiled, lived, had ambitions for themselves, made sacrifices for their children very much after the fashion of other Americans not colored. But at no time could the incubus that weighted them be wholly ignored. Emancipation accomplished, they naturally looked forward to a future in which they could thrive and expand under the sanctity of law; be protected and sheltered in the exercise of those citizen rights upon the concession of which the fate of the republic had hinged. The gradual revelation of the true inwardness of the actual state of things dismayed many, disheartened not a few. Still the majority of thinking persons with tightening of lips and squaring of shoulders met the plain indecisions of deferred hope with a composure almost amounting to stoicism. These could discern a practical policy, that of aiming to stand erect under the most disabling conditions, that of attempting to advance in the face of apparently insuperable obstacles. They were sustained by the conviction that to live life faithfully, if not fully, lies within the power of every self-respecting individual. Georgiana Putnam was one who understood this and applied it and the life she developed during a lengthy series of busy fruitful years was rich and enduring in its aspiration and its accomplishment.

In the retirement of advanced age, hampered by physical disability, she could find respite and consolation in her memories of well spent periods of activity during which her benign influence dropped in garnered fullness upon those who came in contact with her.

ANNA ELIZABETH HUDLUN

1840—1914

Anna Elizabeth Lewis was born a child of joy. Shortly before her birth in Uniontown, Pennsylvania, February 6, 1840, her slave mother was set free by the Quaker family who owned her, and all of the happiness and joy of the mother's realization of freedom was breathed into the soul of little Anna Elizabeth.

As Anna grew older her mother had to assume the responsibility of a woman lone in the world with the little girl child to support. She was fortunate in finding another devout Quaker family of Pennsylvania willing to take Anna to rear, while the mother traveled with one of the prominent families of the country. A background was thus formed for the fine, spiritual life which she ever manifested in her work, and no one who knew her, failed to love and honor Anna Elizabeth for it.

When the mother realized that Anna Elizabeth had reached the period in life where her distinctive attractions might bring her in contact with matrimonially inclined youth, she joined her daughter and together they came west, stopping in St. Louis, Mo., for a time, finally locating in Chicago, in 1854. While in the city of St. Louis, Anna Elizabeth met a young man, Joseph Henry Hudlun, and although the meeting seemed a casual one, fate seemed the directing hand, and 1854 found young Hudlun also located in Chicago. In 1855, after a brief courtship, they were joined in wedlock.

During the years of great growth and development of the city of Chicago, the lives of both Anna Elizabeth and Joseph Henry Hudlun blossomed with kindly impulses and good deeds. Hand in hand, they walked through life with a devotion that never wavered.

They realized that to become substantial citizens they must acquire property, and they owned the first house, a little five room cottage, contracted for and built by colored owners. This little home, at 279 Third Avenue, not far from the Dearborn Station, soon became the Mecca toward which the old pioneers and the strangers alike wended their way for social life and civic betterment. In times of distress, as that of the Chicago fire of 1871, the doors of the Hudlun home were thrown open to colored and white alike and as many as five families found refuge therein at that time, and all lived in harmony and good will, subsisting on hard tack furnished to the sufferers by the city and water from Lake Michigan drawn to the home by Hudlun in his little buggy. This sufficed until roomier guarters and better fare could be provided.

This one act endeared them to all Chicago and not to know the Hudluns, was to be denied the best in the city.

While Anna Elizabeth Hudlun was busy rearing the family, working in old Quinn Chapel A. M. E. Church where her mother was among the earlier members and with which Anna herself connected in her very early years, working to keep the mixed schools of Chicago open, and ministering to the needy of all groups, Joseph Hudlun was likewise serving the Master.

He was born a slave, in Culpepper Court-house, Virginia, October 4, 1839, but through frugal habits and conscientious labor, he amassed considerable property by the time of his death in what is now a thickly settled part of the South Side. Thirty-nine years of continuous service on the Chicago Board of Trade, where he did his duty well at all times endeared him in the hearts of every Board of Trade man. How well and conscientiously he served them was brought out on the night of the fire of 1871. Leaving his little family, he went to the Board of Trade in the thickest of the conflagration, opened the vaults and saved many of the valuable books and papers of the institution. At the father's death, as a testimonial of his worth, the institution placed in his stead, his younger son, Joseph Henry, Jr. so that Anna Elizabeth whom they had come to know, love and respect, might always feel their protection through his son. To-day the portrait of Joseph Henry Sr. done in oil, hangs in the "Hall of Celebrities" of the Chicago Board of Trade, and Joseph Henry Hudlun, Jr. still holds forth as the trusted successor to his father, although the father has finished his loving mission and Anna Elizabeth is laid to rest beside her companion of more than 50 years.

Not alone did Joseph Henry Hudlun serve on that night of the great Chicago Fire. "Mother Hudlun" as she was affectionately called, was seeking out the distressed to give them help and comfort, aside from those who were sheltered under her roof. These deeds gained for her the title of "Fire Angel" which clung to her to the end.

When the second conflagration came in 1874 and swept the homes of the colored neighborhoods into oblivion, again "Mother Hudlun" was conspicuous for her solicitude for the homeless and distressed, supplying good clothing, sheltering and feeding many families. So endeared to the people had she become by this time that another title was added in reverence and affection. "Chicago's Grand Old Lady."

Anna Elizabeth Hudlun would have been called one of the foremost social welfare workers of her day had her work been classed. She was an ardent supporter of the work done by her children along that line, and week ends found several of the dependents of the Juvenile Court, who were under the supervision of her daughter, Joan, finding change and recreation under her hospitable roof. She was an enthusiastic club member and organized a club for the purpose of placing needy old people in the Home for Aged and Infirm, which Joan helped to found, officer and support, when it was very unpopular. To her last day she was still soliciting to place one more needy person in the Home. She believed in organized effort and her club was a member of the Federation.

On November 21, 1914, she passed on to that sweet rest which the dear Lord has provided for them that serve Him.

Anna Elizabeth Hudlun left behind her beautiful memories in the hearts of all classes of Chicago's cosmopolitan people who honored and loved her for the Good Samaritan that she was.

"Tis hard to take the burden up,
When these have laid it down;
They brightened all the joy of life,
They softened every frown.
But oh! 'Tis good to think of them
When we are troubled sore;
Thanks be to God that such have been
Although they are no more!"

MISS MARY J. PATTERSON

1840—1894

In these days when our women for the first time in history are taking the degree of Doctor of Philosophy, it is interesting to recall that about sixty years ago our women began to take the collegiate degree of A. B. Miss Mary J. Patterson was, we believe the first colored woman in America to take the degree of Bachelor of Arts. This degree was conferred by Oberlin College in the year 1862.

Miss Patterson's father was one of the far-sighted colored men of North Carolina, who, having obtained his freedom was desirous of securing for his family the benefits of education, and in pursuance of this object, removed to Ohio in the early fifties and settled in the little village of Oberlin, where was located Oberlin College, one of the few educational institutions that then enrolled colored men for Collegiate degrees and the only one that enrolled colored women for the same honors. Here Mr. Patterson lived to see four of his children complete college courses.

Miss Mary Patterson became a teacher and taught many years in the City Schools in Washington, D. C. Later she was the first of our women to be appointed to the Principalship of the Washington High School. Miss Patterson held this position with success until failing health necessitated a change.

Miss Patterson had in the school-room a vivacity of manner and a sympathetic interest that gave her a strong influence over the youth with whom she came in contact and many successful men and women of to-day remember with gratitude her influence on their lives.

Miss Patterson was an educated pioneer, in her own

student life and in her life as teacher. She blazed a trail that many have followed and will follow, ever choosing the highest and hardest courses and ever overcoming.

She passed from this life to a higher in 1894 at Washington, D. C., but her friends think of her as still faring on from height to height in the Great Beyond.

MRS. ANNA ELIZABETH HUDLUN
"Mother Hudlun"

MRS. JOSEPHINE ST. PIERRE RUFFIN
Founder of Colored Women's Clubs

MADAM ELIZABETH KECKLEY
Modiste to Mrs. A. Lincoln

MADAM ELIZABETH KECKLEY

1840—1900

Elizabeth Keckley was born a slave. To her came a full measure of the horrors and torture of slavery. In spite of this her spirit was unbroken and the serene calm, so characteristic of her rare personality was unruffled.

It is said that every cloud has a silver lining. Many years passed ere Madam Keckley caught sight of the gleam. After years of arduous labor, wherein by means of her skillful needle she supported the entire impoverished family to which she belonged, she finally realized her true commercial value. With the realization she borrowed the necessary money, purchased her freedom and by dint of great concentration of effort repaid the debt.

Although bitterly opposed to the great injustice of slavery, nevertheless, in speaking of those earlier days, Madam Keckley never failed to recognize the true value of the friendship she had formed with those by whom she was held in bondage.

At the time of her emancipation Madam Keckley was living in St. Louis, Mo. Soon after, however, she moved to Washington, D. C. where her skill as a modiste was soon recognized.

Although her patronage was largely among the congressional circle, it had long been her ambition to serve "The first lady of the land." After a time even this was realized when she became la modiste for Mrs. Lincoln.

Situated as she was "behind the scenes" it was possible for her to learn much not only about the Lincoln family but also about the affairs of state which were generally hidden from public view.

She became a staunch friend and confidant of Mrs. Lincoln and was greatly respected by the rest of the family. As time passed by and the bonds of friendship were deepened Madam Keckly became a participant in all their joys and sorrows. She prepared the President's wife for gala and formal functions, comforted her on the occasion of the death of her son and of her husband and later when Mrs. Lincoln was in adverse circumstances she continued to be her friend through all her adversities. When the two were forced to part they corresponded regularly.

The above period of her life is very vividly portrayed in "Behind the Scenes" a book published by Madam Keckley in 1868. This book was censored by the authorities hence could not receive the circulation it deserved. In closing her preface Madam Keckley says, "Had Mrs. Lincoln's act never become public property, I should not have published to the world the secret chapters of her life. I am not the special champion of the widow of our lamented President; the reader of the pages will discover that I have written with the utmost frankness in regard to her—have exposed her faults as well as given credit for honest motives. I wish the world to judge her as she is, free from the exaggeration of praise or scandal."

Mrs. Lincoln had given Madam Keckley several souvenirs belonging to herself and the President. These were later donated to Wilberforce University and were lost when the College was destroyed by fire on the night of Lincoln's assassination. The motive which prompted her to do this was not merely that of sympathy but also of tender association. Her son had attended Wilberforce up to the time he enlisted in the army in the service of which he lost his life.

Later Madam Keckley went to Wilberforce as director of Domestic Art.

Her exceptional personality, dignity of bearing, graciousness and love for youth made an abiding impression.

It was shortly after the death of a beloved mother that the writer met Madam Keckley.

The tender expression of sympathy, cheery smiles and final charge when departing for Philadelphia are now cherished memories.

Several years later we met again in Washington where she spent her declining years living in retrospect the events of her remarkable and romantic career.

A GREETING

All Hail,
  Women of America,
    A darker type!
Thy night of traffic, scourge and gloom,
Hath now become the op'ning day—
A rosy, bright, effulgent noon.
Grim Darkness hides his face away!

All Hail,
  Women from every state,
    A stronger type!
From homely scenes with haste we come—
Yet think of distant fields to roam—
Builders of wastes, with honors won,
Makers, keepers of hearth and home.

All Hail,
  Women of worth and power,
    A Nobler type!
Thy field doth lie from sea to sea.
Go forth in all humility,
The weary, fetter'd heart make free
Through Christ to all eternity.

JOSEPHINE ST. PIERRE RUFFIN

1842—1924

Josephine St. Pierre Ruffin was born in Boston in 1842. Her mother was an English girl, coming straight from Cornwall, England, to Boston where she married John James St. Pierre. The latter was a native of Taunton, Massachusetts, and a descendant from a long line of Indians, Negro and French antecedents, the Negro forebears coming originally from Africa. Because there were separate schools in Boston, Josephine St. Pierre was sent to the public schools of Charleston and Salem and later to a private school in New York, coming back to Boston at the opening of the public schools to colored pupils. She went to the old Bowdoin school which was the finishing school for girls as no high school had been started for girls up to that time. In 1858, Josephine St. Pierre married George L. Ruffin at a very youthful age. His family came from Virginia in the 'fifties' to seek opportunities for their children. Immediately after the wedding the young people set sail for Liverpool, England, planning not to rear children in a land which recognized slavery. Soon after their marriage, agitation for freedom for the slave was gaining headway, and they soon returned to America in response to the fighting spirit which was a prominent part of Mrs. Ruffin's endowment, and often asserted itself in matters where justice and equity were concerned. From the time of her marriage until her death she was always identified with public movements.

The following were some of her many activities: She recruited soldiers during the Civil War; worked with the

Sanitary commission after the war. She early connected herself with Julia Ward Howe, Lucy Stone, Abbie May, Edna Cheney and others in the Suffrage Movement,—being one of the charter members of the Massachusetts School Suffrage Association, and cast a vote for over fifty years for school officers under this body.

She was invited into the New England Women's Club; was a volunteer under the Associated Charities for eleven years. She was organizer of the Boston movement for the "Kansas Exodus" sufferers. She formed the first Colored Women's Club in Boston and possibly the first in America. This was known as the "Women's Era Club" and she also called the first convention of colored women ever held in America which resulted in the formation of the first "National Federation of Colored Women's Clubs."

With her daughter Florida, who was associated with her in much of her public work, she founded the "Women's Era," a monthly magazine for club women, which was issued for ten years. Through the publication of this she became a member of the Women's Press Club of Boston, being the only colored member. She was also a charter member of the Moral Education Society. She founded the Northeastern Federation of Women's Clubs and went into the General Federation of Women's Clubs on the invitation of Mrs. Howe and Mrs. Cheney. She went into the famous Milwaukee Convention, after this invitation had been extended to the Women's Era Club, to meet the great opposition of Mrs. Rebecca Lowe, the southern President. Until eighty years of age Mrs. Ruffin was an active member of the Calhoun Club and the Sedalia Club, and was chairman of the League of Women for Community Service.

It is not forgotten today that this woman of many interests founded an association to help Mrs. Sharp's African School and that she also served as vice-president in this association with Edward Everett Hale as president.

Mrs. Ruffin has two children living, George L., and

Mrs. Florida R. Ridley. Mrs. Ridley has been associated with her mother in many of her activities.

In closing the life of Mrs. Ruffin, the writer wishes to quote some facts from a letter received from her daughter, Mrs. Florida Ridley, to whom she wrote for intimate facts concerning the life of her distinguished mother. Mrs. Ridley writes as follows,—

"My mother in her eightieth year attended 'Women's Day' at the Copley Plaza Hotel, November 16, 1921. On that day she headed the receiving line composed of distinguished women of Massachusetts. On our 'Founders Day,' in Massachusetts, celebrated nearly three years afterwards, on February 10, 1924, she was present and although the day was a frightfully stormy one, she went in a taxi by herself to a hair-dresser before she came to the reception, as mother was most particular about her personal appearance, retaining her good looks to the last. In February she was elected to the Board of Management of the Sedalia Club of Boston. In recently looking over the Manual of the Massachusetts State Federation of Women's Clubs, I found that my mother was one of the founders, her name is linked with those of Mabel Looms Todd, Ada Tillinghast and others as incorporators. This puts her not only as a pioneer in colored club work, but also as a pioneer in white.

"Mother was a member of Trinity Church of Boston, and her funeral was held from this church with three clergymen officiating, and the full-vested choir taking part. She was active until the very last, for it was on February 28, 1924, only a short time before her death, that she attended the annual meeting of the League of Women for Community service, where she cast her vote and waited with the rest of us until one o'clock in the morning for results. The end came March 13, 1924, after she had taken to her bed only a few days."

MRS. MARGARET E. REID

1846—1923

To a large number of the present generation of Wilberforce students this short life sketch will bring personal interest.

Margaret Elizabeth was born in Maysville, Kentucky, in 1846. Her parents were John and Anna Norris. At the early age of eight years she was converted and during her entire life was a shining example of piety and truth. At the age of eighteen Margaret Norris was married to George W. Reid, who preceeded her in death.

For several years they lived in Kentucky, then moved to Osborn, Ohio, and later made her home in Springfield, Ohio. The couple were industrious and frugal and accumulated sufficient to purchase a beautiful home. In 1895 Mr. Reid went on a bond for a friend who proved false and their property, representing years of toil and sacrifice was swept away. In that year Mrs. Reid moved to Wilberforce and kept a boarding house which was opened to the public for twenty-eight consecutive years. Not blessed with children of her own Mrs. Reid reared two children who died soon after reaching their majority. Later she adopted her sister's three children, Anna, Margaret, and John Gillard. For this kind act she was liberally rewarded with deep affection and unusual loyalty and devotion on the part of her name-sake Margaret.

Mrs. Reid was a member of Holy Trinity Church, Wilberforce and was active in all good work. Her life was one of service. Hundreds of students who attended Wilberforce University during her life, were the recipients of her bounty. She was never known to turn one from her door or her table. Not only the cup of cold water, but many good meals, and other creature comforts, she gave with a sweet smile in "His Name."

To all who knew her, students, faculty, neighbors, and friends this sweetly-disposed, unselfish, never-tiring woman was lovingly called, "Auntie Reid." So when she fell asleep on August 11, 1923, at the age of seventy-seven, the flame of love and appreciation burned on the heart altars of thousands scattered throughout America, the islands of the sea, and far off Africa.

It was a privilege to know her and to be one of those whom she helped, for her example was above reproach—her life beautiful, and although she did not accumulate much of this world's goods, she laid up for herself treasures in heaven where moth doth not corrupt. This image of this friend, soft-spoken, kind and generous with hands outstretched to the poor and needy will live in the hearts of those who knew her, for none knew her, but to love her.

MATILDA J. DUNBAR

1848—?

"Sad days were those—ah, sad indeed!
But through the land the fruitful seed
Of better times was growing.
The plant of freedom upward sprung,
And spread its leaves so fresh and young—
Its blossoms now are blooming."

—Dunbar

The subject of this sketch was born in Shelby County, Kentucky. She had many thrilling experiences during the time spent in slavery. In her own language she tells some highly interesting facts concerning her life. She pondered over her condition, wondering why she was not permitted to learn to read—why she was compelled to work for people who gave her few clothes and no wages—why she could not live with her mother and grandmother—in fact why she was a slave—dangerous thoughts for a young woman in bondage—but these and other thoughts kept obtruding until she found resentment against her condition had filled her bosom. The crisis came one day when Matilda, house maid and cook for fourteen persons, was accused by her mistress of an act of which she was not guilty. She denied it and—"Miss Matt slapped me in the face, causing the blood to flow. I was peeling an onion, I threw the onion across the kitchen and with the knife in my hand walked out. She ordered me back. I did not go. She called me all the pet names such as you will not find in the unabridged. I knew I had violated a law which meant the whipping post. I did not know which way to turn. Night

MRS. MATILDA J. DUNBAR

Mother of Paul Lawrence Dunbar

was coming on—I sat on the steps and wept. I was not yet fifteen years old—no one to help me—father, mother, sister, no one near. I hid near the stile. How frightened I was! Milton, the house boy passed. I called him. 'Go up stairs, I said, and get my buff calico dress, my shoes and shawl.' He went and came right past Miss Matt, who did not see him. I rolled them up and started. Milton said, 'Come back! You're hurtin' yo'self.' I said 'Hush!' 'Yo' bettah come back.' I said 'Hush!' I went up to him and said, 'If you open your mouth I will murder you.' I went past Miss Matt's room window, up a corn field fence, hiding when I heard the clash of horses feet on the hard road, then on for seven miles to my sisters Ellen's. 'Matilda, go right back,' she said. 'I'll die first' said I. Her son said, 'Mother, "Tid" don't haf to go back.' A heavy snow had fallen, but at midnight the boy went with me five miles away to old Aunt Doshy's cabin, but she could not keep me, so on we went five miles further to Binie Redden's cabin and then for four weeks hid in the loft where I stayed with fear and trembling all day, stealing down at midnight for something to eat."

It is interesting to follow her from Binie's cabin until her fetters were broken. When emancipation came she was told that only soldiers' wives were free, but soon she learned that she too was free and when she gave vent to her feelings was told to pack her things and leave. Again she says—"Early that morning I sang, my heart was so full! I had a fine voice for singing. At four o'clock I sang like a mocking bird. I sang the whole house awake. I was in the kitchen getting breakfast. The word came—'All darkies are free.' I never finished that breakfast! I ran 'round and 'round the kitchen, hitting my head against the wall, clapping my hands and crying, 'Freedom! freedom! freedom! Rejoice, freedom has come!' I hurried to Louisville and on January first there was a great celebration. As the parade passed on Broadway near Twelfth street some one turned a wild bull loose. For a time there was a panic, but soon the vicious animal was captured and the parade moved on. O, how we sang and shouted that day! The very memory "Happifies" my soul and I must honor and praise His High Name."

She did not long continue in Louisville as her heart yearned to see her mother who was in Dayton, Ohio. The narrator continued, "I was permitted to care for my mother in her old age—although deprived of her love and affection in my childhood. Well do I remember how we little ones, peeking through the logs of the cabin, saw our poor, little mother ready to be whipped for an act she did not commit. 'Who did it if you didn't do it?' 'I don't know, Massa David,' she cried. His wife Miss Sallie, said, 'If you know about it Liza, tell him.' 'I don't know, Miss Sallie.' She could not stand the sight of that poor tearful mother, but turned to her husband and said, 'Mr. Glass, I did that'."

Mrs. Dunbar resides in the Dayton home from which her poet son fell into "that last dear sleep whose soft embrace is balm." That comfortable, commodious home, shaded by magnificient elms, where he fought his losing fight, watched over and tenderly cared for by the devoted mother —those last days or any of his days and years would have been impossible without that mother who faithfully fulfilled a heavenly misson during the weary months and years of her son's illness. At the open door she greets the visitors with a smile. They come to talk of Paul—her one great theme—then she conducts them to his sanctum sanctorum—"Well, his den," she says—he named it "Loafingholt"—the walls lined with book shelves filled with his own works and choice bits from noted authors—photographs of eminent men and women of both races and dainty bits of bric-a-brac. Here is his desk with pens and ink wells, his caps and boots—his couches piled high with gay sofa pillows, inviting one to "loaf"—a violin made by Captain Stivers of Steele high school—all cherished by this loving mother who delights to show them, these silent remembranc-

THE DUNBAR HOME, DAYTON, OHIO

es of a dear departed one—"the soul of a summer day, the breath of a rose, but the summer is fled and the rose is dead." It is a privilege to visit that mother who struggled to give to the world a song-bird, who toiled that he might have the advantages of an education—a boon she so greatly coveted— a birthright out of which she was so cruelly cheated.

In her presence one gets the impression that here is a woman of uncommon native ability. At an advanced age she is fluent in conversation which often sparkles with wit. She possesses, to a remarkable degree, the gift of story telling, accompanied by great drollery and mimicry—in fact she dramatizes, as she relates, by act and tone. It is not difficult to trace the poesy of Paul to this mother who, given a chance, would have been as great a woman, in the field of literature, as her son was a man.

Go on and up! Our souls and eyes
Shall follow thy continuous rise;
Our ears shall list thy story
From bards who from thy root shall spring
And proudly tune their lyres to sing
Of Ethiopia's glory.

DR. SUSAN S. (McKINNEY) STEWARD

Born, Brooklyn, N. Y., 1848
Died, Wilberforce, Ohio, 1918

The life story of the subject of this sketch is the unvarnished narration of a full fruitful finished career. Its unfolding is ample refutation of vile slanders that like deadly upas branches have again and again cast blighting shadows over the contingent of American women with whom she was identified by race extraction. It is also a confirmation of the latter day contention that woman can succeed and in strictly conventional fashion, in any endeavor which appeals to her upon which she concentrates attention and in the prosecution of normal conditions, thus furnishing a practical example of women alert enough to apprehend the privileges and comprehend the responsibilities that are at once the glory and the burden of womanhood.

One among the countless host of young women, obscure though ambitious, Susan Smith grew till physically and mentally she attained a harmonious maturity. At the time of her translation she had loomed up a conspicuous figure among even the exceptional women of her day and rank. She laid down mortality crowned with the success that is the legitmate result of intelligent, applied, strenuous activity.

The importance of the doctor's life history is enhanced by the stress of that extraordinary period of awakening on the part of women during which she lived. It was then that women were beginning to select their own life plans instead of tacitly accepting those arranged for them; when they were beginning to scrutinize and criticize the time honored and conventional, to discover to what extent their adoption or rejection would impede or forward the desire to live in the fullest sense of the term.

What induced Susan Smith to choose a medical profession cannot be difinitely stated; this is to be regretted for it would be highly interesting to trace her process of thought from the initial suggestion to the final conclusion. A sentiment is cherished by her family as one of the influences that, subconsciously it may have been, directed her natural bent toward a life of service. Upon an invalid neice she lavished the tenderest care in a sympathetic attempt to lessen the suffering of one afflicted in earliest youth. In this ministry of affection she was probably influenced to decide upon what later proved to be her proper place among the world's workers. Whatever the impelling cause the result amply verified the wisdom of her decision.

A woman who today enters upon professional life does a casual ordinary thing; it was vastly different a half century ago. The bugbear of that period was the fear that a woman would unsex herself. Only level headed, self reliant, determined women then ventured upon a course of action certain to elicit unfriendly criticism, likely to induce disparagement if not alienation.

It must be conceded that "our women" have always striven to keep abreast of the times; none have been more progressive, more aggressive. Whenever and wherever they have entered the arena of competition, while they have met equals, they have never been forced to retire before superiors. It is therefore more gratifying than surprising to find Miss Smith no exception in this respect. She studied at the New York Medical School for Women and Children and concluded an arduous course with success and distinction. The faculty gracefully recognized her merit by choosing her to be the valedictorian of her class, the strongest one then sent out.

Then followed a post graduate course at the Long

Island College Hospital. She was the only female student in the class to which she was assigned. This involved no embarrassment. Though young she had acquired a measure of dignity and some common sense. These, joined to intense absorption in her studies, ensured the proprieties and rescued the situation from being humiliating as well as unusual.

She commenced practice in her native city. Business grew slowly but steadily and experience kept apace. Certain endowments of temper and temperament helped to abridge the probationary period, and in a few years she became a popular, properous family physician. Friends became patrons with growing confidence in her skill and devotion; strangers having solicited her services remained clients upon realizing she was capable and reliable. Her practice was unrestricted by race or sex discrimination and consultations brought her in frequent contact with leading New York practitioners. At the zenith of her Brooklyn career she maintained consulting offices in two widely separate sections. During this period she became the wife of the late Rev. Wm. G. McKinney. Her professional obligations were not less satisfactorily discharged by the addition of the duties of the home maker. Two children survive her, a son, Rev. William S. McKinney of Saint Stephens P. E. Church, Jamaica, L. I., and Mrs. James Carty, one of Brooklyn's successful school teachers.

The doctor had a talent for music; this she cultivated making is a source of both pleasure and profit. She studied under John Zundel, of Plymouth Church, and for years was organist and choirmaster in the Bridge Street African Methodist Church.

Dr. McKinney was a model of an "all around" woman; trained to routine in business, as a manager of a home, she pursued a plan in which the results of system in the economy of thought and strength were apparent; she succeeded in becoming an animating influence in her family circle, and adequately performed her social duties. She was one of the founders of the "Woman's Loyal Union" of New York and Brooklyn and for years was on the board of managers of the Brooklyn Home for Aged Colored People.

The doctor was an active member of the Kings County Homeopathic Society and a close student of the history of the rise and progress of women in medicine. In a monograph she pathetically wrote: "The earliest women physicians, a noble band of heroic, energetic women, through discouragements deep and dark, by hard work and with personal sacrifice, opened up the road of opportunity to the great army of women who are now following in the footsteps of their pioneer sisters."

The same article contains an eloquent tribute to the "beloved physician" who was to all her pupils, friend as well as preceptor. "Dr. Clemence Lozier was a most remarkable type of noble, energetic womanhood. She was firm though generous; kind though judicious; she attached very closely to her those fortunate enough to receive training under supervision. The college founded by this Christian lady is said to be the best women's college in the world to-day."

After Dr. McKinney became Dr. Steward by a second marriage to Rev. T. G. Steward, a former Chaplain in the United States Army and a professor at Wilberforce University, Brooklyn ceased to be her place of residence though it never ceased to be her home in the broader sense of the term. Her identification with it has survived her decease.

Any account of women in medicine would be incomplete without reference to Dr. Steward, any record of "our women" would be unfinished, lacking a resume of the salient points of her character. Her message to the world is, that no normal woman should neglect to seek opportunity for self-betterment. To women specially she has left the valuable bequest of the power and courage of an illustrious example. "To our women," the Colored Women of America, her eloquent though mute advice is, to take stock of resources available and limitations that restrict; learn to distinguish between proper ambitions and sordid greed. Cultivate a desire for a full life, one of selection and expansion to the limit, keeping ever inviolate the purity and prestige of womanhood. Glorify the life individual and claim scope for that free full development which is the birthright of every human being.

The manner of passing out of earthly existence is by no means of necessity an index how one has passed through it, yet the "ceasing to be" is occasionally in marvellous correspondence with what one has been. Her change from "activity to repose" was singularly befitting a person of the doctor's orderly ways and methodical habits. Never disabled by bodily infirmity or wasted by protracted sickness, with her life mortal blended almost imperceptibly with the life immortal. By some this co-called "sudden death" is regarded only as a ready willing response to the call of the Master, "Arise, my love and come away!"

Dr. Susan S. McKinney Steward

KNOW YE NOT THAT A GREAT WOMAN HATH FALLEN THIS DAY IN ISRAEL?

Address of Miss Hallie Q. Brown on the occasion of the death of Doctor Susan Maria Steward, at Wilberforce, Ohio, March 7, 1918.

I come not to deliver a studied euology on our lamented Doctor Steward, but rather to pay a heartfelt tribute to one who was a very dear friend and a very close friend.

Her passing was so sudden and unexpected that it is a shock to each one of us. It is one of the many instances that remind us of the uncertain tenure of human life. And so today we meet to pay a tribute to the memory of a great woman.

She was great in the estimation of those who knew her capacity, her ability, her real worth. She was not a spectacular woman. She was modest. She did not indulge in the modern methods of advertising those qualifications that fitted her so preeminently for public service.

A woman absolutely self-reliant, honest to herself and to her friends. She acted upon her own judgment and when she had made up her mind that a thing was right and ought to be done, SHE DID IT. She had the courage of her convictions; a faithful, reliant woman, honest in all the relations of life; loyal to her family, the public and her friends.

A great woman has departed from among us, great in intellect, great in heart, great in all things that make for better conditions in the world. She scorned to rise upon the shoulders of others. Rather would she put her own shoulder to the service of some less fortunate. She was one of those generous natures that love peace, order, and harmony.

But she could strike, and strike hard, in what she believed to be a righteous cause. With her it was justice on the one side, and injustice on the other. The line was sharply drawn. There was no middle ground of expediency or compromise.

Her success in life did not arise from accident. She was a student. She applied her mind with all the intensiveness of her nature.

She was a model housekeeper, and wisely ruled her household ever holding the admiration of her husband and family.

She was a musician of note, understanding that master of instruments, the pipe organ, and served as organist of the Bridge Street A. M. E. Church in Brooklyn 28 years, and in a Baptist Church of that city, two years.

She identified herself with every good movement in the communities in which she lived. Coming to Wilberforce as a stranger, she set about to cooperate, to build constructively. She despised the idea of rule or ruin.

We find her engaged in the following activities:

College Aid Society, of which she was president;

Mite Missionary Society, of which she was treasurer;

Young Women's Christian Association, member of the Advisory Committee;

Neighborhood Club, of which she was treasurer;

Stewardess Board of the church, a member;

Temperance Union, active member;

Red Cross Society, active member;

Negro Soldiers' War Relief League, active member, giving not only of her earthly substance, but the energy of her soul.

And now I come to speak of the strong bent in the character of this notable woman—Physician-Friend. Not even the ministry of the gospel bears such close relationship to a family or an individual as does the physician.

Graduating with honor from the New York Medical College and Hospital for Women and taking post-graduate work in the Long Island Medical College, and practicing continuously for 45 years, she was thoroughly equipped to stand beside the highest in this land; and when in after years the search light of history is thrown full upon her work, it will be shown that she was one of the great physicians of her generation. Her record at Wilerforce is phenomenal. When given complete control and left unhampered, Doctor Steward never lost a case. I very much doubt if any other physician in the county or state can show such low mortality record as can be produced by the case books of Doctor Steward during her splendid career of twenty-one years at Wilberforce. More still, during her long practice of forty-five years there has never been so much as a hint toward dishonorable practice aimed against this Mother in Israel.

Ah! In these twenty-one years, how she has stood by this community! And how happy we are, we who knew her worth, that stood by her!

We see her entering the darkened chamber and in sympathy go down in-to the valley of motherhood, rescue the young wife from her peril, and fan the flickering spark of babyhood into the bright and healthy flame of life. We see her, hopeful and confident, as she enters our halls and dormitories and brings to health and happiness the fever stricken boy or girl. We see her tear of sympathy and feel the pressure of that kindly hand as we stand by the bedside of father, mother, brother or sister, and see the life ebb away and hear her say: "God's will be done."

We cannot think of her as gone!

"I cannot, and I will not say—
She is dead. She has passed away.
With a cheery smile and a wave of the hand,
She has wandered into an unknown land,
And left us dreaming how very fair
It needs must be, since she is there."

Wilberforce can never be the same without Doctor Steward. Many a fond mother will start out of her sleep at the midnight hour to hear the moan and stand helpless before her little one, and cry with the poet:

> "O, for the touch of a vanished hand,
> And the sound of a voice that is still!"

Doctor Steward often said that she had no patience with pain. She had relieved so many sufferers by her knowledge and skill that the Great Physician decreed that she should suffer no pain. So He laid His hand upon her and took her unto Himself.

We are not at this time reconciled or comforted. But if our grief be great, how much more so must be that of her beloved husband, her idolized son and daughter. How she loved to talk about them! They were her jewels.

Grieve not dear ones. Look away from the tomb to that land of fair delight. If Doctor Steward could speak she would say to us:

> "When I am gone,
> Above me raise no lofty stone
> Perfect in human handicraft.
> Say this of me and I shall be content,
> That in the Master's work my life was spent.
> Say not that I was either great or good,
> But, Mary like, 'She hath done what she could'."

HENRIETTA CORDELIA RAY

Born in New York City—1849

Died in Brooklyn—1916

A tiny rill has its mission as well as a majestic river. Aggregated rain drops unite to form mighty billows. The faint flush of dawn though lacking the resplendence of cloudless noon, is none the less a direct emanation from the primal source of light. Any record of good repute attached to lives of even the obscure, embraces much that is illuminating that contrasts gracefully with the follies and foibles incident to humanity. Such details are worthy of narration for their forceful, healthy influence over every day folk who in so large a majority comprise our work-a-day world.

"As a stained web extended to the sun
Grows pure by being purely shone upon,"

so human beings grow more enduring in spirit, more stable in principle by the contemplation of careers finely illustrative of human possibilities, in attempts to climb the ladder of patience and devotion to duty up to the great heart of the infinite Creator.

It is a fact equally gratifying and indisputable that many, many, of "our women," under most untoward conditions, have lived lives, the persual of whose details cannot fail to interest, should not fail to kindle or intensify a longing for better things. Most of these women had during their existence reputations that were limited and local; it is their due that a wider circle than that composed of reflective personal friends should become familiarized with the diverse yet undeviating admirable traits of character they developed. Most were matrons; a fair minority being however unmarried. Neither class allowed the confines of the hearth to limit the extent of their reasonable ambitions. Each in spirit lowly, in aim lofty, aspired to become an animating influence, to rise above the dead level of an automatic drudge. The experience of life may have brought, probably did have for them, seasons of unrequited toil, undue anxiety, and devastating pain; yet, each had her moments of compensation. These were the treasured times when hope seemed to weave her loveliest tissues. Then she could act or wait with uplifted eye and serene brow sustained by the firm belief that "love is stronger than death" and that the Lord of life is the source of deathless love.

The hall-mark of good woman, and all consistently good women are truly great women, is reverence for humanity and faith in God, that benign Father who can transmute pain into peace and who will eventually blend all earth's discords into one grand heavenly harmony.

Once, long ago, a woman sang of her sex in these lines of gloomy prophecy:—

"* * * her lot is on you
To make idols and to form them clay,
And to bewail that worship."

The subject of this sketch, herself a poet, caroled her lay of faith and hope in these gladsome words:—

"With vision clear and purpose true
Humanity's broad scheme will trace;
* * * thus life expands
To sweet fruition, till the waves
of Time are lulled on golden sands."

In the world's great output of poetic literature expressed in our noble English language, a few, a scanty few productions stand unrivalled, unapproachable; for the great singers, those touched with the burning coals of the divine afflatus, are exceptional, each the marvel of his age. But the muse of fancy has many poetical gifts varying in degree but not in satisfaction. Each minor bard is content to have a place more or less lowly at the foot of the divine heights inaccessible to ordinary mortals. He is competent to give and receive joy in proportion to his ability and his opportunity. Between the casual stringers of prosaic rhymes and one who has drained the silver rill of imagination, there is no connection. The poet is he whose cadences are touched with that mysterious boon that:

"Like an Aeolian's wind played tune,
Makes perfect all the psalm."

Among those who have been responsive to this simple yet unique test are three of our women whose songs have made music during three successive generations. Phyllis Wheatly who carolled at the dawn, was endowed with the highest degree of intellectuality; Frances Ellen Watkins Harper in later times was most prolific in tender thoughts and graceful expression. Her verses brought cheer, stimulated hope and revived faith even when their minor undertones suggested soul conflict through tense and trying experiences. Cordelia Ray's poetry, with less exuberant fancy may be likened to the quaint touching music of a shell murmuring of the sea—a faint yet clear note sounding all the pathos and beauty of undying life. It is the peculiar share of clarity and elevation combined that glorifies and makes so rich the quiet flow of music in her songs.

In the dedication of her book of poems, Miss Ray refers to the memories of a household "made beautiful by the presence of loved ones who have entered the Life Immortal." The tender and delicate appreciation may with propriety be applied to her personally, for in her home she moved serenely, diffusing all the light, warmth and beauty of a sunny presence. The even tenor of her way was apparent from her earliest youth. Her daily walk and conversation, her attitude toward the various affairs in which she took an intelligent and willing part, are well remembered. There was a transfiguring light that radiated from her, for she bore herself as one endowed with an innate sense of things divine.

The home so highly prized by Cordelia was a lovely one both in the material and in the immaterial sense of the term. In it she passed a sheltered childhood growing and developing under the fostering care of a refined, cultured mother and made steady by the inspiring example of a vigorous, energetic father whose natural puritanical stamina were neutralized by deep sense of justice and sincere deside to aid, uplift and make better. Miss Ray came of the primitive Massachusetts stock, being a direct descendant of aboriginal Indian, English and of the first Negroes of New England. To find an ancestor of hers with unmixed blood, one would have to trace back from four or five generations. Emphasis is made of this fact as a vital disproof of the theory that a mixture of blood deteriorates all the component elements. Miss Ray had all the qualifications of a gentle woman. She was well-born, well bred and enjoyed all the advantages accruing to her position in a family where birth, breeding and culture were regarded as important assets. The parents of the Ray Children could afford to give them all the intellectual advantages of the time. Those who lived were well educated and three of the girls were college graduates. Cordelia became proficient in French, Greek and Latin and was an English scholar. By opportunity, habit and inclination, she was essentially a student.

Her life long companion was her next older sister Florence who was an accomplished teacher and a brilliant conversationist. In society, Florence naturally attracted immediate attention but no one who ever met Cordelia could entirely forget her. Her curious air of detachment from things ordinary, her entire absence from affectation, her genuine self-forgetfulness, made her charming. A classmate once said of her that she appeared as one unspotted by the world. Always affable she dispensed only kindness and looked for nothing but goodwill. To describe her in her own words: "Her soul was trust, her eyes a prayer!"

When Florence undertook teaching, Cordelia, ever desirous to imitate and emulate the dear sister whom she regarded with an affection tinged with admiration, applied and secured a similar position. But the dull routine and drudgery of the school room became distasteful to the girl fresh from the atmosphere of a home where taste and good will ruled and high ideals and affluence combined to "draw life's finest issues." She decided to take up a life for which she felt most fitted. In this resolve she had both the sympathy and assistance of her sister. As her wants were simple and her taste equally so, an arrangement was made to enable her to do a comparatively rare thing, to live tranquilly and pursue unhampered her literary work. In time she became an indefatigable student, a humble worshipper at the shrine of the muse, and her work grew in beauty and value as her inner vision became more distinct and clarified.

Yet she was far from unpractical. She enjoyed imparting to others the knowledge which so attracted her. She almost always had some pupils individually and in small groups whom she taught music, mathematics and the languages. At one time for two successive seasons she conducted a class in English literature composed of teachers. With such a grade of pupils the course was extensive and thoroughly enjoyed.

That such a woman should be accurate, precise, and methodical may seem contradictory; yet she certainly was an example that ideality is not an impracticable adjunct to painstaking. She made an admirable secretary and served in that capacity in several organizations. Her work and her worth were duly recognized and appreciated by friends to whom such help as she was able and willing to render seemed invaluable.

Happy with her friends, her books, her writings, her charities, she lived a simple, blameless life. Her wide range of reading, her habits of sustained and elevated thinking aided to lift her literary efforts far above the ordinary. Gradually she attained an exquisite sense of fitness which purified her tastes, restrained her imagination, directing her with broadening experience toward fuller knowledge and increasing grace of diction. Her gifts were exceptional, her advantages unusual and her poise exquisite in its constancy and its adjustment. Among a generation of brainy New York women, she was probably the most accomplished, yet outside her immediate circle the least known. Her modesty was excessive, she never boasted nor appeared self-conscious, nor did she talk fluently unless in the unreserve of her home with intimate friends. One's knowledge of her came from frequent contact and by personal observation. She rarely unbent to talk freely of her pursuits, her aspirations, her ideals.

It was fortunate indeed for her to be able to love a life she so enjoyed and for which she was so well fitted. When the closing hour became apparent, she shrunk from the crisis not from fear or selfishness but because it entailed separation from that beloved Florence, long a confirmed invalid whom she had watched and tended with a devotion surpassing the love of a mother. But she rallied to her support that faith that had never failed and meekly said farewell to her whom she has mortalized in verse as her dear "Heart-Sister."

Were it as discreet as agreeable, a critical reading of at least one of her poems would form a fitting conclusion; but such an indulgence may to an extent defeat the intent of this volume. The immediate purpose of this book is to be something beyond a vehicle for information or a source of casual enjoyment. It is designed to arouse that admiration that leads to emulation, to emphasize the doctrine of personal responsibility. The number of talents a person has is of minor importance compared with the realization that each human being is accountable for the development and exercise of all powers and faculties with which he is endowed.

Mention should be made of Miss Ray's filial and fraternal feelings. With Florence she collaborated a memoir of her distinguished father. Her verses to her mother and a younger sister who died in early childhood are models of tenderness and enshrine an affection and a faith deep and enduring.

A volume of her poems was published in 1910, a copy of the same would be a valuable addition to any library. It displays as reflected in a mirror, her versatility, love of nature, classical knowledge, delicate fancy, an unaffected piety. She sings like a gladsome child basking in the sunshine of earth's cheer and beauty; again, like a serious maiden she stands with quiet reverent feet at the edge of sealed mysteries. Whether gleeful or sober, carolling or crooning she is intensely feminine and her flights of fancy, not unduly elevated are always steady.

One of her poems is an unconscious portrait of herself; only two slight verbal alterations have been made to make the picture perfect:

"Her ringlets glistened like the bronze of morn
And framed an oval outline statue fair,
Somewhere a faint blush lingered for awhile,
Sending its ripples to the wavy hair.
Upon her features grace had shed its charm
And in her soul sweetness to naught gave way;
'Twas like a streak of sunshine thrown across
The motionless repose of early day,
No sorrow rested on the calm pure brow
But thought held undisputed empire there,
Eyes like the dusky brown of woodland tree,
Gazed in a dream or in a quiet prayer,
And through her aspect something noble shone
That proved the soul in charity had grown."

MRS. LUCY SMITH THURMAN

1849—1918

Mrs. Lucy Thurman, the daughter of Nehemiah Henry and Catherine Smith, was born October 22, 1849 at Oshawa, Canada. Her educational alvantages were obtained in the schools of Canada. At the age of 17 she went to Maryland to teach school and was associated with Frederick Douglas and many of the leaders of that day. In 1875 she entered temperance work and was among the first of the band known as the "Blue Ribboners." When the Woman's Christian Temperance Union was formed she immediately joined. For years she was one of its most successful lecturers, her work being largely in Indiana, Illinois and Michigan and wholly among white people. In 1893 at the World's Fair during a convention of the W. C. T. U. she was elected Superintendent of Temperance Work among colored people, the first person to occupy such a position. In the performance of her duty she traveled in every Southern state and as far west as California. She made a specialty of the schools in the South. She attended the World's W. C. T. U. Convention which met in England in 1896, and was the guest in the home of Lady Henry Somerset while there. Was active in club life, having organized the first club among colored people in the state of Michigan. Organized the Michigan State Association of Colored Women's Clubs in 1900 and was its first president and served for several terms. Was elected President of the National Association of Colored Women's Clubs in 1907. When the body of Miss Francis Willard lay in state in the Temperance Temple at Chicago, Mrs. Thurman was called from the far South where she was lecturing to be one of the guards of honor. Mrs. Thurman was twice married, the first marriage taking place at Cleveland, Ohio, in 1847. Two boys were of this union, and are now living at Jackson, Mich. In 1883 she was married at Detroit, Mich., to Mr. Frank Thurman. Two children were the result of this union, one of whom survives, Dr. F. S. Thurman, St. Louis, Mo. Mrs. Thurman died at Jackson, Mich., March 29, 1918, and was laid to rest in the family lot in Evergreen Cemetery of that city.

JOSEPHINE SILONE YATES

1852—1912

Josephine Silone Yates came of a family with rare and remarkable race pride in their pure African descent, coupled with a strong intellectuality. To this was added the New England environment with the ethical and religious elements which have made this section the Cornerstone of the American Republic. Blessed is he who was reared in New England.

An old legend of the family tells of a slave-ship with its cargo of African slaves that was driven ashore on the rocky coast of New England and its human freight scattered to various parts of the country where freedom came to them nearly a century earlier than to the slaves of the South.

Among these thus fortunately placed were the ancestors of Josephine Silone. For several generations they lived on Long Island, esteemed as men and women of sterling worth. To Alexander and Parthenia Reeve Silone were born two daugters, Harriet and Josephine; the older showing a taste for manual industry developed into a superior dress-maker; the younger, showing a taste for books and study was given every opportunity to secure a good education. Their training started at the feet of an intelligent, christian mother—so that when Josephine was old enough to enter the district school—she was admitted to advanced standing.

At the age of eleven, she was invited by her maternal uncle, Rev. J. B. Reeve of Philadelphia to his home, that better opportunity for education than that afforded by the district school might be hers. Here she came in contact with a large number of cultured people and especially with Mrs. Fannie Jackson Coppin, a woman of rare qualities, and in attending her Institute for Colored Youth, Josephine made rapid progress. When her uncle was appointed to a charge in Washington, D. C., she accepted the invitation of a maternal aunt, Mrs. Girard, who lived in Newport R. I., that beautiful "City by the Sea," to live with her and attend the high school there. Her brilliant qualities as a student soon attracted the attention of such men as Colonel Wentworth Higginson, a member of the school board. She was not only valedictorian of a large class, but was the only colored member of her class, and the first colored graduate of the school.

To fit herself for the work of a teacher, she entered the Rhode Island State Normal School at Providence and graduated in 1879, again the only colored graduate.

In 1880 she came West and began teaching in Lincoln Institute, Jefferson City, Missouri, as head of the department of science and held this position with marked success until 1889 when she resigned to marry Professor W. W. Yates, principal of the Wendell Phillips School of Kansas City, Missouri.

A warm welcome was extended by Kansas City to a woman already known in educational circles as one of the best teachers in the state, and she was soon called for as a private teacher by a host of young and old aspirants for more learning. In later years she was called to teach again in Lincoln Institute and in the High School of Kansas City.

For the greater part of her life she had been writing for the press and now enlarged her work in that line, often writing under the *nom de plume* of R. K. Potter. As a writer she had a clear, incisive style and a wide range of thought. She wrote often in verse, as "The Zephyr," "Royal To-day," "The Isles of Peace" and others.

With the beginning of the club work among our women, she became a zealous club worker, and was one of the organizers and the first president of the Kansas City Woman's League in 1893, one of the oldest clubs among the colored women. Later she became one of the State Presidents of the federated clubs.

When the National Association of Colored Women was organized in 1896 she became one of its earnest supporters and later served four years as its treasurer and four as president—at the fourth Convention in St. Louis in 1904, and in Detroit, Michigan, at the fifth Convention in 1906 she presided with a quiet dignity, grace and tact. At the close of the Convention in Detroit the members of the Convention expressed their appreciation of her faithful service and impartial ruling by presenting her with a large silver loving cup.

Mrs. Yates was a woman of rare intellectual power—she delighted in study and passed with distinguished success every examination she entered. She had a wonderful capacity for work, and it was no unusual thing for her to write or study all night and teach the next day.

She never allowed the duties of the home to encroach upon the time set apart for study or literary work, and in many lines of work, husband and wife continued side by side, for Mr. Yates also was ever a student.

Hers was a nature to make and hold friends, of strong moral fibre, of keen insight into human nature, of broad, deep sympathies, that knew friends in every rank of society and every race. To the many hundred students with whom she came in contact, she was an inspiration—showing them the heights that could be reached without wealth, beauty or favor, by steady concentrated work.

Two children were born to Mr. and Mrs. Yates, whose education she carefully superintended, never feeling that her responsibility ended by "sending them to school." The daughter, Josephine Silone Yates graduated from Kansas University and is a successful teacher in the schools of Kansas, City, Missouri; the son William Blyden Yates also graduated from the University of Kansas, and then took a medical course at Northwestern, in Chicago and is now practicing medicine in that city.

In November, 1910, Mrs. Yates was left a widow by the death of Mr. Yates whom the Board of Education esteemed so highly that they renamed the school of which he had been principal, the W. W. Yates School.

Mrs. Yates was later appointed a teacher in the high school where she taught with all her former success, until Sept. 3, 1912, when she suddenly departed after an illness of two days.

To her children and her friends she left a priceless heritage, the memory of a woman who stood on a height in usefulness, character and culture.

MARIA LOUISE BALDWIN

1856—1922

Once a great teacher called a little child unto Him and set him in the midst of His hearers and said, "Whoseoever shall humble himself as a little child the same is greatest in the Kingdom of Heaven, and who shall receive one such little child in My name receiveth Me." These words are spoken reverently and applied to the subject of this sketch. Her gentle manner, her brave simplicity, her loving recognition of children in the name of her own Master manifested her greatness and prompted grateful memories of her service.

Miss Maria Louise Baldwin was born September 13, 1856 in Cambridge, Massachusetts. She was the oldest daughter of Peter L. and Mary E. Baldwin.

All of her school days were spent in Cambridge. At the age of five years she entered the Sargent Primary School. She attended the Allston Grammar School and finally the Cambridge High School, graduating from there in June, 1874. She entered the training school for teachers in the same city and graduated from there in June, 1875. Her first teaching experience was in Chestertown, Maryland where she did excellent work for two wears. In 1881 she was appointed as teacher of primary grades in the public schools of Cambridge. In 1889 after teaching in all the grades from the first to the seventh, Miss Baldwin was made Principal of the Agassiz School. She hesitated about accepting this position for a long time, her native modesty making her feel herself not worthy to step into the place held by so fine a person as her predecessor. But upon being urged she decided to take it on condition that if at the

Mrs. Mary Ella Mossell

Miss Maria Louise Baldwin

Mrs. Susie I. L. Shorter

Mrs. Victoria Earle Matthews

end of a certain time the Board of Education was not satisfied with her, or she was satisfied that she was not the one for the place, she would return to her former position. Evidently every thing was satisfactory for she remained Principal for four years.

In April, 1916, when the school was torn down and a new building was erected at a cost of $60,000, its grades made higher and a Master was needed instead of a Principal, Miss Baldwin was made Master of the new Agassiz School, a position of great distinction, as there are but two women Masters in the city of Cambridge. The position of Master she held for forty years. The school, including all grades from the kindergarten to the eighth, is one of the best in the city and is attended by children of professors and many of the old Cambridge families. The teachers under Miss Baldwin numbering twelve and the five hundred pupils were all white. Miss Baldwin thus, without a doubt occupied the most distinguished position achieved by a person of Negro descent in the teaching world of America. Miss Baldwin was always a student. She took many courses from professors at Harvard and other colleges. She was a great reader intensively and extensively to which her fine library bore witness.

Miss Baldwin numbered among her many friends from whom she had autograph letters such noted persons as Elizabeth C. Agassiz, Alice Freeman Palmer, Thomas Wentworth Higginson, Mrs. Ole Bull, Alice M. Longfellow, Edward D. Cheney and Edward Everett Hale. Miss Baldwin passed very suddenly and unexpectedly from this to a better world on January 9, 1922 "The Agassiz," the school paper has a Memorial number in which tributes from teachers and pupils acknowledge her worth and work and the high regard in which she was held by the community where she had so long rendered unselfish service.

A Sister's tribute:

"With a heart big enough and warm enough to embrace all with whom she came in contact, she gave of her love unstintingly to her "Children" of the Agassiz School. Her understanding was keen and her sympathy deep for the young people whom she knew and her happiness was inextricably bound up in them.

Their successes were her joy; their failures her sorrow. What an empire is to a queen and what a family is to a mother that was Agassiz School to Miss Baldwin.

* * * * * * *

Said a Senior Pupil:

"The news of Miss Baldwin's death came to our school as a shock, an impossibility. Such a hush and reverent solemnity fell over it that all life seemed stopped for the minute. Laughter died on the lips and eyes that were dry filled with tears.

Miss Baldwin, our friend, our teacher had passed from this world to a far, far better one. We at school will realize more and more as we grow older that Miss Baldwin was one of the greatest beings that ever breathed. Her memory will always be a thing sacred. We loved her, loved her with a love that will never die."

* * * * * * *

About a year after her death the Agassiz School people unveiled a tablet to her memory. The tablet was the gift of the Class of 1922, the last class she taught.

The ceremony was conducted under the auspices of the Agassiz Parent-Teachers Association of Cambridge. The inscription on the tablet reads:

"In grateful memory of Maria L. Baldwin, 1856-1922. Forty-one years inspiring teacher, wise and beloved Master of this School. A scholarship has been founded and this room has been named Baldwin Hall."

The subjoined testimonials are culled from many that were voiced at the Memorial meeting:

Said one:

"Baldwin Hall in Agassiz School,—I love to think that these two names are hereafter to be associated in the minds of all pupils of the school of which she was principal so long. The names of two great persons, two great teachers.

From the first day I saw her I realized that she was a rare character. I was then serving on the Cambridge School Board and she was teaching in one of the lower grades in the Agassiz School which was in my care. Her poise and dignity, her calmness and beautiful voice struck me at once and I felt that her mere presence must be a valuable lesson to all the children. Several parents told me their children realized this and always spoke of her in admiration and affection, but never spoke of her color.

When the principal of the school was changed the superintendent told me it would be my duty to appoint a new principal. "Why," I said, "you know as well as I do there is only one suitable person, Miss Baldwin." "I think so too," he said, "but I was not sure about the color." "It is not a question of color," I said, "it is a question of the best." So she took the place and for forty years filled it with gentleness and capability, and in all those years, with all the changes that come in city governments, I am not aware that there was any dissatisfaction or any suggestion of change. With such a record it is most fitting to honor her memory and to hope that her memory may always remain to serve as an example to all future teachers in the Cambridge School."

* * * * * * *

She was conscious of her ideals. She was conscious, too, of her powers and of the difficulties that were around her and around the people of her own race. Yet it never led to any self-consciousness and bitterness. She would take no praise for herself, no recognition in this or in any community which could not be given to every one of her own race. She was like the Shunamite woman, who, when asked, "What can I do for you?" answered, "I dwell with mine own people." That was her spirit all through life.

Many a time I have talked with her in regard to those deep and tragic problems of all of us. I never found her to flinch in her idealism, in her thoughts of what ought to be. Never, on the other hand, did I find in her any bitterness, but just biding her time for the great changes, which must take place in this and every community. I have seen Miss Baldwin under circumstances when it seemed very hard for her to accept what was going on in this country, the deadness of public opinion, the lack of real idealism inadequately manifested in our public life, and the shock of that was very crushing to that quick understanding which made her take her part in the work which she aand all of us had to do.

I am glad she lived in Cambridge, for her sake, for the recognition she received here, and glad for our sake that we had her with us. She gave herself to teaching, teaching the young, but she was more than a teacher of the young. She had a civic spirit, a high idealism, which inspired to that nobler America being wrought out of all the races here, slowly wrought out, but through infinite sacrifice actually working.

I cannot think of her as passed out of life or ever forgotten by those who have come under her influence. Her radiant personality, her ready sympathy, deep wisdom, are a part of our civic possession. This school must ever be connected with her name and her example. Her death was just what she would have asked—the completing of her life without break or absence from her place. She dropped as a good soldier on the battlefield. She had "fought the good fight"; she had "kept the faith."

Miss Baldwin always made us believe more and more in the ideal America. I never heard her say anything harsh, but once she did say something which revealed her deep feeling, her sensitiveness to the wrong done to those to whom she belonged and loved. It was during the time of the presentation in Boston of the "Birth of the Nation," and she felt an insult had been offered to the race itself. I asked some of the colored race to meet with me one afternoon just for an expression of good-will and so I said to

Miss Baldwin when I asked her to read from Paul Dunbar's poems, and we will just sing at the end "My country, 'tis of thee." She said, "Please do not sing that then for it would break my heart when I know of the feeling of so many in Boston and throughout the country, who do not recognize truly the fact that this is our country. I might sing it another time, but not now."

I knew how she felt, the deep restraint, the strong sense of duty, which kept her from giving way in moments of depression.

It is our duty as citizens, proud and glad for what she did for our children, to acknowledge our debt to her. Among the great citizens of Cambridge there are few that have been greater and no one who held such a unique position; and I am glad that we are here to testify that we are aware of that great soul, great mind, beautiful spirit which for so many years ministered to the children of this community.

* * * * * * *

The death of Miss Baldwin came as a shock not only to the people of Cambridge but to the people of the United States, for she had become well-known as a result of her activities in behalf of teaching. I believe Miss Baldwin is a severe loss to the people because of the great work she accomplished since she has been in charge of the Agassiz School. She was one of the most lovable women whom God ever sent to this earth with a mission to perform so well.

As a member of the Common Council I became acquainted with her in behalf of education. Later, when my children were attending the Agassiz School, I had the opportunity of meeting Miss Baldwin as principal and noted the spirit of the school expressed between Principal and teacher, teacher and pupil, teacher and parent. When the discussion of a new building for the school was under way, I discovered the great executive qualities of which Miss Baldwin was possessed. In many ways the building was a tribute to Miss Baldwin, there was a distinctive atmosphere in the Agassiz school due to her personality. I feel as if I had lost an intimate acquaintance.

Miss Baldwin's profession is one of the most honorable in the world,—educating our youth—because that which they receive when young makes or breaks them in life. Americanization was taught here by Miss Baldwin long before it was taken up by the state. The outstanding features of Miss Baldwin's character was her strict adherence to duty and her loyalty to teachers and pupils. I never heard of a serious difference arising between teachers and pupils in the Agassiz School. I never heard Miss Baldwin say an unkind work to boy or girl. Her lovable and amiable qualities commanded respect. Those who have attended the Agassiz School are a standing monument to Miss Baldwin's efficiency. I trust she will always be embodied in our memories to the end that we are better for having known her.

* * * * * * *

We parents can be unfailingly reached through our children. The poignant hold Miss Baldwin has upon our hearts takes on a special tenderness in our gratitude for the devoted service she gave our children. My first thought, when the news of our loss came to me, and it was probably the first thought of every mother here, was, "How can I bring up my children without her help"? It was not their intellectual training I felt the loss of, a hundred people could give them that, but it was the moral training which she was able to give in such measure, discipline in honesty, loyalty, devotion to duty, it was that that we mothers know cannot be easily replaced.

I have chanced to be in the office at the school when children were brought in for discipline, and have marveled at the wisdom and gentleness with which she dealt with each problem. She always brought out in the light any differences between the teacher's and the child's attitude, and then with sweet reasonableness set the matter right and sent the child back to his room readjusted and serene.

She had a remarkable power of enlisting the child's co-operation in any disciplinary problems. She never felt, and she never failed to tell the child so, that it was any victory to impose her will upon him. The child must make the decision and take the action himself. She always made him feel that he and she were only partners in the effort to make the school one worthy of complete devotion. I never left her presence without wishing I were a better mother, that somehow I could be as wise and tender a mother to my five as she was to her five hundred.

* * * * * * *

It was my great privilege just before the completion of this building to nominate Miss Baldwin for principal of the Agassiz Grammar School. And it was the only nomination by any superintendent, so far as I know, that was instantly received with applause from the School Board, and not put over till next meeting but unanimously approved within two minutes from the submission of the name.

When I think of Miss Baldwin, I am reminded of the young soldier mortally wounded in the service of Sir Philip Sidney, who, when asked if he had any special desire for an epitaph, said, "Say I was a friend of Sir Sidney." It is our greatest honor to say that we were friends of Miss Baldwin. We have lost a great, sympathetic friend, a great adviser.

Just a little instance to show her wonderful quiet forcefulness. One day I was in the building when something happened in one of the rooms in the teacher's absence, and when I went into the room Miss Baldwin said to me, "Mr. Fitzgerald, we are sorry you are here today. Please don't ask us why."

Looking around the room I noticed a little boy trying very hard to get out of my sight. Miss Baldwin continued, "When you come in next week we will have all nice boys and girls." Afterwards I learned that the little boy came to her room and said, "You won't let Mr. Fitzgerald know I was that little boy, will you, if I promise never to do it again?" And she promised and he promised and they shook hands.

The parents have lost a very wise, sane counselor and friend. Believing absolutely in her integrity the School Board had the utmost confidence in her and any suggestion that came from this district was very readily received. I have never known a destructive criticism to emanate from Miss Baldwin or from her teachers. We know that her memory will be christened and cherished in this district.

As a father, proud in the true sense of the old word, to have his children go through the classes of the Agassiz School, as a teacher and as a friend, I am glad to be here tonight and join in the words of tribute to Miss Baldwin.

I think I may claim to have been a friend of Miss Baldwin's for thirty years. It is exactly thirty years this month of February since I was invited by Colonel Thomas Wentworth Higginson to a small dinner party as he called it, in honor of a young teacher of English in whom he had become interested. I had just come from Scotland, being called to give some lectures in literature at Harvard College by my old friend, Professor Child, and to give one on English in reference to my old teacher, David Masson.

Colonel Higginson said to me, "I have a young teacher in English to meet you tonight who is carrying on her work very much in the spirit in which Masson seems to have carried on his."

He said nothing about Miss Baldwin, and shall I ever forget my feelings when I first met her—feelings of infinite interest which very soon deepened into infinite regard, which continued to deepen and strengthen through the thirty years we knew each other.

After Miss Baldwin left Colonel Higginson's that night, he turned to me and said, "I feel that she is bound to be one of the living forces in our Cambridge, for she has to a remarkable degree the gift of fruitful service," and all I have heard tonight is but an illustration of what dear old Colonel Higginson had read in Miss Baldwin—that gift, that marvelous gift of fruitful service.

That was the secret of her extraordinary power over our children, a power that has, in many cases, been an ennobling inspiration. In the deepest, truest sense of the term, she was one of the most religious women I ever met. Without ever speaking about it, she simply lived it through and through, just as she became one of the potent influences for the upbuilding, as we have heard tonight, of a true ideal of citizenship. Without any talk about, one way or the other, by simply being, under those conditions and difficulties which have been referred to tactfully tonight, one of the truest and noblest specimens of womanhood you and I have ever known. That is the thing through life, more than talking that is going to break down all these barriers connected with race and denominationalism—to live a worthy life from day to day, from week to week, throughout the years. We are all talked to death. What we want is the good quiet living up to the highest and noblest ideals.

There is one word used by St. Paul with reference to his ideal of living, that again and again occurred to me when amid all the trial and talk and amid all the racial difficulties and church matter brought forward up and down the world. She realized the Pauline idea of studying to be quiet, and the great serenity she ever had in her heart was after all the secret of the wonderful influence she had over these children of ours.

The last time I ever talked with Miss Baldwin I told her I had found an epitaph for her. It comes to me now when I think of what happened so soon after. "Well?" she said, "You have found many things for me. What can the epitaph be?"

"It is a dedication that I came on long ago in a little book: "To him who first early in life's morning awoke me!" That is what hundreds of children think about you."

Nothing could be more wonderful, full of help and significance than that. I should like it to be said of me. I should like it to be said of every teacher.

Who early in life's morn awoke me—first opened the way to me! That is exactly what Miss Baldwin did. She awoke in the young that dormant spirit, the angel which is within us all.

* * * * * * *

Once I lived in another city in New England, and it was my habit in the morning and evening to pass another school, and over the portal of that building were the words of a master teacher: "Come, let us live with our children." And I have been thinking these last few days of a paraphrase of that immortal inscription, since we parents are lacking in ability to fulfill that meaning, "Come, let Miss Baldwin live with our children."

You are parents as I am a parent, and I give you my testimony that next to the immediate home surroundings the influence of Miss Baldwin has been the most potent influence, the most beautiful and inspiring influence in our home and household, and no words could possibly be spoken that could give more than a shadowy idea of the substance of feeling in my heart when I think the most beautiful of Miss Baldwin's special gifts was that she lived with our children.

The greatest thing that can be said of her personality is that that personality had power. Power is the sun of our ambition, it is the object of all our creeds, even up to our adoration. Power is the ability to persuade people to do what you wish them to do, and the more silently and subtly and indirectly one exercises that power, the higher is it to be praised, the nearer is it to be called immortal.

Miss Baldwin had order without discipline because she loved the children. To have abundant love of children is to have the most powerful thing in the world. It was the privilege of Miss Baldwin to give that namelss quality to every word, deed and every attitude she took in life. She had marvelous power, the power that "Cometh not with observation," "The Light of the world," "The salt in the meal," but by means invisible, intangible and yet invincible.

This life, this power, this permanent spirit that has dwelt among us has made us think only of things that are permanent. It seems to me entirely desirable and inevitable as the natural expression of our common wish that we do something that will serve as a memorial, to this immortal personality.

MARY ELLA MOSSELL

1853-1886

"Hail, Sister of the Skies, and Farewell"

It should be a pleasant task to write of one's mother, but when the most vivid impression is that of her martyrdom, the emotions are not unmixed with sadness.

I should like best to tell of the impressions Mother made upon me as a child. I thought her the most beautiful little lady in the whole wide world. I loved to watch her comb her glorious wealth of hair, to hear her voice, and, best of all, to have her clasp me in her arms and tell me my daily story. I should like to tell of my hour, "The children's hour," the best of the day that Mother gave to me.

Of the facts I shall state here, a few I know from actual contact and experience but most of them I learned as I grew older, from the lips of Father, the writings of Hon. John M. Langston and President Solomon of Hayti, from chats with Grandmother and a few notes of Mother's own.

May Ella Forrester was born in Baltimore, Maryland, May 22, 1853. Her parents were free people and versed in the three "R's." Miss Forrester graduated from the Baltimore Normal School, receiving three scholarship prizes. She commenced the study of music when in the lower grades and continued the subject until her marriage. Miss Forrester was married, in 1874, to Rev. C. W. Mossell and two years after her marriage accompanied her husband, who was appointed a missionary of the A. M. E. Church to Hayti.

It was on this mission field that Mrs. Mossell was to find her hardest trials, her richest blessings and her martyrdom.

Mrs. Mossell had studied the Latin, Greek and German languages but the speech of the Haytians is French and a native patois both of which it was necessary for a successful missionary to master together with Spanish which one frequently needed in daily travels. The climate had discouraged many, and caused the failure of more than one attempt to establish missions on this West Indian Isle. The customs too were to be reckoned with by one who must reach the people. Hayti, had its cultured groups but the masses were primitive. Superstition and ignorance were the heritage and the sanitary conditions were such, at that time, that pestilence and climate seemed leagued in an effort to discourage the foreigner who attempted to establish himself upon this otherwise beautiful Island.

President Solomon, in his writings marvels at the fact that our little missionary mastered the languages complex to the country in so short a time. She soon became so proficient in French that she was an recognized authority. She mastered Spanish also. The native patois quickly ceased to puzzle her and when she could use it helped greatly in her unceasing efforts to reach the masses.

The customs, though strange, were met with tact and a keen insight into human nature. The suspicious native women were won over through the medium of some brightly colored yarns which Mrs. Mossell collected, and sitting on her veranda, in plain sight of the street she proceeded to work the brilliantly colored yarn into patterns. One by one and then in small groups the native womn overcame their suspicion and superstitions dread of the foreign woman and came cautiously at first and then freely to watch the miracle of blending colors and design. Soon a large group of these women were on friendly terms at the mission house and many were brought into the school and into the church. Through the town of Port au Prince went this little woman carrying intellectual enlightenment and Christian comfort where it had not been before.

In Hayti the more enlightened people were Roman Catholics, "politicians"—and therefore careful to avoid any religious entanglements, or they were men whose business relations with the interior natives made it seem necessary to subscribe to the superstitious cults of the island. It was difficult indeed to reach this group but Mrs. Mossell found her musical talent and her linguistic ability to be the devices here and she was soon accepted in the homes of the cultured upon whom she drew for converts and for pupils. Her musical talent was not limited to the piano; she was a composer of no mean ability. Her compositions that counted most on the mission field were "La Grande Marche," dedicated to President Solomon, and "Le Bouquet," to General Ligitime, another was "La Grande Marche Patriotic," some songs in patois that are lost should be added to the list. The songs and music, the brilliant mastery of the language were accounted by this little woman as merely gifts meant to help in God's work.

Mrs. Mossell and her husband succeeded in creating enough interest in Hayti and at the home base to send five young Haytian gentlemen to the States for higher education at Wilberforce. The wisdom of their selection of these men is evident from the fact that each one of them became a staunch workman in the A. M. E. Church. One returned to his country as secretary of the legation after he had served the church in Hayti and he is now counted with the staunchest and strongest on the episcopal bench.

The inhospitable climate of Hayti was the most trying obstacle our missionaries had to meet. With the exception of the Revolution horrors, it was their deadliest enemy. Both claimed their toll. Both were equally deadly. The climatic severity was enhanced by the miserable sanitary conditions in the town of Port au Prince. Before the onslaught of plague and pestilence our Missionaries faltered but buried their dead, succored their wounded and marched on. Rev. Mossell, returning to the states on the death of his mother, brought back to the mission field another volunteer in the person of his sister, Miss Alveretta who contracted the dread yellow fever and thus untimely came to the end, the first to fall. Mrs. Mossell was to fight the ravages of the fever upon each member of the family and to be brought low herself but Alveretta's was the only fatal case.

The plague of smallpox came next and skillful nursing was all that saved an only daughter, scarred but otherwise unharmed.

Pestilence, dangerous native superstitions, revolutions, and death were always near but this little woman faced them, kept the faith and performed her work to such an end that one Haytian gentleman writing of her said: "Her death was the glorious counter-part of her magnificent life." President Solomon, in his memorial address said: "But how shall we estimate our loss when we recall that, perhaps, no one among us has accomplished larger labors in this field of dignified, useful and indispensible service, and who has been more successful?"

Having survived the climate, mastered the languages, and, with delicate tact penetrated the native prejudices, destroyed, in some cases, the superstitious dreads and worships of the people Mrs. Mossell and her devoted husband brought many to Christ and to the mysteries of letters. They risked their all, giving it freely and they had won— but the zero hour was to come in the revolution of 1883. "Contemplate a frail American woman, of Protestant Methodist faith, educated in the language of her own country with some knowledge of Latin, Greek and German, in hand-to-hand struggle against such ignorance, superstition and mental inactivity as existed in Hayti," remarks one writer when recounting Mrs. Mossell's trials in the revolution.

On the twenty-second and twenty-third of September, 1883, the notorious Bazelias Revolution was brought to a terrible and terrific close in an awful tragedy of blood and flames. In these two horrible days, scenes of outrage and murder were enacted and more than ten acres of homes and shops destroyed in the city of Port au Prince.

"Ah! A sad day! Black as night in the life of a great nation,' writes Mr. Langston, "But what proves to be the Black Day of the nation," he continues, "is the glorious, effulgent one of a humble, delicate woman, who shrank in natural diffidence and Christian modesty from public gaze or display. It is a day fraught with duties and consequences which a trying, cruel emergency would bring upon her. Whence comes now the physical strength, the moral fortitude, the conscious sagacity equal to the responsibility of this hour?"

Mrs. Mossell had seen every house, neighbor to her own go down in flames; the small American Flag on the gallery was of no avail for, "the moment made haste when her own house must go................and the family was left to make their way as best they might against the fast devouring flames and the furious mob now forcing their way into the house with bloody intent. Revolvers, guns and swords were freely used; many of those who had taken refuge in the mission house being shot down, wounded or killed upon the spot. Threatened with death, Mr. Mossell was rudely forced into the streets and forced to march at point of revolvers to what he was told was to be his death. Now came the supreme hour of Mrs. Mossell. She alone could, and, she alone did, by her courageous and heroic conduct, prevent the assassins' foul purpose upon her husband's life. Her imploring words, her womanly, earnest efforts; her whole appearance and manner, so impressive and subduing, as, clinging to her husband, she was borne on as he, by the mob through the streets, pulled, hauled and pushed under the direst threats of personal violence, could but draw to her and her husband, in such sore condition, at least a friend or two who would seek their relief. So it happened and they were saved."

"The emergency came and it was met in an heroic manner. All the beauty, and excellence, and nobility, and dignity which it revealed in the character of Mrs. Mossell will ever remain our glad heritage. The amplest justification of our deep admiration for her as a true Christian heroine."

The effects of those terrible days and nights took heavy costs from our missionaries. It brought about the untimely birth of a daughter who survived but a short while and left their only remaining child lost for four days, in fact to be given up by all but her mother, as having perished. It left the mother to linger through a little more than two years of much suffering thence to go, amidst eulogies and grief, to her own reward.

AGNES JONES ADAMS

1858—1923

Mrs. Adams, a native of Baltimore, Md., was a member of a family there well-known and highly respected. She received the usual training afforded by the city public schools, and in addition being studiously inclined and being associated with cultured persons, her ambition incited her to gain proficiency in some of the higher subjects of learning.

In early womanhood she joined the Methodist Church and became a devoted church worker. She adopted the profession of day school teacher and besides discharging her regular duties did welfare work as opportunity offered. In an unassuming way she continued active and absorbed until her marriage. Her wedded life though happy was brief. While yet a young woman she found herself responsible for the rearing of a son, her only child. This led her to remove to Boston, Mass., that the lad might have all the advantages of an atmosphere conductive to normal, unhampered development.

In this new home she did not remain long unnoticed; for through church and social affiliations many shortly came to know her and to learn of her worth. Her estimable qualities of mind and heart caused acquaintances to become admirers, then friends, according her an affectionate regard. A race devotion won for her a conspicuous place among those working for race uplift. She joined the Women's Era Club, the National Association for the Advancement of Colored People and similar organizations. Useful, steadfast, led by the highest convictions of duty she in time attained prominence among a group of women drawn toward her like aspirations.

In July, 1895, the "National Federation of Colored Women" held its preliminary session at Boston. The Women's Era Club as hostess naturally took the lead, issuing the call, arranging the program, and, through the indefatigable exertions of its executive board, making a signal success of what in some of its phases had of the necessity the nature of an experiment.

The body of our women has expanded normally with garnered experience, and, with accessions of superior women, today it stands for an impelling force of great magnitude. Its successive biennial sessions have been graced and vitalized by the wit, culture and wisdom of countless self-sacrificing members, loyal to keen apprehensions of duty and responsive to the finest impulses inciting human activity. The meetings like mile-stone, have outlined the progress of American colored women along the path of upward trend. All the gatherings have been significant. many of them notable; everything taken into consideration, the initial one may be designated as the most famous.

The pressing urgency of a coming together for conference was made clearly apparent by the circulation abroad of a scurrilous letter. This offensive document was designed to arouse animosity and to accentuate race hatred. It bore evidence of a lack of appreciation both of truth and justice and marked its author with the unenviable reputation of lacking in chivalry and honor, of being afflicted with that dense ignorance upon which insensate race prejudice is founded.

On the second day of this meeting of protest Mrs. Adams presided. She delivered a fervent opening prayer and then took up the subject allotted for consideration. It was the delicate yet pregnant theme of "Social Purity." This she treated in detail with reserve and care yet with firmness and clarity; her utterances were followed with closest attention. Before this she had attained a reputation locally as a well-informed logical speaker with a pleasing address. In this latest venture, gripping as she did the interest of women from fifteen states—many of whom were ready popular speakers, she received a baptism as an ardent eloquent advocate of every endeavor to develop our womanhood and to extend concerted action in "forlorn effort" to secure for them the chance so often ruthlessly denied to them. From that time on Mrs. Adams was regarded by circles, clubs and federations as invaluable in all altruistic movements. No one has ever spoken more convincingly than she in behalf of that contingent of Americans than whom none have ever made a more uniform record for patriotism, than whom none have ever been treated by the powers that be with greater ingratitude through a callous ignoring of the common justice certainly their due.

The earnestness and enthusiasm aroused by Mrs. Adams kindled a lofty spirit of devotion and loyalty in the hearts and intentions of her auditors, that has never been allowed to die out. Remaining active it has intensified and helped others to aid in the accomplishment of the ulterior object of her speech—the amelioration of the condition of colored women by securing for them that fair play which enables any accused to defend himself against treachery, snap-judgment and wholesale incriminations.

To this woman belong the honor of, at a most critical time, the time when she and women of the same descent were publicly and brutally attacked, of voicing an unanswerable appeal to justice, culture and civilization. And her heroism in "standing on the breach," without stopping to count the cost in her endeavor to right a flagrant wrong, entitles her to the highest praise for fidelity and fearlessness.

The conference fully demonstrated the wisdom and efficacy of a national "getting together." The advantages of council were briefly and clearly outlined in the thoughtful address of the president, Mrs. J. St. P. Ruffin. She emphasized the necessity for so doing for both women in general and our women especially. The latter she described touchingly as "those who were bearing peculiar burdens, suffering untold hardships, enduring oppressive provocations."

With a seriousness at once pathetic and dignified, Mrs. Ruffin struck the keynote of the intention of the gathering: "It is meet, right and our bounden duty to teach an ignorant suspicious world that our aims are identical with those of all good aspiring women. With an army of organized women standing for purity and mental worth we open the eyes of the world to a state of affairs to which they have been blind, often wilfully so. We break silence not by noisy protestations of what we are not, but by a dignified showing of what we are and what we hope to become."

The ultimate result was the formation of a sisterhood in which Agnes Adams and others like her found congenial work. This included the establishment of reforms, the cementing of bonds of unity, the defense of the dignity of our women, and the refutation of unjust and unfair accusations—charges often so audaciously and flippantly made and of so humiliating a sort they tended virtually "to force the accused into a mortified silence, especially in sections where the scales of fair play and verity are not evenly balanced."

In July, 1922, the death of a brother recalled Mrs. Adams to her former home. While there she decided to make her birthplace again her abiding place, and so resolving took up again in a near by village the work of teaching. The April following, attacked by a serious illness she succumbed in a few days.

Her life work was unfinished only in seeming, her influence is still paramount as a guidance to those who knew her and loved her, those who, still active and inspired by her lowly spirit but lofty aim are striving to emulate her unselfish, courageous example.

Mrs. Adams thought, decided, acted from a conviction

she had something definite to do in the strenuous endeavor to uplift while she essayed to climb. This made her vigilant, patriotic and steadfast toward those with whom she was allied by sex and race extraction. Good women like Agnes Adams have a value not to be estimated. And of such women among us countless numbers are in daily evidence. Uusually they are ordinary, everyday women, wage-earners, bread-winners or home conservers, saved from obscurity by that spirit of service which transfigures and glorifies. To know of such is indeed a "liberal education." It leads to the basic conclusion that what a woman thinks of herself, does for herself and with herself, may be the silent but effective means of aiding character development in many others less fortunately situated.

"For us is the seed time, God alone
Beholds the end of what is sown;
Beyond our visions weak or dim,
The harvest time is hid with Him.
Left unforgotten where it lies,
The seed of generous sacrifice
Though seeming on a desert cast
Shall rise and bloom with truth at last."

SUSIE I. LANKFORD SHORTER

January 4, 1859—February 27, 1912

In the progressive town of Terre Haute, Indiana, on January 4, 1859, a little daughter was born to the Pastor of the A. M. E. Church, Rev. Whitten Strange Lankford and his wife Clarrisa Carter Lankford.

The first of the five children was named Susie Isabel.

When Susie was fourteen years old her father took her to Wilberforce University that she might be instructed by Bishop Daniel A. Payne and the other noble educators there, whose ideals were high and their motives for teaching pure and unselfish.

Among the subjects Susie studied in the two years spent at Wilberforce were botany, rhetoric, French, music, algebra and arithmetic.

And it was the Professor who taught the last two subjects who afterward became her devoted husband.

Her school life was cut short by the death of her mother, and when only sixteen years old this young girl became a teacher at Rockville, Indiana, and later in Richmond.

It was at Christmas time 1878, in her second year as teacher in Richmond that Susie Lankford became the wife of Professor Joseph Proctor Shorter.

To them were born eight children, of whom three are living. They are Lee Shorter, Joseph Shorter, and Susie Pearl Shorter Smith. She was exceptionally kind and considerate, always lending a helping hand in church, state and community. The small shop known to-day as the College Inn, over which she presided, was filled with articles both gay and useful, so dear to the student heart.

She was not only a faithful wife and devoted mother in sickness and in health, but she was interested in all mankind and that interest was shown by her articles written for the "Ringwood Journal,"—by her poems, and by her joy in missionary and club work.

The paper she wrote and read before the gathering of friends in Jacksonville, Fla., at Bishop Payne's eightieth birthday celebration was published as a booklet and named "Heroines of African Methodism."

This, and the poem used as the "Ohio Federation Song," are the best known of her writings.

She was not perfect, we know of none who are.

She was not renowned. But like her dear husband, she had so many fine qualities that not only her children rise up and call her blessed, but the many students to whom she sent a bowl of soup, or a dainty meal when they were ill; and the little children of the neighborhood she lovingly gathered into her home to give free kindergarten lessons and the hosts of visitors who year after year found cordial hospitality at this Shorter home, all would have joined in the resolutions from the Young Men's Christian Association at her funeral when the soul of "Mother Shorter" as they tenderly called her, had peacefully passed from a suffering body to that happy land, where all is joy and perfect understanding.

It was on the 27th day of February, 1912, soon after her 53d birthday, that Susie Lankford Shorter went to that other world to join her beloved husband who had died two years before.

But to their children, and others who really loved them, it is but yesterday. For their sweet, inspiring spirits still abide with us.

FEDERATION SONG

(*Tune—"Glory, Glory, Hallelujah"*)

We are a band of women, from the
National we come,

We are marching into battle 'tho
We've neither fife nor drum,
The Ohio Federation, lifting others as
we climb,
Our motto, "Deeds not words."

CHORUS

Deeds not words shall be our motto,
Deeds not words shall be our motto,
Deeds not words shall be our motto,
We're "Lifting as we climb."

We represent the women who were
once denied a place,
In the National Convention of the
highly favored race,
Nothing daunted we have struggled
and we've made ourselves a place,
Our motto, "Deeds not words."

Our race must be enlightened, we must
earn our daily bread,
We must give our time and talent—
and the hungry must be fed,
We must root up sin and sadness,
planting good and joy instead,
Our motto, "Deeds not words."

All hail The Federation! And may
others join our band,
May the torch that we have lighted,
shine in this and every land,
Till the women of all races, will be
glad to take our hand,
Our motto, "Deeds not words."

VICTORIA EARLE MATTHEWS

1861-1898

In an humble cottage, May 27, 1861, at Fort Valley, Ga., was born Victoria Earle. She is described as a bright, lovable child, always planning some new game or leading her playmates in some new sport. At school, she easily led her classes, and we are told she often asked questions that startled her teacher by the depth of thought they expressed. All who knew her affirm that while she was high-spirited, quick to resent an injury, especially to her playmates or a cruelty to a dumb creature, she was gentle, respectful to her elders, affectionate and most helpful to all who seemed to need her services.

One can readily imagine that her opportunities for development in the small southern town in the early sixties were meagre enough. She, however, learned almost automatically not only the "knowledge learned in school" but a lover of the woods and fields, she was prone to wander far, far away into the depths of the forest and "list to Natures's teaching."

Observant, resourceful, likely to think things through she came to New York with her mother and sister about 1873, wise beyond her years, a tall, lank, straight haired girl, with large, soulful eyes that hinted of the high-strung romantic nature of the girl.

In the public schools of New York she seemed in her element and making good use of her opportunities she was soon well known for her ready responses to questions that puzzled the others. Being a great reader, she had fuller knowledge than many who had far superior home advantages.

The child grew rapidly and was truly happy, preparing her lessons, reading whatever she could lay hands on, and stealing away whenever she could into the parks to commune with the birds and flowers so dear to her and with whom she seemed to have a weird understanding. She was a bright, happy, studious child.

Truly Victoria might have uttered Tom Moore's plaint —"From childhood's hours, I've seen my fondest hopes decay." In the midst of her happiness came what was to her a real blow. She was obliged because of family difficulties to leave school and go to work. Nevertheless, with the courage and cheerfulness that characterized her later life, she entered upon her duties and performed them in a highly satisfactory manner. Life was made much happier for her when she found that in the home in which she was employed there was a wonderful library. She longed to get to those books, yet feared to touch them or even ask permission to read one.

At last, one never-to-be-forgotten day, she was sent to the library to dust the books. Her task accomplished she could no longer resist the temptation to open just one. Her attention was fixed immediately. Unconsciously she slipped into a chair and as the day light began to fade she dropped to the floor near a window. So absorbed was she that she did not hear her employer enter the room. He did not see her and in the semi-darkness, he stumbled over her. Great was her confusion, but the kind-hearted man feeling that any child so eager to read should be encouraged, gave her permission to read the books in the great library whenever she could find time. It is unnecessary to say that the book-loving Victoria made good use of his kind permission.

It seemed that she never lost an opportunity to improve her mind, and by means of lectures, special studies, constant contact with trained persons, she gratified to some extent her thirst for knowledge and became in spite of untoward circumstances an educated, cultured woman.

Victoria Earle was married to William Matthews in New York when she was eighteen years old. Her interest in her studies continued, and to the end of her life she was possessed with the desire to know that she might the better serve her race for which she had a devotion that amounted to a passion.

For many years she wrote for children's papers and was a contributor of stories to the Waverly magazine. Her culture, pleasing personality and intelligent grasp of ideas made a great demand for her as a reader for invalids and others who needed such service.

While still a very young woman, Mrs. Matthews manifested a keen interest in all matters pertaining to her race, and early became active in club work. In 1892, the Woman's Loyal Union of New York and Brooklyn was formed with Mrs. Matthews as President. She worked with rare intelligence, persistence and enthusiasm for this organization. Writing about her work in those days, the secretary of the Union said, "To her much of the success of the Union is due."

Mrs. Matthews was one of the leaders in that splendid movement to honor, encourage and assist the intrepid Ida B. Wells during her stay in New York after her bitter experience in Memphis, Tenn. Mrs. Matthews' energy and exceptional executive ability went far towards making the demonstration to Miss Wells a brilliant, instructive and profitable affair.

She was one of the group of courageous women who responded eagerly to the call made by Mrs. J. St. Pierre Ruffiin, President of the Woman's Era Club of Boston in July 1895; the call to our women all over the country to gather in Boston for consultation for conference and to band ourselves together for our protection and the welfare of the race.

Truly interesting and inspiring are the reports of Mrs.

Matthews' unselfish devotion to the cause for which those brave women labored. Her suggestions in the general meetings, her indefatigable service on committees, her resourcefulness and courage tended to make her services invaluable to the new organization which later became the National Association of Colored Women. She served as Chairman of the Executive Board in 1896 and later, as National Organizer.

The beginning of the life work of this unique character may best be told in her own words. In answer to the question of a reporter for the *New York Sun* she said: "Nearly three years ago I lost my only child, a sixteen year old boy, and immediately my heart went out to other people's boys, and girls too, for that matter . I went down to Alabama, visited Tuskegee and several other places, and became much interested in the work that is being done for the colored race in that State. I was being persuaded to go into the work there when a minister here wrote, begging me to come back here and start practical work among my people. In this district, lying between 59th and 127th streets, from Park to First Avenue, there are about 6,000 Afro-Americans, who have mostly been driven away from Bleecker Street by the influx of Italians. I found that this was my field so I began to visit the families. I selected the ones I thought needed me most and tried to be a real friend to the mothers.

When I went into a home to call and found an overburdened mother preparing a meal in an unpalatable way, I helped her, showing her the right and easier way. If I found a woman doing her laundry work, I turned in and helped her do her rinsing. Then I began to hold mothers' meetings at the various homes where I visited; and you may not believe this, but one day at one of these meetings we prayed especially for a permanent home where we might train the boys and girls and make a social center for them where the only influence would be good and true and pure. Almost immediately Mr. Winthrop Phelps, who owns an apartment house, offered us one of it flats, rent free for three months to make our experiment. We opened here Feb. 11, 1897."

Because there were no places then in New York where colored girls could go for training in domestic work, cooking classes were organized and were taught by that large hearted, faithful servant of God, Miss Mary Jane Bevier assisted by Miss Victoria Coles. There were sewing classes too, conducted by Mrs. S. E. Wilkerson, Mrs. Mary B. Pope, Miss Mary Lewis and Mrs. H. G. Miller. Dressmaking classes were taught by Mrs. Armand Miller and Mrs. Thomas Jackson. Thus many a young, untrained girl learned something of the "art of doing things" before she ventured out "in service." The colored women stood by the work through every hardship. Miss Lewis and Mrs. Pope are still in the fore front of the work.

The writer remembers too, visiting these little mission rooms and speaking to the large group of eager, restless boys and girls ranging from three to fifteen years of age. Most interesting was the kindergarten class taught by Miss Alice Ruth Moore, later Mrs. Paul Laurence Dunbar. It was a joy and an inspiration to see the enthusiasm with which this attractive young woman, recently come from her home in the South, gave herself to the work of teaching these neglected little ones, using her own means to purchase many of the numerous gifts and games and aiding by her charming personality in training the children and making them happy in their beloved "mission." The children were truly a varied group, some neat, clean and orderly, giving evidence of careful home training, others sadly neglected, some rude and boisterous, but all learning to love Mrs. Matthews and her faithful helpers and little by little learning important lessons in decency, order, thrift and love for each other.

Being by nature a leader and a teacher, Mrs. Matthews won the most incorrigible of all the boys in taking him aside one day and asking him to "please take charge of those boys, Kim, Henry and Al especially and see that they keep quiet and give attention." As proud as a major, at being trusted and given responsibility, he not only became orderly and obedient himself, but being the ring leader, kept the others in order, and peace reigned.

At the parting hour, Mrs. Matthews who lived in Brooklyn always went out with the children. It was a pleasing picture to see the black robed, pale woman surrounded by these little ones, each clamoring for a place next to her, as she passed to them with her own hands the flowers, chiefly daisies, which she and her helpers had gathered from the large open spaces then to be found in the Bronx. To these, the Master's "little ones" she was the embodiment of patience, gentleness and love, giving herself not from a sense of duty but giving to that which "is out of sight, that thread of the all-sustaining beauty which runs through all and doth all unite," and who can estimate the influence upon the lives of those poor neglected children? Many of them grown into manhood and womanhood will tell you today that they are serving well their God and their race because of the invaluable lessons in "Mrs. Matthews' White Rose Mission."

In 1900, a girl in the far south desired to come to New York and a friend of Mrs. Matthews wrote and asked her to meet the girl. Every precaution was taken and Mrs. Matthews was at the steamer promptly but one of those unprincipled men who haunted the incoming ships in those days lured her far away and the most diligent search failed to discover her for several days. When found she had passed through a terrible experience and had to be sent back home, a perfect wreck of her former self.

Deeply grieved by this sad incident, Mrs. Matthews and her little band of faithful women resolved that they must take immediate steps to try to prevent similar occurrences and by dint of Mrs. Matthews' earnest solicitation, by newspaper articles and by the united efforts of the workers, a house was secured at 217 East 86th Street and a "Home for Colored Working Girls" was established. Brave woman! She undertook a mighty task, going forward "not knowing what would befall her," but she builded better than she knew. God in His infinite wisdom and mercy led to her friends both white and colored. Among them were Mrs. C. P. Huntington, the Misses Stillman, Miss Grace Dodge and that faithful adviser and friend who gave years of unselfish devotion to the cause and is still giving of her best, Miss Mary L. Stone, at one time president of the White Rose Industrial Association.

For years, the colored women mentioned before met the boats at the Old Dominion and other piers and directed and helped the strange girls and women, many of whom came wholly unprepard to grapple with the problems of the great city. Thus, as far as we know, Mrs. Matthews was the pioneer in the now extensive work of the Travelers' Aid Society. Later, Miss Dorothy Boyd, then Mrs. A. Rich, sister of Mrs. Matthews took up the work at the New York Docks and after a year or two Mrs. Proctor was engaged to meet and direct the girls at Norfolk, and a perfect chain was established, a chain as it were of "White Roses." "Let us call it White Rose," said the founder in her romantic way, "and I shall always feel that the girls will think of the meaning—purity, goodness and virtue and strive to live up to our beautiful name."

And so as the years rolled on the White Rose grew and flourished, thousands of girls being sheltered, guided, fed, clothed when necessary, many taught to work acceptably in the homes of the Metropolis and many others saved from lives of shame. All sorts and conditions of girls found their way to the White Rose, the illiterate, the needy, the destitute as well as some of the fine specimens of young Negro womanhood, all found a welcome—often without money and without price, and thousands now bless the day when they were guided to the White Rose.

As to the woman, she is best revealed in her work. Writing of her at the beginning of her work in the "mission," a reporter for a daily New York paper thus described her: Mrs. Victoria Earle Matthews is a Salvation Army field officer, a College Settlement worker, a missionary, a teacher, a preacher, a Sister of Mercy, all in one, and without being in the least conscious of it."

Perhaps because in her ideas she was far in advance of the times in which she lived, possibly no woman was more greatly misunderstood. Her enthusiasm and quick grasp of any situation, together with a certain dramatic quality gave her a forceful, decided manner of speaking that was not always understood. Urged on by her eager, restless spirit and that foresight which enabled her to see the end, she could not always wait for others to see, but seemed impelled to carry out her plans immediately, as if there might not be time enough to do all that had to be done. This was because she saw that the need for earnest, practical work was so great that she could not wait—perhaps, too, in some mysterious way she realized that for her what was to be done must be done quickly; and so she worked tremendously, overtaxing her strength and ofttimes with her extraordinary influence sweeping others along with her until she accomplished a sufficient amount of her work to show the world what was burning in her heart—the desire to do a practical, useful and at the same time cultured work for her race.

Her utter devotion to the race was shown in all that she did. Long before the interest in Race Literature became general, she was an enthusiast on the subject and placed in the White Rose Home a choice collection of books written by and about the Negro in America, forming, as a white reporter wrote, "One of the most unique special libraries in New York." The books of this library were used by Mrs. Matthews as a basis for her class in Race History. An inspiring sight it was to see this frail woman, her life slowly ebbing away, as she sought eagerly, almost impetuously, to impart to a group of intelligent young men and women the knowledge of the work and worth of the men and women of their race—a knowledge with which she was completely saturated. Thus she hoped to inspire in them confidence in their group and in themselves—confidence and a hope that she believed would incite them to noble thoughts and great ideas and deeds. Who dares to estimate to what extent her dream was realized?

It was the writer's privilege to serve as assistant superintendent of the Home with Mrs. Matthews for several months and later to be elected superintendent of the Home. During the months of close association, the inner life of the woman was revealed, and her faith in God and her race, her courage, her sympathetic understanding with all phases of human life were a revelation and an inspiration. Her spirtual life was far deeper than many of her closest friends realized. The six years spent in the work after her "shoulders had dropped the load" were among the most interesting and helpful experiences of the writer's life.

Infinitely greater, however, than anything that can be said of her was the life that she gave for the cause that was her dream, her passion, her love; and "Greater love hath no man than this that a man lay down his life for his friends." She did what she could, she gave her all and the White Rose Home is her monument. Not the institution alone, but that which it represents. The fuller, richer lives of thousands of Negro girls and the enriched lives of their children's children shall bear witness through the ages to the vision, the courage, the willing sacrifice of a Negro woman with a frail body and a mighty soul.

George Eliot's poem seems to breathe her prayer:

"May I reach the highest heaven.
Be to other souls a cup of strength in some great agony,
Enkindle generous ardor, feed pure love,
Beget the smile that knows no cruelty,
So may I join the choir invisible,
Whose music makes the gladness of the world!"

MRS. MARY B. TALBERT
Hon. President of the N. A. C. W.

MARY BURNETT TALBERT

1862—1923

Following closely the ties of blood are those of friendship and association. Involuntarily one gives a warmer clasp of the hand to a person coming from his section of the country or state, and the fellow-feeling is still more intensified when one hails from the same city or town. Mary Burnett and the writer were from the little educational village of Oberlin, Ohio, in the northern part of the state near the city of Cleveland. After early child-hood we passed out of the lives of each other. My family moved to Washington, D. C., while she continued to live in Oberlin, graduating from the college at an early age. Later she went to Little Rock, Arkansas, where she made a most acceptable teacher for several years, until she married William H. Talbert and located in the city of Buffalo, New York. Mrs. Talbert possessed a kind, thoughtful, generous nature. She did not hesitate to do the smallest deed to the humblest person in any possible way. For if one does not possess these qualities in the small things in life she can never fully expand to the greater ones. Her personality was most charming, her smile an object of beauty. She possessed a ready and versatile tongue and pen. A letter from her was almost equal to a face to face conversation. She was at once graceful and gracious. By her ability, her oratory and her pleasing personality, she held the undivided attention of an audience when she appeared as a speaker. In 1916 she was elected President of the National Association of Colored Women which post she held for four consecutive years. During the first two years of her incumbency she called upon the women of the country to redeem the Douglass Home and restore it to its former condition. She was so optimistic and drew so upon her imagination as to what could be accomplished, that she aroused great enthusiasm when she traveled, planned and wrote and addressed large meetings, all of which required bodily and mental energy until her dream was verified. In 1918, two years after the movement was started, when the Biennial of the N. A. C. W. met in Denver, Colorado, the money had been raised and the mortgage on the Douglass Home was burned. The next two years Mrs. Talbert spent in securing funds to restore, rehabilitate and beautify the Home, which was dedicated in August, 1922 at the close of the Biennial held in Richmond, Virginia. This event brought together many men and women representing culture, refinement and appreciation for what had been accomplished for the race through this great-hearted woman. In 1920 she represented the N. A. C. W. at the sixth quinquennial meeting of the International Council of Women in the Storthing at Kristiana, Norway which was presided over by the marchioness of Aberdeen and Temair. When the great world war began Mrs. Talbert was called into active service in this country and abroad to cheer and hearten the brave boys who were defending our liberties on a foreign field.

When peace was declared she at once began working for the passage of the Dyer Anti-lynching bill. To this she gave the vitality that may have cause the undermining of her health. She realized her physical condition but was willing to lay down her life, not only to perpetuate the deeds of Frederick Douglass and other leading characters for the inspiration of our youth but her large sympathy extended to the unprotected and the unfortunate in all avenues of life. The awarding of the Spingarn medal was the stamp of appproval which was bestowed on this fearless leader for what she had so nobly accomplished.

The writer's association with Mrs. Talbert in the

affair of the Douglass Home and the Anti-lynching movement will ever be a most satisfactory and delightful memory. As an untiring worker, full of energy and ingenuity we will miss her more greatly than we dare permit ourselves to realize.

Her going has left a void which is felt by her numberless associates and friends. Those who admired and loved her are legion. "Our ways are not God's ways," or Mary Burnett Talbert would still be among us performing her own invaluable service. "She cannot come to us, but we can go to her." Her spirit can be with us, inspiring to greater things. In that spirit of love, consecration and ambition, we can commemorate her memory in no better manner than to complete the work that she has already carried to so great a state of advancement.

The Douglass Home, with her plans carried out, will then be a monument, as she had intended it should be, to men and women of mark who have gone before her. Let us join hands with renewed vigor and inspiration to carry on her work.

MADAM C. J. WALKER

1868-1925

December the 23d, 1925, marks the birthday of the late Madam C. J. Walker, born fifty-seven years ago of slave parents at Delta, La. The late Madam C. J. Walker by remarkable common sense, determination and will power made for herself a name that is now a household word and occupies a place in the hall of the immortals.

The oustanding thing in the life of this remarkable woman is not the fact that she built up a large and successful business, but is her largeness of heart, great vision, loyalty of race and sweet simplicity. Madam Walker was one of those whole-souled christian characters that saw in the development of a larger business but another avenue and opportunity to serve her race. She realized that the great need of her time, and this is equally as true to-day, was avenues of honorable employment for developing young manhood and womanhood of the race. Keen of observation, she noted that millions of dollars were spent by our people annually for toilet requisites, that nearly all of these millions were going to the man who did not help colored charities or employ colored boys and girls. Madam Walker realized that in this as well as other fields the Negro could make jobs for himself by establishing his own institutions and patronizing them and thus bring his dollars to his own pockets. Sensing this, and realizing yet a bigger thing that if the Negro is to move forward as a desirable citizen he must have a care as to his personal appearance, she stepped out on the firing line and gave to her race the great company that bears her name and to-day stands out as foremost among the best. A great soul never dies. This

MADAM C. J. WALKER
Founder of The Madam C. J. Walker Mfg. Co.

is preeminently true of the late Madam C. J. Walker, for she not only lives to-day in the institutions and individuals that she has helped, but under the provisions of her will, her bountiful hand yet stretches forth from the grave, touching and influencing almost every phase of our race life and institutions. Because of this provision and because of her bigness of soul, it is no exaggeration to say that Madam Walker belongs to the immortals and will be better known and loved tomorrow than she is today, and tomorrow and yet tomorrow her name will be whispered in terms of love, inspiration and hope.

SUSAN ELIZABETH FRAZIER

1864-1924

Miss Susan Elizabeth Frazier was born in the city of New York, May 29, 1864. She was the daughter of Louis M. and Helen Eldridge Frazier. She attended the public schools and graduated from Hunter College in 1888. She was named as a substitute teacher in the public schools of New York and served in that capacity until appointed as an additional teacher in 1895.

She was the daughter of a noble father whose ancestors fought in the Revolutionary War and the subject of this sketch exhibited many of their fine characteristics of patriotism and loyalty. It was reserved for Miss Frazier to contend for justice and equal rights for herself and many women who followed her.

Thirty years ago as a graduate from the Normal College, Miss Frazier became eligible for appointment as teacher in the public schools. For no apparent reason except the fact of her color the appointment was from time to time deferred. She retained an attorney who applied to a Supreme Court Judge for a Writ of Mandamus against the school authorities to act in the matter. The Judge refused to issue the writ upon some technical point and stated his convictions that the school authorities would not refuse to appoint an eligible candidate for teacher because of her color. Miss Frazier refused to carry the court proceedings any further. A few months later she received her appointment which she held until her death. She was the first colored teacher in a mixed school in New York.

Her appointment caused a wave of opposition, which soon subsided when the character and ability of Miss Fra-

Miss Susan Elizabeth Frazier

zier became known. She proved to be one of the most successful teachers in the whole system and won a high place in the estimation of the school authorities during her long term of office.

Miss Frazier had an ideal home life. She possessed a charming personality which attracted many to her side who admired her as a model woman and a loyal friend. In a quiet and cheerful manner she assumed great responsibilities. She organized and became the enthusiastic president of the "Woman' Auxiliary to the Old Fifteenth National Guard" during the World War and served until her death. Under her administration this organization did splendid work in the interest of the colored soldiers serving in France and continued this work afterward with the 369th Infantry New York National Guard, successor to the wartime regiment. The organization rendered to the wives and relatives of the soldiers valuable assistance and endeared her to the hearts of the destitute and bereaved.

After the World War, the *New York Evening Telegram* inaugurated a contest among teachers of the public schools for trips to the European battle fields to be awarded to the most popular contestants. Miss Frazier was one of the winners and made the trip to France and other countries with the winning teachers.

For many years she gave her efforts toward Social Uplift work by serving as president of the Woman's Loyal Union. She was an active member of the congregation of St. Phillip's Protestant Episcopal Church, for many years a teacher in the Sunday School and served as president of the Church Missionary Society.

In recognition of her unswerving exertions, as a fitting close to her splendid career, full military honors were held in the 369th Regiment Armory and fitting eulogies were declaimed by the commanding officers. The casket was draped with the American flag and taps were sounded by the Regiment bugler. This is said to be the first time in our country's history that full military honors were paid at a funeral service of a colored woman. A day later St. Phillip's Protestant Episcopal Church was crowded to capacity to pay tribute to the beloved teacher and friend. On June 21, 1925 a tablet in her memory was unveiled at St. Phillip's Church with the following inscription:

To the Glory of God and
In Loving Memory of

SUSAN ELIZABETH FRAZIER

May 29, 1864—February 6, 1924

A graduate of Hunter College and a teacher in the Public Schools of this City.

Her life work was performed with an unselfish devotion to duty. In every undertaking she gave her best. Her unfaltering courage under conviction, graced by a kindly spirit, earned for her many treasured friendships.

This tablet is placed in her Parish Church by her friends, teachers of Greater New York, as a tribute to her worth and character.

Requiescat in pace

"Until the day break and the shadows flee away."

MARGARET MURRAY WASHINGTON
(Mrs. Booker T. Washington)
Hon. President of the N. A. C. W.

MARGARET MURRAY WASHINGTON

1865-1925

Mrs. Booker T. Washington was born in Macon, Mississippi. There were five children in the family, of which she was the third. Strange how guiding angels or powers of unseen forces manifest themselves in directing the affairs of many of our great men and women from the beginning, for when but a child she went to live with a Quaker family, whose careful teaching and thorough training influenced her life during those impressionable years, and of those friends she always spoke in warmest terms. Catching a glint of the possibilities of little Margaret Murray they sent her to Nashville, Tennessee to be educated. Entering Fisk University, she stayed and studied and worked for eleven years. As she became more experienced, there developed the determination to thoroughly fit herself that she might help challenge the cause of the Negro woman , in whom she had abiding faith. More and more she felt confident that if the Negro woman was given a chance like other women, she would gain and maintain in the world a place for herself.

The vision of the Negro women came to her as a student at Fisk. She never lost sight of it, and during her last years in the University she quite decided that her life would be consecrated to the work of setting before our people high standards and developing race pride, always with the assurance and guarantee that in the end the Negro would triumph. And thus the early years of her life were filled with intensive work and study, in the preparation for greater service, with an ever passionate desire to help where she was most needed.

General Armstrong had recommended Booker T. Washington at the inquiry of a southern gentleman, Mr. George W. Campbell, for a teacher in the Black Belt of Alabama. Mr. Washington came to Tuskegee and pitched his tent on barren ground. With such scanty means he started the Institute that only a magician or believer in miracles would have attempted such an undertaking. Having been married twice to women of good training, high standing and with the keenest desire to help him in the struggle for his race, Mr. Washington found himself again in 1887 alone with three little children,—an attractive little girl, Portia, and two dear little boys, Booker T. junior and Ernest Davidson named for his mother. How discouraged he must have felt, with a great vision before him, the development of the Tuskegee Normal and Industrial Institute,—with no money, few influential friends, and three small children the youngest being only two years of age when his mother died.

Mr. Washington visited Fisk University, at which time he spoke in his characteristic way, laying down his practical, solid and constructive program. To the graduates of Fisk it was a challenge. Who was convinced that Booker Washington was doing a work worth while? Who knew better than she the conditions in the south? Who was eager to render real service? Who was strong enough not to let difficulties stand in her way? Margaret Murray, of Macon, Mississippi, who had until this time planned to teach in the State of Texas. At Mr. Washington's invitation she came to Tuskegee in 1889 as Dean of the Woman's Department, doing classroom work, and anything else she was called upon to do. She was never afraid of working too hard or doing too much.

Being able to study Margaret Murray at close range, Booker Washington recognized her strength of character, her unusual ability to direct affairs, and loved her for her sterling worth. After three years' work at Tuskegee, she entered more intimately into his life as his wife, mother of his children, and his strong and constant support in the development of the institution. How they planned and worked together! How they opened avenues of employment for well educated Negro men and women who had been thoroughly trained in schools, colleges and universities all over the country and who wanted employment! How they inspired hundreds of unlettered young men and women who came from all over the southland seeking a more abundant life, with nothing but their desire to do, and their firm belief in God to become useful citizens,—can only be interpreted in the wonderful way Tuskegee grew by leaps and bounds from year to year.

Mrs. Washington was a keen, energetic, magnetic, forceful executive. Underlying these characteristics was a lovable, sympathetic disposition, qualities she did not always display unless the appeal was very deep.

Largely through her strenuous efforts at Tuskegee, a home for girls' industries was erected—Dorothy Hall—and she was made director of that phase of the work. For twenty-six years she inspired young girls as well as the teachers who worked with her, with the importance of learning practical things,—the necessity of knowing how to make the home attractive, how to properly prepare and serve wholesome meals,—the importance of sanitation and good health; and all matters that were so vital in the development of womanhood of our race.

Located in a community where social service work was a crying need, she visited rural homes, schools and churches. Into these places she always carried sunshine and words of encouragement, with the assurance that a better day for the Negro was ahead if he would only improve his home and conditions around it, send his children to school, and seize the opportunities that were at his door. This message was received by large numbers of rural folks and in many communities improvements were evident. Women's clubs, night schools and mothers' meetings were agencies set in action, and teachers at the Institute were detailed here and there to keep close supervision over each newly started interest.

Thirty years ago Mrs. Washington organized the Tuskegee Woman's Club. It is composed of women of the faculty and families of the Institute. At the time of organization she was elected president and held that position until her death. This is one of the best known groups in the South, and has done a magnificent work, first, in bringing the women of the Institute in close touch with one another, together with helping the poor and dependent in the commuity, and inspiring high ideas and ideals in the women generally.

With the full years her vision broadened and her interests extended. She was one of the few in a group of women who met in the north and agreed to organize clubs all over the country, which finally resulted in the National Association of Colored Women. She was made National President at Hampton Institute, Va., in 1910, a position she held for two terms. It is customary that the ex-presidents of the National Association be made honorary Presidents at the expiration of their term of office. This gives them lifetime membership on the National Executive Board. Mrs. Washington, therefore, continued to give much of her thought and time to this growing power for good.

Largely through her untiring efforts, the women of the state of Alabama were organized and federated clubs started that have done constructive and far-reaching work all over the state. Mrs. Washington was president of the Alabama State Federation for a number of years. At this time Negro boys, young and old, were sent to the jails for petty offenses as there was no place provided for the confinement of such cases. Mrs. Washington, with a number of influential women of Alabama, realized the need of a reform school for colored boys where they might be sent and given a chance to be taught the right way of living. Clubs all over the state responded liberally to this cause.

Individuals, North and South, made generous contributions, and the school became a reality. The officials of the state were glad to recognize this creditable work of the colored women. Seeing its growth and knowing the need for such an institution, located at Mt. Meigs, Alabama, is now the home of three hundred and more boys who are cared for, controlled, taught and loved. It has done great good, and many a wayward boy has gotten a new lease on life and taken a fresh hold.

A similar school for girls has been started at Mt. Meigs, Alabama, under separate management. This was another seed planted and nurtured by Mrs. Washington and the club women of the state. The little seed has sprung up, as yet tiny plant, but never to be crushed, for it is the determination of the women of Alabama to have as good an institution for the girls as the one already established for the boys, with the satisfaction and assurance that the State will come to the rescue when the time is fully ripe.

In Richmond, Virginia, a few years ago, Mrs. Washington organized the International Council of Women of the Darker Races of the World, and inspired here at Tuskegee a course of study on conditions of women in foreign lands. She thought and spoke of them as our sisters, and it was her hope that this Council would bring together the women of the darker races in a close and sympathetic contact.

Very recently she was appointed Chairman of the Colored Women's Work for the Inter-Racial Commission of Alabama. She was a member of the general commission with headquarters in Atlanta,, Georgia. Her opinions and advice were sought on the subject of race relations, a study in which she was profoundly interested. So great was her faith in both races that she firmly believed the question of interracial co-operation would ultimately be adjusted.

Mrs. Washington is asleep, not dead. "Can a woman die whose ideals live?" Tuskegee and our country have lost a great character in her passing, but her memory and influence will live always. I was glad it was my privilege to have been intimately associated with her for the past nine years. She has rendered real service in helping the women of our race realize they have a definite place the world will respect, that no other women can fill.

MADAM EMMA AZALIA HACKLEY
Noted Lyric Soprano

preaching that the gray matter—the brain—was the same color and texture in every head. The child was not only inspired with the thought that she could do anything that anybody could do, but she was cautioned that if she failed to excel where other races were concerned that no excuse could prevent a speedy home accounting.

At the beginning of her school life the young Azalia was the only colored child in the Miami School, which was attended by children of the better class of white people, and she soon believed that it was her duty to make her mark as a race representative. At thirteen she was in the high school; at eighteen she began teaching in the public schools of Detroit, having finished both high and city normal schools. She was the first colored girl to appear upon the high school commencement program. At this time she appeared twice to play the class march which she had composed and to sing a solo.

Night after night, while attending high school and even after teaching she played with orchestras until the wee small hours of morning, and also gave piano lessons after school hours, to obtain the extra money for music study. She studied both voice culture and the violin, but never had a piano lesson, although she absorbed music from her musical mother.

After about five years teaching, when first assistant of the Clinton School, she married and went to Denver, Colo., although the next year she expected to be made principal. Detroit was proud of its talented, energetic daughter, and called her the "pet of Detroit," but it was in Denver, where she became popular along broader racial lines. Here she conquered every kind of prejudice and opposition until both white and colored believed she would be a good candidate for State Senator. Madam Hackley declared that it was in Denver where she "found" herself and developed and it is Denver that she wanted for her last "camping place" in the long, long rest.

In this western city she received her degree as Bachelor of Music of the University of Denver, and in the summer she taught the voice pupils of the Dean of the Music Department to help with her tuition. Both white and colored claimed her musical service as a singer and teacher. All her recitals and choral concerts drew crowed houses and the music critics were so enthusastic about her really remarkable achievements, that her fame spread from coast to coast.

During all of her professional life the color question has played a tantalizing temptation. Immediately after graduation, while abroad and even recently offers have been made for our singer to cross the color fence and lose identity with her race. But the loyal race woman wittily remarked that she was "pre-natally marked for everything black and she gets color hungry when she is among pale-faces."

This is one reason why we loved her. She loved her race, and has proven it, time and again. The race has done what it could for her and she has clung to it and has given its offerings over and over to those who have been struggling for a chance in the arena of life.

When the altitude of Denver affected her health, she started East for more study and fell into the groove of a concert singer, an occupation for which she had no preference or liking. How well she fulfilled this position for years as the leading artist of the race will go down as race history. She is one singer who made and held her position by sheer merit. She dignified the profession. She directed her whole career alone and made a success of every effort she put forth.

Believing that no amount of professional singing by herself or by all the artists of the race combined would instruct audiences to a proper degree of appreciation, in order that the race might benefit musically and that future musical audiences might result, she changed her programs from the old-fashioned rule of one or two showy songs, to lecture-recitals and demonstrations. From school to school, city to city, she traveled to teach the masses of our people. In one day in Norfolk she taught two thousand students, and in Chattanooga in one day nearly three thousand students were instructed in her unique convincing method. It is easy to see how she reached about sixty-three thousand in a little over a year. The effect of this musical stimulus and instruction began to bear fruit at once, for schools and audiences demanded a new standard of teacher and entertainer. She repeatedly used her earnings to give free recitals and demonstrations in localities that were termed musically hopeless and she left the Hackley stamp of uplift and enthusiasm which generally has benefitted other artists who have followed her visits.

THEN CAME HER VISION OF FOLK SONG FESTIVALS, AND THE REVIVING, DIGNIFYING, AND PRESERVATION OF THE NEGRO FOLK SONGS to educate the masses of the people through mammoth entertainments planned along the line of logical musical development.

She developed into our national vocal teacher and her tremendous success because she studied her people musically and knew what they needed. While the Normal Vocal Institute in Chicago was her headquarters, the whole race was her school, for she taught from ocean to ocean. Her pupils and protegees are passing on her ideas and she lived to see the fruit of her efforts and sacrifices.

Negro posterity will owe her a lasting debt, not only musically, but for her love and faith in the race and her unceasing efforts to inspire the race with faith in itself. She also stands as an example of what a handicapped colored woman can accomplish for herself along musical lines, all by her own efforts, and how much can be done by one person for race musical uplift.

A prominent club woman in writing of Madam Hackley says, "It is impossible to describe this gifted woman of our race. Words fail." She was a woman of the highest ideals and was a born leader. So successful was her teaching and influencing others that some of the envious have called her a mesmerist. Her personality was one of her strongest points. While splendidly gifted by nature and while honors were showered upon her she was simplicity itself. She was the kind of a woman that mothers point to as an example for their daughters, and she was the idol of young girlhood and children. Strange to say, she was a queen among woman admirers, who everywhere adored and followed her.

She was a born humanitarian following out St. Luke's instruction, "If you have two coats, give one." The best of herself, the best she had, she always gave. Not only did she make her life count, but she pulled up others and made their lives count also. Possessed of great business instinct and judgment, she not only managed her own business affairs, but repeatedly burdened herself with the care of others. Her decisions generally proved prophecies.

She was so dead in earnest about musical social uplift that sacrifices and total self-effacement were a pleasure to her. She was an optimist and had many visions for race progress, many of which she helped to fulfillment. Her versatility and energy were remarkable. While always busy she was never too tired to help out a plan for race uplift. She did not rust out but wore out beautifully.

People marveled at her wonderful energy, but she received strength from many unseen sources, besides the "Great Source," which had chosen her as a handmaiden to lift a gifted people from musical bondage. She was a passionate lover of nature in all its manifestations, and of the beautiful in art. She was artistic in everything, and loathed anything spectacular or sensational, along any line.

When Madam Hackley passed out of her orbit of usefulness, her face bore the reflection of a well spent life and beautiful thoughts and motives. She has not only opened the eyes and ears of the Negroes everywhere to show the relationship between their God-given talents and the every day affairs of life, but she has given an original, simple, practical method of acquiring spiritual, moral and physical power through these gifts.

She has given us a new Philosophy of Emotional Control as it pertains to the Negro, and she has taught Negro children a higher appreciation of their bodies and racial characteristics than any one else has done.

Her creed is " Love." "The greatest of these is love." Cor. 13:13.

She has given us a standard of race musician that is new. She was endowed with spiritual gifts and carried love in her heart for her people, and it was long evident that she was chosen to do this missionary labor. She let her light shine not only to brighten the pathway of the dark race in musical darkness through its singing, but she assisted the Great Purpose which has given the Negro a voice that he may sing his way into the hearts of other races, and through his voice work out the higher, nobler purpose of life.

Madam Hackley gave most of her time toward elevating and dignifying Negro Folk Songs due to her keen appreciation of their beauty, rythm and harmony coupled with their naturalness for many looked with shame upon these soul-stirring songs, ignorant of their spiritual and emotional significance.

She was a pioneer teaching the masses to love their folk songs, hence she had little time for composition, yet she has given us "Carola" a song of beauty, art and love.

She has also contributed to literature in her book entitled "The Colored Girl Beautiful."

Madam Hackley's life is a story of lofty purposes and brilliant achievements.

"Exalt her and she shall promote thee, she shall bring thee to honor." Prov. 4: 8.

Mrs. Laura A. Brown

MRS. LAURA A. BROWN

1874-1924

Laura A. Brown was born in Gettysburg, Pennsylvania, November 8, 1874. Her parents, Reverend and Mrs. Frank Penn were devoted christians who reared their daughter in a home of comfort and religious influence. At an early age she was united in marriage to Mr. George Brown of Pittsburg, Pennsylvania, in which city she made her home.

To this union was born a daughter. Mrs. Brown was a devoted wife and mother. She was not only a home maker but her life, both eventful and beneficial, led her into wide fields of usefulness.

She possessed a sweet voice and soon became the recognized leader of church choir.

Her activities extended into public life, and she became an earnest, devoted member of the Pennsylvania Federation of Colored Women's Clubs, working to foster its high ideals and principles. In this work she demonstrated a strict adherence to integrity and was never known to sacrifice right for expediency. During the World War she was in charge of the war savings stamp campaign and raised thousands of dollars for the relief of soldiers, in camp, at home and in France.

During the Harding Campaign she was appointed a member of the Executive Board of the Republican Women's Committee of Allegheny County under the Chairmanship of Mrs. Leonard Wood which position she held during her life. In 1922 she announced her candidacy for the legislature from the First District, Allegheny County, being the first colored woman to run for the legislature. Her earnest, serious purpose attracted attention throughout the state and although defeated made a commendable race and had the support of her staunch friends.

As organizer of the Woman's Christion Temperance Union in Pennsylvania she seemed to have found her happiest work. She gained religious fervor by studious application to the study of the Bible and carried its message of truth and love into every company she addressed. She traveled through the state winning many adherents to the cause of temperance, attending conventions and addressing large congregations. At a district convention she was decorated with the meritorious gold ribbon.

Her work in the State Federation of Colored Women's clubs attracted national attention and she was appointed, by the late Mrs. Mary B. Talbert, acting president of the National Association of Colored Women, as director of the Douglass Home at Anacostia, D. C. Through her splendid efforts in this movement she was made a member of the advisory board of the Home which place she held till her death.

She was an active member of the Warren M. E. Church of Pittsburgh, affiliated with the Red Cross, the Army and Navy Union of America, of the Frances E. W. Harper League, Pennsylvania State Federation of Clubs, National Association of Colored Women Advisory Board of Douglass Memorial and Historical Association, Republican Council of Women, City-County Federation of Allegheny.

She passed away at the home of her parents at Gettysburgh very near the spot where the martyred Lincoln delivered his memorable address and where on November 8, 1874, she first saw the light of day, where she first found joy, where she first knew sorrow.

"The world will little know, or long remember what she said here, but it cannot forget what she did here." A Co-laborer has written:-

"Laura A. Brown, a leader among women has passed

on. By her own efforts, she forged ahead to a place of trust and honor in the state and nation. No flowers, however beautiful, can express our love; no wreath of laurel, our respect for her character and achievements, nor can the greatest monument surpass that which Laura Brown has left in the hearts of her bereft co-workers.

So will we remember her, as one who answered the call to public service, through the agencies of church, club, Red Cross and W. C. T. U. endeavors, giving unsparingly and unreservedly of her time and energy to the work of race advancement.

May the realization that another leader has fallen, causing an irreparable loss, strengthen us in the resolve to stand firmly, shoulder to shoulder and accept the greater responsibility, which is ours."

CALIFORNIA COLORED WOMEN TRAIL BLAZERS

—extract from—

"NEGRO TRAIL BLAZERS OF CALIFORNIA"

The following will give the reader a short survey of the splendid women of color who have blazed a trail for other women of the race in California. The Native Sons and daughters of California are very proud of the pioneer mother; but for some reason the pioneer Negro mother has received little or no attention from California writers. The Negro Pioneer mother, of all women coming into this state, was truly a trail blazer. There are instances where a few were free, but many came with their masters and drove the cattle and other live stock across the plains into California.

Nevertheless these Negro pioneer mothers, with all the hardships, ever kept burning within their breast a ray of hope for a better day. The writer has been told that very few of the free women of color went astray during the wild days of the gold rush. This is especially remarkable because of the large amount of lawlessness among the men and women of the opposite race. There was no Volstead law, life was held of little value because of the lack of established law and authority. The reader must not lose sight of these facts, and ever remember them when thinking of these women, even those who were free and had been educated in the east previous to coming to California. There were no public libraries, or anything else to entertain them except their self respect and lofty ideals. And yet among this group of women there are some characters that stand out in bold relief, as the following will show.

During the gold rush there came to San Francisco, California, Mr. and Mrs. Joe Scott, coming across the Isthmus of Panama from New Bedford, Mass. After spending a short time in this city they proceeded to Hangtown, Placer County, where "good diggings" were reported. Both had been well educated, since they were free born people of color. Mrs. Elizabeth Thorn Scott was born in New York City, but educated in New Bedford, Mass., where she was married. After coming to California, and becoming widowed, she decided to move to Sacramento, where she established the first school for colored youth May 29, 1854. This was just one week after the first school was opened for colored youth in San Francisco. Later Mrs. Scott married Mr. Isaac Flood, of Oakland, California. Moving to that city, she soon established the first colored school in Alameda County.

The Board of Education selected Mrs. Priscilla Stewart as teacher of the Broadway School of that city. This lady had been well educated and had taken an active part in every uplift movement for the race in California.

During 1858 there was a bill before the California Legislature to banish from the state all Free Negroes. This lady immediately wrote a poem and personally had it printed and distributed. Her object in so doing was to encourage her own race, to enlist the sympathy of the other race, and to gratefully acknowledge the kindness shown the race by the British government. The ruler of British Columbia, at Vancouver, sent his Harbor Master to San Francisco to invite Free Negroes to come to that country and make their homes. Mrs. Stewart recognized the call as coming from Queen Victoria, then reigning ruler of the British Empire. Queen Victoria, has been quoted as having said she "would not be crowned as Queen if any of the Empire held slaves." Mrs. Stewart named her poem "A Voice from the Oppressed, to the Friends of Humanity," composed by one of the suffering class, Mrs. Priscilla Stewart.

Later we find Mrs. Stewart addressing a group of men who were holding a meeting, the object of which was to recruit a regiment of colored soldiers and offer their services to the United States Government, to help win the War of the Rebellion. Among others she spoke to them on the value of united action. She was a trail blazer in many ways. Her poems have received much praise for their spirit of hope.

There were other pioneer colored women living in San Francisco who did much to keep alive a ray of hope for better days for the race. Among this number must be mentioned Miss Cecilia Williams, a Shakesperian tragedienne. She was free born and had been well educated in New Bedford, Mass. She would train men and women in giving concerts. She wrote splendid poetry, and wrote a poem commemorating the passage of the Fourteenth and Fifteenth Amendments to the Constitution of the United States. It was called "The Glory of the Coming Man." It is truly a masterpiece, a song filled with hope and courage to persevere until the race obtained their full rights. There was Mary Ann Israel Ash, who lived in the mountains, who upon being awakened in the night discovered a band of Negro slaves passing her home on their way to San Francisco to take a steamer back to the southland, to become slaves in a slave state. The master wanted one thousand dollars for their freedom. She mortgaged her home and gave them their freedom.

In speaking of slavery in California, and the colored women who came as slaves, there is none who holds more of interest and inspiration than the life of the late Biddy Mason and her family of three little girls. California was admitted to the Union as a Free State in 1850, and yet this woman, Biddy Mason, and her family were held as slaves in San Bernardino, California, from 1851 to 1854! They came to the state with their master from Hancock County, Georgia, by ox team. There were three hundred covered wagons in this train, and at the end of the train

Biddy Mason drove the live stock across the plains into California.

She also cared for the children of her mistress, and her own three little girls, enroute. It was when the master decided to leave the state with his slaves and go into Texas, where he could still hold them as slaves, that word reached the Sheriff of Los Angeles County who stopped him. The slaves and their master were taken into court; later the court gave them their freedom. After their free papers were duly recorded Biddy Mason secured work as a confinement nurse. It was then that she made a solemn vow to God that she would save her money and purchase a home for her children.

The *Los Angeles Daily Times* published a Lincoln Edition of their paper February 12, 1909. This issue was most remarkable because it gave the history of the colored people then living in that city. The Negro women were given a full page, which was edited by the late Mrs. Kate Bradley Stovall. In speaking of Biddy Mason, among others things she said, "Following the occupation of nurse Mrs. Mason accumulated sufficient means to buy a share in a large lot in what was then represented as the "Map of the Plains"; later, through her business tact, she purchased the remaining interest in the property, and secured for herself and children a clear title to the land. With surprising rapidity she acquired other property, but often said, "This first homestead must never be sold." And now in the center of the commercial district of Los Angeles, on this very old homestead, stands the Owen's block, owned and controlled by her heirs. Biddy Mason was well known throughout Los Angeles County for her charitable work. She was a frequent visitor to the jails, speaking a word of cheer and leaving some token and a prayerful hope with every prisoner. In the slums of the city she was known as "Grandma Mason" and did much active service toward uplifting the worse element in Los Angeles. She paid the taxes and all expenses on a church property to hold it for her people. During the flood of the early eighties she gave an order to a little grocery store which was located at Fourth and Spring streets. By the terms of this order, all families made homeless by the flood, were to be supplied with groceries, and Biddy Mason cheerfully paid the bills.

Her home at 331 South Spring St., in later years became a refuge for stranded and needy settlers. As she grew more feeble it became necessary for her grandson to stand at the gate each morning and turn away the line which had formed awaiting her assistance. At the age of seventy-three Biddy Mason passed to her reward, leaving to her surviving daughters, Ellen and Harriet, and to her two grandsons, Robert and Henry Owens, the nucleus of a vast estate."

Mrs. Stovall has given a splendid summary of the life of this grand trail blazer of California pioneer women. The reader must not lose sight of the fact that Biddy Mason was born a slave on the plantation of Robert Smith, in Hancock County, Georgia, August 15, 1818; and as a slave was denied the privileges of acquiring an education, and yet at her death, which occurred June 5, 1891, she was rated a millionaire! She taught her children and grandchildren the value of money and property holdings until, you will find, at this late date, 1924, her fortune in a large measure has been retained by her heirs in the city of Los Angeles. This city has produced many colored women who have been of great service to the race. Among this number was a Mrs. Sessions, whom the writer has been told was greatly responsible for the organization of the club that built the "Sojourner Thruth Home" for working girls in that city. A most interesting account of this lady has been given by the late Mrs. Stovall, in the edition of the *Los Angeles Daily Times* previously mentioned. Among other things she has said, "Mrs. Lucy Sessions of Los Angeles, held the first diploma received by a Negro woman in America, graduating from Oberlin College in 1850. Mrs. Sessions' eyes grew dim with tears as she told of being driven from every public school in Toledo, Ohio, on account of her color; and of her struggles to please at each succeeding school. Then forcing a smile, she said: "But never, my dear, did a teacher send me home; it was only the visitors that did not know me, who objected to my presence." When she returned broken hearted from the last school in the city, her mother assured her that she should have an education. With the assistance of friends Mrs. Sessions was finally taken into Oberlin College, on trial, as she was too young to be admitted. Her record was such that she readily gained permission to continue her studies. After her graduation she taught school in the south during reconstruction days. She died February 18, 1910, in the city of Los Angeles, California.

No doubt the reader would like to know something concerning the late Mrs. Kate Bradley-Stovall, who has furnished such splendid accounts of so many pioneer women of California; the following account of her funeral, as it appeared in the "New Age Weekly":— "She was the daughter of Mr. and Mrs. Allen Bradley of Austin, Texas, born August 4, 1884, and at a very early age came to Los Angeles and was reared and educated in that city by her aunt Kate." Continuing it said, "Carefully this aunt trained her for womanhood, and with loving interest watched and encouraged the progress she made in her educational work. Upon graduation in 1903 from the Commercial High School, on account of her excellent record she was commented upon in the *Los Angeles Times,* and among other things said; "Colored lass eloquent, Commercial High School striking oration. The four orators to represent the graduating class of the Commercial High School...............it was a distinguished honor the class conferred upon itself by its magnanimous action. Kate Bradley, in the execution of her trust did it with distinguished honor to herself and the class. She is a tall, lithe, good featured colored girl; her oration eloquent, concise and strong. Her topic, "The New South," was one that enlisted her sympathy and brought out the warmth of her nature toward her race, though no mention was made of any race. Miss Bradley talked warmly of the progress in the South and its rapid strides toward a place of greater importance in the commercial world. "This progress, she said, may well be termed wonderful, for it did not begin with the Constitution of the United States." This sentence brought the first applause, and it was the nearest reference she made to the problem. Her summary of the industrial progress and coming commercial importance of the New South was worthy of a statesman, both in subject matter and manner of delivery." "Miss Bradley received no bouquets as she stepped back to her place but the audience perceiving the probable thoughtless omission, redoubled its applause, and no more fragrant nor complimentary bouquet could have been tendered her, in the numberless mass of bouquets that banked the stage. No doubt there were a goodly number for her as well as for the other graduates.."

On November 1, 1904, Kate Bradley became the wife of William Stovall, a young man of excellent family and sterling worth, who has proven to the community his high qualities in the way he has stood up under the strain of illness and affliction. Two especially bright children, Wilalyn, and Ursula, brightened the union of these young people. Mrs. Stovall became a factor in race progress in Los Angeles, being intensely interested in fraternal, religious, and secular affairs. Her first thought was always toward the work of educational uplift among her people, and especially did she wish to inspire hope and enthusiasm in the minds of the young. Working on this line and acting upon the suggestion of her husband, she organized the "Southern California Alumni Association" in 1909, and served that body as its president for four years, until forced by ill health to resign. At the time of her death she was president emeritus of the organization, and her thoughts and hopes were always for its progress. She died at the age of thirty years.

SARAH G. JONES

Dr. Sarah G. Jones was born in Virginia soon after the close of the Civil War. She attended the public schools of Richmond, Va., and graduated from the Richmond Normal School. For a number of years she was a teacher in the public schools of her native city. She resigned her position as teacher to enter Howard University, Washington, D. C., to study medicine. After pursuing her studies there for a number of years she received her degree and was the first woman to pass the Virginia Board to practice medicine. She founded the Richmond Hospital and Training School for Nurses. Together with her husband Dr. Miles B. Jones, she enjoyed a most lucreative practice for many years. At her death a few years ago she was still the only colored woman to be practicing medicine in the state of Virginia.

MARIETTA CHILES

Miss Marietta Chiles for 46 years a teacher in the public schools of Richmond was a woman of lovable qualities. Her father was a messenger in the state capitol during the Civil War and carried the message to Jefferson Davis that Gen. Grant was near Richmond. This splendid woman served for a number of years as the Grand Secretary of the Grand Court of Calanthe and died as the honored and respected incumbent of that office. She was active in all efforts of uplift among her people.

ELIZA P. FOX

Mrs. Eliza P. Fox was for more than a quarter of a

century the President of The Woman's Baptist Association of Virginia. As the wife of a Baptist minister she knew what hard work meant and together with her husband she was active in every Christian organization. After his death she still maintained her interest in Christian work. The Convention of which she was President raised thousands of dollars for missions and education and to perpetuate her memory they erected a splendid stone building at the Virginia Theological Seminary and College, Lynchburg, Va., and called it the Eliza P. Fox building. Although not a woman of superior educational attainments Mrs. Fox was a splendid type of the consecrated Christian worker, a mother in Israel whose many daughters call her blessed to this day.

Mrs. Sarah G. Jones
Present Poet Laureate
Ohio Federation of Colored Women's Clubs

CONTENTS

CONTENTS—Concluded